3rd. Edition
SAN DIEGO's
BEST
FREEBIES & BARGAINS
(and surrounding areas)

by Sally R. Gary

Pacifica Books, Etc.   San Diego

San Diego's Best Freebies & Bargains

Sally R. Gary

ISBN 0-933-717-06-7
Copyright © 1995. All right reserved.

No part of this book may be reproduced or transmitted in any form or by any means, electronic or mechanical, including photocopying, recording or by any information storage and retrieval system without the written permission from the author; except for the inclusion of brief quotations in a review.

Previous Editions: Copyright © 1991, 1992, 1993 Revised 1994

The content herein is based on the best available information at the time of research. The publisher assumes no liability whatsoever arising from the publishing of material contained herein. If a phone number is not working, please call information, 411; then, leave a message for me. Thanks.

Dear Reader,

The benefits from reading this book will be equivalent to receiving a pay raise! You'll have more money left over at the end of your pay check!

Whether you want to save up for that down payment on your house, pay off the mortgage early and get out of the rat race sooner, or just have a few thousand left in the bank at the end of the year, you'll be glad you read this book. It will save you tons of money and increase the quality of your life.

Please feel free to leave messages on my answering machine regarding your successes in bargain hunting, new discoveries you have made, or perhaps a favorite bargain you want to share.

If you have a club or organization you would like a program speaker for, please contact me. I speak on how to "Live Better For Less With San Diego's Best Freebies & Bargains." I give presentation for businesses: brown bag lunches, staff appreciation luncheons, professional growth day and staff development day; also, for professional organizations, social organizations, church groups and PTAs. It's a great fun topic. Everyone benefits.

Til then, enjoy.

Sally ☺

TABLE OF CONTENTS

Chapter 1
GOODS & SERVICES *FOR LESS*

The face of the marketplace is changing as we head into a new century. The malls of the last decade are now competing more and more with general merchandise warehouses, discount and off-price stores, factory outlets and clearance centers. Sales are up at wholesale by mail catalog outlets.

The "used" market is experiencing a "boom." Clothing from some of the best closets in San Diego and furniture and household items from all over the world are being recycled through consignment shops, resale stores, antique stores, thrift shops, auctions, estate sales, swapmeets and yard sales.

In this chapter, you'll find the best bargains on the market in local goods and services with all the shopping options just mentioned. (The other chapters are devoted to shopping tips; free things to do; cultural events for less; discount and free travel; health; quick money makers; job info and how to raise quick cash; credit and legal good deals; free and bargain classes; restaurants for less; and in the last chapter, important money saving resources you should know about.)

Check out all your options. The bottom line is, if you shop around (get six to ten price quotes), you can almost always find someone who is ready to offer you a better deal! You're gonna love what's ahead for you in this chapter. . . enjoy! Ask me if I had fun putting this together!

Antiques & Collectibles

Ya' like antiques? Practically everyone has at least one if not a whole house full. When you buy new furniture, about 50% of it's value is gone the moment you take it out the door of the store. With most antiques, though, the value remains; in many cases, it goes up! So, whether you're an addict or a novice, if you want to spend a day browsing for that treasure (or cash in that old heirloom), here are the places to check out:

Newport Avenue in Ocean Beach has become an antique haven! After browsing, take a walk out on the O.B. Pier to the cafe for lunch or coffee and enjoy that great fresh ocean air. Go on a Wednesday around 3 p.m. when the Farmer's Market is there.

△ **Ocean Beach Antique Mall**, 4878 Newport Avenue, 65 booths, 222–1967. **Decades Antique Mall**, 4873 Newport, 226–6711; **O.B. Collectors Mall**, 4847 Newport, 523–1262; **McDonald's Antiques**, 4861 Newport; **O. B. Attic**, 4921 Newport, 223–5048; **Mallory & Sons Antiques**, 4926 Newport, 226–8658; **Newport Avenue Antique Center** (over 100 booths), 4864 Newport, 222–8686; **Newport Avenue Antiques** (over 60 booths), 4836 Newport, 224–1994.

△ **Unicorn Antique Mall**, 704 J Street, downtown, 232–1696. Three floors of antiques and collectibles, American and European furniture, jewelry, clocks, deli. Over 80 dealers, 30,000 square feet.

△ **Olde Cracker Factory Antiques**, 448 W. Market near Seaport Village downtown, 233–1669. Large complex of antique shops, including Bert's Antiques, 239–5531 (Bert and Olga are great people who also run estate sales. Ask to be on their mailing list. Tell them Sally sent you.

△ **Antique Mall**, 452 8th Avenue, downtown, 239–6255; many shops, restaurant and deli. Open everyday.

△ **House of Heirlooms**, 801 University, uptown, 298–0502. Comprehensive selection of antiques, including 18th C. English.

△ **Adams Avenue Antique Stores include the Kensington Antique Parlor**, 4222 Adams, 563–6440; Antique Seller, 2938 Adams Avenue, 283–8467; Adams Avenue Consignment, 2873 Adams Ave, 281–9663; Quartermaster Military Collectibles, 3039 Adams, 281–2648; From Time To Time, 3287 Adams Ave., 284–4795.

△ **West Sea Co.**, 2495 Congress, Old Town, 296–5356; large selection of fine quality marine antiques and art.

△ **Mission Hills/Hillcrest Antique Association includes House of Heirlooms**, 801 University, 298–0502; Mission Gallery, 320 W. Washington, 692–3566; Papyrus Antiques, 116 W. Washington, 298–9291; Private Collector Enterprises, 800 W. Washington, 296–5553; Whooping Crane Antiques, 1617 W. Lewis, 291–9232.

△ **La Jolla Consignment**, 7509 Girard, La Jolla, 456–0936. Over 9000 square feet (2 floors) of antiques on consignment. Quite a place; some things are quite elaborate and pricey. (This is La Jolla!)

△ **Grossmont Antique Mart**, 8379 Center Drive, La Mesa, 466–2040; 65 shops, open every day.

△ **Rocking Horse Antique Mall**, 8772 La Mesa Blvd., 469–6191; 24 shops, closed Tuesdays.

△ **Years of Yesterday**, 7895 Broadway, Lemon Grove, 464–3892; 10,000 square feet. Buy and sell.

△ **T&R Antiques Warehouse**, 4630 Santa Fe, Pacific Beach, 272–0437; over 15,000 feet of fine furniture and accessories, specializing in French, Italian. Appraisals, about $25.

△ **Antique Warehouse**, 212 S. Cedros, Solana Beach, 755–5156; 100 dealers; antiques, collectibles, memorabilia. Closed Tuesdays.

△ **Escondido Antique Mall**, 135 W. Grand, Escondido,

743–3210; 60 dealers; antiques and collectibles. Open daily.

△ **Hidden Valley Antique Emporium**, 333 E. Grand, Escondido, 737–0333; 52 dealers; complimentary coffee, tea and popcorn. Open daily.

△ **San Marcos Antique Village**, 983 Grand Avenue, San Marcos, 744–8718; 50 dealers, consignments,

furniture, collectibles. Open seven days.

△ **Temecula** has become another mecca for antique browsing. Don't miss Home Crafters, 18475 Front St., Ste. B2, (909) 676–6712. Specializing in Flo Blue, Blue Willow and other fine porcelain, furniture and decorator items.

△ Whether you want to buy or sell an antique, check the *Union–Trib* classified ads for Garage Sale/Moving #707, Antiques & Art #735, Thrifties #780, Auctions #700, Collectibles #730, Estate Sales #701, Furniture/Accessories #815, Miscellaneous #705 and Wanted To Buy #825. Very interesting stuff for sale!

△ To find an antique appraiser, look in the *Yellow Pages* under appraisers. Some appraisals are free; others are $10–15 and up, depending on the article and its value.

△ For a list of buyers willing to pay cash for all kinds of collectibles, check out the "Wanted To Buy" column in the *Union–Trib* classifieds, or order *Wanted To Buy,* available from Collector Books, below.

△ For a free catalog of hundreds of books on antiques with pricing guides for furniture, pottery, porcelain, china, stoneware, Occupied Japan, dolls, Barbie, Disney, jewelry, Indian, Depression glass, etc., call: Collector's Books, (800) 626–5420 or L–W Books, (800) 777–6450.

Apparel for Women

San Diego offers a wide assortment of places to shop for great clothing with affordable price tags. We have the traditional malls with their fabulous sales (and clearance centers), factory outlets where you can buy factory direct and save 20–30% and up, the discount and off–price chain stores that sell overstock (the same merchandise you find in malls for more), and the new trend for the new century: the resale market. The truth is: you can dress like a million for as little as a few bucks.

Here's a tip: many department stores offer a discount on your first day's purchases when you open an account. For example, Broadway gives a 10% discount, and they frequently offer a 10% off coupon during their advertised sales which you can also use (now you're at 20% off). Women planning and buying whole wardrobes for the season *on sale with a 10% off coupon*, and an additional 10% off for opening a new account!! With each purchase, you will earn bonus points toward a free gift. Bullock's gives 10% off the first day's purchases, and when your Bullock's card arrives, it is accompanies by another 10% off coupon. Mervyn's gives 15% off your first day's purchases. Some stores allow 90 days deferred billing with no interest, and you'll be put on their mailing list to receive advance notice of sales. These policies are subject to frequent change. (Check with other stores for their policy on first day discounts for new accounts!!) Most stores give "instant credit" with a Master Card or Visa. If you buy an item that goes on sale within 2 weeks (varies with stores), they will refund the difference with receipt.

△ **Anne Klein Factory Outlet** (you'll have to travel to Barstow for this one, but it's definitely worth the trip! There are 95 outlets!), 2837 Lenwood Road, (Barstow), (619) 253–5690; also at Cabazon, near Palm Springs, (909) 849–1114. If you like the upscale designer Anne Klein, whose fashions carried at Neiman–Marcus and Bullock's,, you're gonna love this place. Blazers, $149 (were $300), suits, skirts, sweaters, turtlenecks, denim pants, regular sizes plus petites and missy sizes. Accessories including handbags, wallets, scarves, fashion jewelry, sunglasses and perfume at least 40% discount for openers, some with an additional 10% or 25% off. $75 earrings for $22. Lot of petites. Clearance racks marked 40% off discounted price.

△ **Apparel Designer Zone**, 931 Garnet Avenue (Pacific Beach), 483–5150; 6335 El Cajon Blvd (College), 287–1850. Closeouts from department stores, specialty stores and catalogs at 40–80% off. Designers include Bill Blass, Limited, Express, Catalina, Tweeds, Nordstrom, Victoria Secret, more. Fashions include casual wear and business wear. New selections weekly. Frequent sales. Most inventory includes all four seasons. Liquidation sales called "shows" at the Convention Center a few times a year with big name brands. Get on the mailing list for these sales.

△ **Artwear Fashion Designers** offer original wearable art by some of San Diego's top designers. To get on the mailing list to be notified of showings, call 297–3030.

△ **Ashworth Factory Outlet**, 4410 Camino de la Plaza, San Ysidro, golfwear for women (& men), 690–5000

△ **Beeba's Creations**, local manufacturers of Body Drama sleepwear, Ulterior Motives rayon dresses (and other fashions sold at Target, Mervyn's, Sears and Walmart) closed their factory outlet in San Marcos, but they have a big annual factory sale. Call 549–2922 and ask to be placed on the mailing list.

△ **Benetton Outlet**, corner Revolucion at 6th in Tijuana. Benetton has over 1000 outlets in the U.S., with casual, colorful, trendsetting fashions. Women's, teens and children's clothing at discounts typically starting at 30% off retail. Prices are reduced as needed with progressive markdowns until the merchandise is sold. Another Benetton is at the Citadel Factory Outlets. See "Factory Outlets" this chapter.

△ **Bon Worth Factory Outlet**, 1050 Los Vallecitos Boulevard #141, San Marcos, 591-3459. Bon Worth labels are sold only at factory outlets. Ladies, misses and plus size sportswear in "budget" priced quality. Practical blends. They also carry a line of coordinating accessories.

△ **Broadway Clearance Center**, 555 Broadway Avenue at H Street, 427-1161. The entire basement is the clearance center for all 47 California Broadway Stores. They carry all the fine Broadway apparel at clearance prices. Items that have "remained on the floor for 90 days" are shipped to this center to be marked down for clearance! Most were marked down before they arrived. Most is regular merchandise, but there are some display samples, discontinued and damaged items. Mainly women's and children's clothing; handbags; (some housewares; domestics; linens; a lot of comforters.) A semi-truck load of new merchandise arrives every few days, so there is a constant turnover of merchandise; however, if the place is loaded with inventory, no trucks arrive for a while. You can hit this place after a sale and it looks empty! So, call first to find out if they are loaded. All articles are half off the original prices when they arrive at the Clearance Center. For example, let's say a $100 dress is marked down to $50 in the regular store before it comes to the clearance center. In the Clearance Center, ticketed prices are reduced from time to time, by colors, as follows: Orange, 25%; purple, 50%; blue, 75%; yellow 90%. You can get some truly incredible bargains here.

△ **Bugle Boy Factory Outlet**, 1050 Los Vallecitos Boulevard #107, San Marcos, 471-9347. Casual clothing, sold at Broadway, Robinson-May, Mervyn's and Wards. Women's (and men's and boy's apparel). T–shirts (to $19), leggings (to $10), sweatshirts (to $23 with retail tag marked $30). Sale items from $2.50.

△ **Charlotte Russe Clearance Center**, Grossmont Center, 462–2060. This is the clearance center for the 30 Charlotte Russe stores in Southern California and Arizona, and is about the same size as their regular stores. Final reductions; drastically reduced prices, everyday. New arrivals on Tuesdays, Thursdays and Fridays. Big store. Lots of separates. Skirts on sale for $6.99–$9.99. Blouses, blazers, very few dresses. Earrings, 2/$6 and $2/8, some 99¢. Sale racks with 50% off.

△ **Christine Factory Outlet Store**, 4466 Camino de la Plaza, San Ysidro casual and special occasion sweaters and sportswear, regularly carried at Nordstrom Town Square, Macy's, Magnins, are sold here for 40–60% off. Sweaters that sell in stores for $68 are $34.99; $180 sweaters, $89.95; $89 sweaters for $34.99. Labels include IB Diffusion, Marissa Christina, Christine. Sales: up to 80% off.

△ **Clothestime**, with 22 locations in San Diego County including 3651 Midway Drive, 223–3958. Call for a store near you. Clothestime, a large chain store with over 500 stores nationally, has discount junior fashions ranging from 30–70% off with an emphasis on casual, youth–oriented sportswear. Lots of stock, including numerous well–known name brands. Jewelry, pantyhose and accessories.

△ **Designer Brands Accessories Factory Outlet**, 4410 Camino de la Plaza, 690–6339; 1928 jewelry, Lauren Kelly, KJL, silver, Black Hills Gold, Jackmal gold, national brands of jewelry, designer handbags, sunglasses and other accessories. Liz Claiborne sunglasses and handbags and many other name brands found at Broadway, at about 50% off most merchandise.

△ **Designer Labels For Less**, 3315 Rosecrans (Sports Arena), 523–9202; 1050 Los Vallecitos #119 (San Marcos), 471–9950; 665 San Rodolfo Drive (Solana Beach), 481–7339; 4470 Camino De La Plaza (San Ysidro), 690–6016; Designer Labels For Less carries fashions from leading designers at 40–80% off. Carried at better department stores, these labels include Carole Little (the San Marcos store carries *mainly* Carole Little), Anne Klein, Christian Dior, Jones of New York, AM Player, Adolfo, Argenti, Armani, Beverly Hills Club, Bill Blass, Lily of France, St. Germaine, CG Designs. There is also a large selection of designer lingerie. The designers differ from season to season and area to area so you may not find all of them at your stores. Most of the Carole Little things I have never seen in department stores, but I recognize her style. (half the San Marcos store is Carole Little apparel.) Names you'll recognize at prices you can't ignore. Evan Picone sportswear separates, $14.96–$29.96, values to $150; Christian de Castelnau lace dress, $39.99, value $120; Carole Little sweaters, $36, value $86. There are 30 stores in Southern California. Their "close-out" center is in Woodland Hills. Call (800) FOR-FASHion to be on mailing list.

△ **Donna Karan Factory Outlet**, Barstow, many things with the DKNY logo: T-shirts, sweatshirts, hats, sunglasses. Carried at Nordstrom (more Donna Karan) and Bullock's (more DKNY), the outlet has stock that is one season behind the stores. Shirts, blouses, some suits, pants, hosiery, everything 40–60% off the store prices; sale rack with 50% off the discounted price. Blazers, $235 up (originally $400 up. The Cabazon Donna Karan Outlet (near Palm Springs) has a better selection, with their couture line: Collection. Another outlet is in Lancaster (Palmdale). See "Factory Outlets", this chapter.

△ **Eddie Bauer Factory Outlet**, 4410 Camino de la Plaza, San Ysidro, 428–7611. Women's pants, wool sweaters, skirts and shirts, overstock and discontinued items from their catalog and 200 retail stores including Horton Plaza, UTC, Fashion Valley and North County Fair. Typical savings are from 30–70%. A wool blazer that retails for $85–90 sells here for $69. There are frequent sales in addition to the discounts. Their stock is more limited in selection than their stores, but the savings are good. Classic styles. Past season clothing, and current. Overruns, catalog overstock, returns, some things that are only in the outlets. Duffle bags ($45 for $29). Belts and accessories, socks, a little bit of everything., clearance prices. For a retail catalog, call (800)426–8020.

◬ General merchandise **discount stores** like Kmart, Marshall's, Target and Walmart have a large selection of mid–range quality sportswear, exercise wear and lingerie, and usually a much lesser amount of career wear. They carry popular brands like Gitano, Brittania, Jordache, and Bonjour, and clothing that is made expressly for their stores. A great place for name brand lingerie at a discount is Walmart (Bill Blass bras, $5.94). Leather purses, $15; 14 karat gold at a discount, costume jewelry and fragrances, too, and when they are on sale, *ooh lala*, the savings! Their weekly advertised loss–leaders are excellent buys as good price comparison shoppers know. See "Discount Stores," this chapter.

◬ **Georgiou Factory Outlet**, 4410 Camino de la Plaza, San Ysidro, 690–3116; Georgiou is a Greek upscale designer with a nationwide chain of stores (one in La Jolla and one in Fashion Valley mall.) This factory outlet specializes in raw silks; there are a few other fine fabrics (some wools, linens, cottons, some polished silk.) They carry a line of coordinates, jackets, skirts, long skirts, blouses, with considerable inventory. Mainly past season, with some seasonal. A jumpsuit that sells in their local stores for $140, sells here for $72. Minimum half off original prices.

◬ **Guess**, San Diego Factory Outlet Mall, 4410 Camino de la Reina, 428–2234. Jeans, shorts, dresses, tops, sweatshirts, bags, glasses, long sleeved shirts for juniors size 3–12. Carried at Broadway and

Nordstrom. Guess retail stores are in Fashion Valley and Horton Plaza. The outlet offers 30% off, up to 50% the store prices.

△ **Janika Designs International Fashion Bazaar,** 2969 State St., Carlsbad, off Carlsbad Village Dr., 729–1840. Wide selection of Moroccan clothing, hand painted silks, batiks from India and Indonesia, trendy gift items. Shoe line: Wild Soles. Imported gauzes from Mexico, reasonable, $29–59. Always a sale rack.

△ **J.C. Penney**, nationwide chain store, carries Jones Wear, a mid-range fashion line by the designer, Jones of New York; Norton McNaughton. Jacqueline Ferrar is Penney's own label (top of the line) and Worthington is another good, stylish mid–line with copies of high–end designers.

△ **Jazzercise**, home based in Carlsbad, has an annual warehouse sale to clear out unsold catalog aerobic wear at fantastic prices. Call (800) 348-4748 to order catalog (which always carries reduced price and clearance leotards, tights, merchandise). Ask when the next sale will be and ask to be placed on the mailing list.

△ **Jockey**, San Diego Factory Outlet Mall, 4530 Camino de la Plaza, 662-1135. Undergarments, sox, activewear, tights, sportswear, sleepwear, hosiery found at Mervyn's, Robinson's–May and department stores around the country. Savings up to 30% on undergarments, more on sportswear.

△ **Jones New York** (you'll have to travel to Barstow, but if you're into this top designer, it's definitely worth it!), 2837 Lenwood Road, Barstow, (619) 253-2544; Jones New York is carried only at better department stores including Bullocks, Nordies. You'll find women's better suits and dresses, blouses, slacks, and casual wear at 25% less than department stores, some sale items up to 50% off. Outlets also at Lake Elsinore and Cabazon Factory Outlet Centers. Labels include Jones & Co.; Jones, career and sports.

∆ **La Costa Resort Products**, 2875 Loker Ave., Carlsbad, 438-2181, (800) 522-6782. Overstock from their boutique and items from the catalog, some returned, are sold at their warehouse, Monday–Friday, 8:30–5 p.m. All very good quality leisure wear including shorts, T–shirts, swimsuits, sandals, etc. at a fraction of the original cost. Some really incredible buys here. $65 sandals, $5; Semi–annual sale. Call for dates. This is a great find!

∆ **Leather Loft**, San Diego Factory Outlet Center, 4498 Camino de la Plaza San Ysidro, 690–5100, San Marcos Factory Outlet Mall, 752–1925. Belts, jackets, bombers, utility jackets. Long dusters were 50% off (clearance). Some items on clearance table. Most items are 10–50% off retail price; Kenneth Cole carried in Nordstrom and private labels.

∆ **L'Eggs–Hanes–Bali Factory Outlet**, 1050 Los Vallecitos Boulevard #131, San Marcos, 736–9212. Hosiery, including Hanes Alive and L'Eggs in 6 colors, lingerie including Bali slips and camisoles, socks, Jog Bras, Isotoner slippers and tights. Kiwi shoe polish, shoe strings and related shoe items. Most items are about 30% off.

∆ Lucky and Von's Supermarkets have sales on **L'Eggs**, first quality, all varieties, up to 50% off several times a year. I always stock up on industrial strength control tops, but you have to go early as they can sell out quickly. If they're out of your size, ask for a Rain Check and you can buy them at the sale price when they are restocked. Discount coupons are available in the Sunday supplemental coupon section, and don't forget to save the coupons in the L'Eggs box (and take them to a double coupon store!)

∆ **L'Eggs Stockings/Catalog**: Slightly imperfects and first–quality merchandise including pantyhose, Bali, Hanes as well as L'Eggs at up to 55% off. Buy 12 pairs of Sheer Elegance control top panty hose $16.08 ($33.98). Bras, tee–shirts, sweats, men's underwear.

Write to L'Eggs, POB 6000, Rural Hall, NC 27098, (919) 744–1790. The catalog has tons more than hosiery: active wear, tights, sleepwear, more.

△ **Levi's Factory Outlet**, 4410 Camino de la Plaza, 662-1244. Here you'll find Levi's 501's, $27.99 ($to $36 in stores), 550, 512's 912's, 950's jeans, $27.99; shirts, shorts, belts, saddles, for men, women and children at a discount. Clearance rack.

△ **Loehmann's**, Highway 78 & College Blvd in Oceanside, 941-4003. Loehmann's is a famous national off–price fashion store chain for those who love fashion and want to save a fortune on the newest designer and name brand clothes. It is one of the 10 largest off–price chain stores in the U.S. for women's apparel. Leisure clothing from Calvin Klein, David Smith, Ann Klein, an occasional DKNY, Donna Karen, Judith Leiber handbags, golfwear. Prices are guaranteed to be at least 1/3 off retail with a reliable quantity always priced at 50% off. Clearance racks with even greater markdowns. There is a much larger store in Beverly Hills store, (310) 659-0674, with all types of clothing from sportswear to cocktail and furs with labels from Geoffrey Beene, Adele Simpson and Bill Blass to Anne Klein, Nippon and others of equal renown.

△**London Underground**, 674 Fashion Valley Mall, 298-6821; progressive, trendy women's fashions; funky, cutting edge of fashion. Labels include Betsy Johnson, Urban Outfitters, Free People, moderate priced tops $18, dress $48-64, (some men's clothing)

△ **Maidenform Factory Outlet**, 4410 Camino de la Plaza, San Ysidro, 662-0388, carries all products that Maidenform manufactures: bras, camisoles, slips, tap pants, control garments (girdles, briefs, body shapers), sleepwear, and panties, reg. $5 each, three for $9. There is a variety of prints and colors, fewer basic colors which is the opposite of most department stores. The usual savings is 30%, with some markdowns to 50%. Clearance items are in the back of store with additional markdowns. To give you an idea of their prices, a basic bra, LetterPerfect, which sells for $18.50 in department stores sells for $13 here; a fashion bra, Chantilly, that sells for $19.50 in department stores, is $13–15 here. Two–for–one sales.

Δ **Marshall's Department Stores**, Fashion Valley West, 260–0891 and 10 other locations. Marshall's is another of the top 10 off-price nationwide chain stores for apparel offering mostly first-quality closeouts and leftovers plus special purchase merchandise. You will find some goods marked "irregular" too. Silk–blend sweaters, fleece wear, dresses, and separates with overall savings throughout the store are 20% to 60%. Marshall's motto is: "Name brands for less," and they carry Evan–Picone, J.H. Collectibles, Carole Little, Chaps, and more. Lingerie, perfumes, leather bags, shoes and boots (9 West and Bandolino reduced 50%!) Occasional buy one, get second product for half off. Great shoe sales (Cole Haan, value $150, $38.)

Δ **Membership Warehouses like Price/Costco** have designer labels (as available) including Christian Dior, Bill Blass, Act II, Playtex, Brittania, Jordache and many more. Of course, they don't have a full line but their buyers buy what is available at the best price negotiable, so what they do get in is at really terrific prices. (See "Membership Warehouses," this chapter.)

Δ **Mervyn's**, with several stores throughout the county including 3345 Sports Arena Boulevard. Call (800) MERVYNS for store nearest you. Over 300 stores nationally, which means they buy in huge lots at discount prices and pass the savings on to you. This is a great place to shop for advertised specials of name brand sports wear, 20–70% off. Gloria Vanderbilt, Bill Blass, Jordache, Bugle Boys, Levi Dockers, Cherokee, and own private label Partners and Ellemeno. When you open an account at Mervyn's, you get a 15% discount on all your purchases that day. Plan to get a whole new spring or fall wardrobe during a sale, and save 15% more when you open an account! All sale periods are from Sunday through Saturday. If you buy an item that isn't on sale, keep your receipts and if it goes on sale the following Sunday, Mervyn's will give you the cash difference if you bring in your sales slips before the next Saturday.

△ **Neiman Marcus** doesn't have a clearance store per se, but their store in Fashion Valley always has sale racks that are loaded with merchandise. Additionally, they have Last Call, their final sale for the season. Even if you don't have an account, you can ask to be placed on the mailing list to be notified of upcoming sales.

△ **Nordstrom,** Horton Plaza, 239–1700; Fashion Valley, 295–4441; University Towne Center, 457–4575; North County Fair, 740–0170. Nordstrom is considered *the* best stores for women's fashions, period. Not because they are a bargain but because they have a great selection of quality fashions and lots of apparel to choose from. Their sales are the *bargain* (markdowns 20–90%) with a half yearly sale in June and November, their anniversary sale in July, a the pre–fall sale with special prices for two weeks (then the prices go up!). Their personal shopper service is free and they will work with any budget. Their Orange County stores are much larger than San Diego stores and worth the trip up: South Coast Plaza, (714) 549–8300; Santa Anna (714) 972–2020.

△ **Nordstrom Rack**, 824 Camino del Rio N., in Mission Valley West Shopping Center, 296–0143. This is the clearance center for Nordstrom's stores, and is the place to find unbelievable bargains in better clothing for women (men and children, too), accessories and shoes, with 30–70% savings and more on everything. You'll need to spend some time here digging through the racks and racks of clothing, but you'll be happy with the price you pay for goodies from Nordstrom, even if the ambiance is a bit frantic. Suits, dresses, separates, sportswear, evening wear, petites, lingerie and more for women. Sportcoats, suits and sportswear for men. Periodic 35%-off Red Tag Sales every couple months with further markdowns to please the avid bargain hunter. I know people who take annual leave to hit these sales. Ask to be placed on the mailing list. Go during the week if you can because this place gets busy. Another Nordstrom Rack is located in Santa Ana at 3900 S. Bristol Street, (714) 751-5901.

△ **The Outlet,** 5600 Kearny Mesa Road, 571-1354. Mainly swimwear by Catalina, Oscar de la Renta, Speedo and Ann Cole with values to $70, prices $10-$30. Some lingerie. Catalina sportswear, T-shirts, pants, jackets. Two other Outlets, formerly known ass Catalina Swim Outlets, are located at 6000 Bandini Boulevard, City of Commerce, (213) 724-4693, and at 1337 S Harbor, Fullerton (714) 738-4476.

△ **Polo Ralph Lauren**, 7th Street and Madero, (Tijuana), 011-52-66-85-13-89. Within walking distance from the border is a Ralph Lauren store which carries a number of polo shirts, turtlenecks, Oxford shirts, sweaters, some skirts. Everything is made in Mexico City but the manager states they have the Ralph Lauren license from New York. You'll find blazers at 25-50% off, and other classic clothing for women (but the store is mainly stocked with men's clothing.) Another Polo Outlet is in Barstow (see "Factory Outlets," this chapter.

△ **Ross Stores**, an off-price store with several locations in San Diego including 4760 Clairemont Mesa Blvd, Clairemont, 292-7415, has name brand clothing and designer fashions at a discount for work, play and an active lifestyle for the entire family. Labels include Carter, Polo, Jantzen, Oleg Cassini, Candies, Cherokee, Diane Von Furstenberg, Vanity Fair, and more at 20-60% discount. Linens, too. Call (800) 345-ROSS for the store nearest you.

△ **Samira's**, 3960 West Point Loma Blvd, 222-0296. Laise Adzer Moroccan cloth knock-offs (look-alikes) at up to 60% off. Frequent sales, and there is always a sales rack in the back.

△ **Sergio Tacchini**, 2837 Lenwood (Barstow), (619) 253-3499, worth the drive for Italian designer leisure wear for women including tennis wear, golf, tennis shoes, ski jackets, and those shiny warmup suits that sell at Caesar's Palace and Nordstrom for $185 and more are under $100. Most merchandise is 20-40% off. Most items are under $100. Cross Fusion, $59-$84; Todd label, $54. They are one season behind, meaning in the spring, they have the last fall's wear. Also, shoes and accessories at factory outlet discounts.

△ **SDI Factory Outlet,** 1050 Los Vallecitos Boulevard #141, San Marcos, designer resort fleecewear, 471-1043

△ **St. John Knits Factory** Annual Sale in Irvine (Orange County) has an annual clearance sale Friday after Thanksgiving. This one is popular: people park in the lot over night to get a number to enter. They issue 7-800 tickets on Friday for the sale which is held on Saturday and Sunday. They let in 100 people every 2 hours. Call (714) 863-1171 and ask to be placed on the mailing list. (There is factory outlet in San Jose, (408) 942-0440. This is the *factory* sale, not an outlet.)

△ **Studio Five**, 1710 Garnet, 483-8557; 5671 Balboa, 576-7075; 6317 El Cajon Boulevard, 582-5659; Escondido, 743-5417; Imperial Beach, 5475-0521. Everything is well under $20. Prices may go up, but for the moment all clothing including dresses, jeans, shorts, T-shirts, body wear, jewelry, hats, sunglasses, handbags, pants, leggings, blazers, skirts, and more are under $20. Fashions for juniors with some amazingly good bargains. Attractive styles. Youth oriented, but much of the casual wear could be worn by anyone. There is a lot of style to be had here for a very small price tag.

Δ **Susie's Deals Factory Direct**, 3325 Rosecrans, 225-8655. Nothing in the store is over $5!! Missy, women's, junior, plus sizes, children. Mostly casual wear, rayon skirts and pants, T-shirts, shorts, mostly cotton. Great for teenagers and the junior set.

Δ **T. J. Maxx**, Midway and Rosecrans; Mira Mesa Shopping Center; Mira Mesa Blvd at Camino Ruiz; and Escondido Promenade, I-15 and West Valley Parkway. Save 20-60% every day on over 120,000 brand name and designer fashions for the entire family. Misses' dresses, skirts, blouses, shirts, sweaters, slacks, jewelry, accessories, luggage. Men's businesswear to activewear to clothes for going anywhere. Plus, underwear, socks, belts, more. Over 10,000 new items arrive every week. Liberal return policy. Individual dressing rooms. Layaways. Some great buys here!

Δ **Trend Club Factory Outlet**, 1050 Los Vallecitos Boulevard #104, San Marcos, 471-7804. Women's fashions and sportswear. Many are the same clothes sold at Clothestime, including the name brand, Bongos, Paris Blues, Beebop. T-shirts, 2 for $18; leggings, $9; career clothing including rayon pants and rayon blazers, $26.99 up. Trendy young styles, but people of all ages shop here. Many sale items reduced further.

Δ **Westport Ltd. Factory Outlet**, 1050 Los Vallecitos Boulevard #100, San Marcos, 471-2750. Women's famous label quality suits, dresses, sportswear and more including Gilmore, Christopher, Sasoon, Sasscom, Westport and Atrium (their own line). An $80 Liz Claiborne gold sweater was $60. Suits range from about $100 to $180, and represent a savings of 40-60% off retail, with 20% off sales.

Factory Outlet Malls:

∆ The **Lake Elsinore Factory Outlet Center** has about the best women's designer fashions around, all at one location, so it's definitely worth the trip (less than 2 hours from downtown San Diego) because we're lucky to have them so close. There are individual outlets for the following designers: Jones New York, Jordache, Koret, Leslie Fay, Levi's, Liz Claiborne, Geoffrey Beene casual wear, He-Ro Group beaded gowns and cocktail wear, Cape Isle Knitters, Leslie Fay, Marika and other designer women's clothing.   There are several excellent outlet stores for shoes including Cole Haan, lingerie and workoutwear. (see "Factory Outlets," this chapter).

∆ **Factory Merchant Outlet Plaza** (Barstow), 2837 Lenwood Road, Barstow,(619) 253-7342. If you drive to Vegas, stop on the way.   There are over 95 manufacturer's outlets including Anne Klein, Barbizon, Brooks Bros., Casual Corner, Danskin, Donna Karan, Etienne Aigner, Jones New York, London Fog, Sergio Tacchini and more.

∆ **Desert Hills Factory Outlets** in Cabazon near Palm Springs, has upscale designers including Adrienne Vittadini, Alpert Nipon!!, Anne Klein, Donna Karen (DKNY!), Harve Benard, He-Ro, John Henry, Jones New York, SpaGear from La Costa Resort, plus mid-priced designers including Duffel, Eddie Bauer, Esprit, Hawaiian Cotton, plus lingerie and shoes. (See "Factory Outlets," this chapter)

∆ Buffalo Breath Costume Co. 1917 India St., 236-0467, has an annual used costume sale in October.   The Old Globe sells costumes then, too.

For more apparel for women, see individual listings, this chapter:
    "Resale Shops"   "Leather"
    "Catalogs"   "Shoes (continued......)

For more apparel for women,
see. . . .
   "Jewelry"
   "Clearance Centers"

   "Factory Outlets"
   "Discount Stores"
   "Membership Warehouses"

Apparel for Children (+ Furniture & Toys)

With children's clothing almost as expensive as adult apparel these days, *my*, how it hurts to pay top dollar for clothing, especially when you know they will be outgrown within a few months and in the hand–me–down pile! Here are some great money savers for you.

△ One of the best sources for kids' clothes, for both quality and price, is **Mervyn's**. Their buyers purchase name brand overruns and sell them at prices way below department stores that carry the identical merchandise. Some items are ordered in especially for a sale; other merchandise may be in the store a few weeks, and then goes on sale. All sale periods are from Sunday through Saturday. If you buy an item that isn't on sale, keep your receipts and if it goes on sale the following Sunday, Mervyn's will give you the cash difference if you bring in your sales slips before the next Saturday.

△ **Carters Factory Outlet**, San Diego Factory Outlet Mall, 4498 Camino de la Plaza, San Ysidro, 690–1106, offers 30–70% off retail on clothing and accessories for newborns to children size 7.

△ **OshKosh Factory Outlet**, 4498 Camino de la Plaza, San Ysidro, 690–2999, namebrand clothing for children to age 7.

Δ Other great places to shop for good prices on kids' brand name clothing for less are: Target, Kids Mart, Kmart, Pic 'N Save, Price/Costco, Fedco, Walmart, Marshal's, Ross, T.J. Maxx, Family Bargain Centers, Tijuana department stores, swap meets (Yes!! Swap meets have four T-shirts with designs for $11!). Also, check out the Broadway and Nordstrom Clearance Centers, red tag sales at all department stores, garage sales. For teenagers, see Susie's Deals and Studio Five in "Apparel for Women," this chapter.

Δ You can pick up great used children's clothing in excellent condition for a fraction of the original cost at yard sales in great neighborhoods (La Jolla, etc.). I've scooped up hand-knit sweaters for 50¢ apiece to give to friends who have infants. One day I saw a couple buy a gorgeous complete layette for a baby girl for $35 at a yard sale at an exclusive home. This couple also bought the crib, stroller, furniture and other items this Little Yuppy-ette had outgrown, the finest quality available. What a score! And, I see Grandmas buying second strollers and cribs at yard sales to have on hand when the little ones come to visit. You can afford to have everything for your kids if you shop at yard sales!! Fabulous toys, clothing, furniture, skate boards, games, bikes, everything!! And, if you don't find it this week, well, there's always next week. My only regret is: I didn't know about the yard sale/rummage sale/thrift store market when my kids were young!!

Δ This one is great!! **The Junior League Rummage Sale** is a huge two-day event, held in October or November (whenever they can get a place) at the Del Mar Fair Grounds. Call 234-2253 for exact date of this year's event, mark your calendar, and be among the first in the door! One year, I saw the most gorgeous little pink ruffly dress for a toddler for $3 that was probably worth close to $100. I know I should have bought it even though I don't know a 2 year old . . . because that gorgeous little dress has caused me to lose sleep! Do you know what I mean? I wake up kicking myself for not getting it!! It was such a "heart connection." I can't afford to lose sleep over the price of a burrito! Not when I thought of the perfect person to give it to three weeks later. Anyway, people grab stacks of children's clothing and sack them up in 33 gallon plastic trash bags! They are getting whole wardrobes for their kids for a song. Actually, there are a lot of pros shopping here too who are buying to resell, so you have competition. I know families who buy for the year at this sale. See "Rummage Sales" later this chapter for more information.

△ **Children's resale shops** are a brilliant idea. Kid's clothes are so expensive, so it's no wonder children's resale shops have become so popular. Not only can you shop there, but you can take your kid's outgrown clothes in to sell. Call first to find out what their days and hours are for buying. Here are some of San Diego's best.

△ All Baby Needs
5119 Cass
Pacific Beach, 581–9339

△ Baby Exchange
910 E. Washington
El Cajon, 441–1210

△ Baby Exchange II
7631 Broadway
Lemon Grove, 462–7238

△ Baby Boomers
1717 Sweetwater Rd.
National City, 477–6612

△ Children's Orchard
4716 Clairemont Square
Shopping Center, 270–8044

△ Children's Orchard
9460 Mira Mesa Blvd
Mira Mesa, 586–7313

△ Children's Orchard
998 W. El Norte Pkwy,
Escondido, 738–7296

△ Children's Orchard
3841 Plaza Drive, Ste 901,
Oceanside, 941–1083

△ Hand Me Ups, 794–7311
12750 Carmel Country Road,
Del Mar

△ Miles to Go, 675–9100
11865 Carmel Mt. Rd.,
Penasquitos

△ Kiddie Kottage, 440–1049
681 Jamacha Rd, El Cajon

△ Jammies and Jeans, 465–3300
4691 Date, La Mesa

△ Janet Jones Baby Resale
5935 El Cajon Blvd.,
College area, 582–9854

△ Katie's Korner, 390–3152
12086 Woodside, Lakeside

△ Little Peeple's, 747–7060
160 W. Mission, Escondido

△ Miles to Go, 573–1526
5949 Balboa, Clairemont

△ Mother's Helper, 224–9960
4810 Santa Monica
Ocean Beach

△ Red Wagon
3652 Voltaire

Ocean Beach, 224-7725
- Reruns, 435-5444
  1015 C Avenue, Coronado
- Stork Club, 287-9449
  4838 Rolando, College Area
- Stork Club Escondido
  331 W. Felicita
    Escondido, 747-3667
- Tot's Spot Maternity
    486-4470
  12222 Poway Road
- Twin's Club of San Diego,
  460-5021
  Bi-annual exchange, anyone
  can attend
- Mercy Hospital Baby-Time
  swapmeet, 686-3776.
- Scripps Memorial baby swap
  meet, 457-6944

Kids' Warehouse, 9720 Distribution Avenue, Miramar, 578-0025 and 1617 Capalina Road, San Marcos, 471-5442; large selection of factory direct furniture and accessories for infants and teens.

North County Kids Center, 830 C Los Vallecitos Boulevard, San Marcos, 591-0222; furniture for babies to teens for less.

OH Baby, 235 Town Center Parkway, 562-6401; 727 Center Drive, San Marcos, 739-0226; guaranteed lowest prices on major brands of children's furniture and clothing for infants.

Children's Parties by Liz, former host of a Los Angeles TV children's cooking show, now a local children's party specialist. Children's gourmet cooking classes, too, 929-0939.

△ **Toy Liquidators**, San Diego Factory Outlet Mall, 4498 Camino de la Plaza, San Ysidro, 428-4826; also, at San Marcos Factory Outlet Center, 1050 Los Vallecitos Boulevard, San Marcos, 752-1418. Name brand toys including Mattel, Hasbro, Fischer-Price, Nintendo, Playskool at 20-40% and more discounts. They buy close-out, overstock and bankruptcy inventories so they don't have all items in a line; it's whatever the truck brings them.

△ Post this on your refrigerator for your kids: **Children's Line 10**, 1 (800) 962-1010. From 2:30-5:30 p.m., your kids can call a Channel 10 volunteer who will talk to them on the phone after school. (That is a very nice service, especially if they are home alone!) Post this one, too: **Children's Story Line**, 24-hour recorded stories, 291-5437.

△ Free parenting classes through San Diego Community Colleges Continuing Education Classes, 527-5242. For parents, children and grandparents. Whole family evenings, too.

△ Pick up children's party favors at the 99¢ stores (see "Clearance Centers, this chapter.)

△ Don't miss two great free newspapers: **San Diego Family Press**, 685-6970, which has a great calendar of events for children and families, and **San Diego Parent**, 624-2770. Both are delivered to supermarkets throughout San Diego. Call for location near you.

Appliances & Electronics

If you're in the market for a major appliance or small appliance this year, here are a few tips: Check the *Consumer's Report Annual Buying Guide* ($6.95), available at Crown Books, newsstands, SavOn Drugs and libraries. It reviews and evaluates appliances according to performance and defects. Make your selection and check prices at six to ten stores. Then call a few wholesale–by–mail stores on their 800 toll–free lines for an over–the–phone quote to see if you can get a better price. Inquire about warranties, shipping (sometimes offset by no sales tax when shipped to California) and return policies.

Here are a few tips: Try to negotiate the price. There is so much competition out there, they are usually willing to work with you to get the sale. Many stores have signs that say: "We won't be undersold," which means that if you find the product advertised for less within 30 days, they will refund the difference, plus 10%. Don't hesitate to ask if a sale is coming up, and, if you can have it for the sale price *now.* Ask if they have any slightly damaged stock with scratches and minor dents (always marked down). Maybe the scratched or dented area is on a side that will be up against your wall and won't be seen. Discontinued appliances are usually marked down. Ask about demos. Floor models can also be a good deal, and if you find any minor damage, you should be able to get a better price. Inquire about refurbished appliances and electronics that have been returned and factory rebuilt. Most have full warranties and you can save a bundle here!

Because discount stores buy in huge quantities, you generally get a better price; however, in many cases, delivery, hookup and removal of the old appliance may cost extra and may affect the overall savings.

The following stores sell **discounted appliances**:
△ **Cousin's Warehouse**, 1691 Hancock Street (Downtown), 293–3137. Open 7 days, M–F, 10–7, Sat 10–6, Sun 11–5. Cousin's Warehouse is an appliance hunter's paradise. You can select from large and small appliances and photo equipment, with all models on display. Frequent blowout sales. Cousins has a 30 day "no questions" return policy and a "no lemon" policy, too. Inquire about their private sales, "garage sales" and "flea market" sales!

Cousin's guarantees the lowest price for *120* days, or give you a refund plus 15%. With approval, pay in 90 days, same as cash (no interest).

△ **Circuit City**, 1608 Sweetwater Road (National City), 477-0093; 3331 Rosecrans (Pt. Loma), 223-2610; 8401 Fletcher Parkway (Grossmont), 589-2030; 1136 W. Valley Pkwy (Escondido; 3998 Clairemont Mesa Blvd, 272-8444; 1715 Hacienda Drive (Vista), 631-8440. Major appliances, (no small appliances), computers, cellular phones, and electronics. Large stores; frequent big sales. Large selection of name brand major appliances, cameras, TV's, phone answering machines, and stereos. They also have a large stock of marked-down scratched, dented, and one-of-a-kind items with full factory warranties. You can return items within 30 days if you are dissatisfied. Circuit City guarantees the lowest price within 30 days.

△ **Silo**, with 9 San Diego stores, carries a full line of appliances including full audio, video and major appliances, TV's, VCR's, washers, dryers, dishwashers, etc. Their El Cajon store, 880 Amele Avenue, 579-0465, and Sports Arena stores, Sports Arena and Rosecrans, 293-7456, are their two megastores. Frequent sales advertised in their newspaper supplements. Returns in 7 days, 30 day exchange for any reason. They guarantee the lowest price for 30 with refund plus 10% over.

△ The **Good Guys**, with 5 locations in San Diego including Sports Arena, 523-2600; Carlsbad, La Mesa, Carmel Mountain Road, and La Mesa. Check out the appliance here, too. Big selection.

△ **Dow Stereo/Video**, 9 stores including 3445 Sports Arena, 226-3500, San Diego. Price guarantee for 30 days, will match the price and give you 15%. Lots of equipment, many advertised specials. Definitely a place to cruise if you're looking for audio/video equipment. Return policy: within 30 days with box and packaging, manual, invoice. Ask about their refurbished audio and stereo at super low prices (sometimes 50% off), with warranties.

∆ **Price/Costco** and Fedco carry a limited number of large appliance models. There may be only one model refrigerator, washer or dryer, but they are at very good savings! You can shop on a one day pass without joining, but you must pay cash and an additional 5%.

∆ **Target, Kmart and Walmart** are good places to pick up small appliances like toaster ovens, coffee makers, blenders, mixers, radios, telephones, cameras, vacuums, etc., when they are advertised as a loss leader. **Kmart** has increased the number of major brands offered. (See "Discount Stores" this chapter.)

∆ **Montgomery Ward's Electric Avenue** now carries a variety of major brands and they say they will match any price you find anywhere else. They will give you the cash difference back if an item goes on sale within 30 days.

∆ **Sears Outlets**, Marketplace at the Grove, College Avenue, 583-9802; 1327 Encinitas Blvd., 942-6021. Major name brand appliances including Amana, GE, Whirlpool, Kitchenaid and their own brand, Kenmore. Everything has been sold once and is considered "used," but has a one-year warranty. Savings of 20-25% off (or more).

∆ **Wholesale-by-mail** stores will give quotes by phone on their toll-free lines. Shop at local stores, find what you want, write down the make, model, color and call for a price quote. Ask about shipping and warranties. You may save sales tax which can be a substantial savings on items that are shipped out of California (depending upon the state). Call Percy's of Worcester, MA, (800) 922-8194, over 50 years in business selling large appliances and more, all major name brands, 30-50% discount; Crutchfield of

Charlottesville, VA, discount up to 60% on name brand stereos, no sales tax outside Virginia, 100–page color catalog of electronics, (800) 336–5566. Damark (liquidation), (800) 729–4744.

Δ For used appliances, check the *Union–Trib* classified ads: "Thrifties #780," "Household Appliances #810" and Garage Sales/Moving " too. Listed are VCR's, refrigerators, TV's, stoves, cameras, and every appliance, large or small, you can think of. I pick up a lot of small appliances (perfect condition) at yard sales including: a Mini–Cuisinart ($1); Rival Steamer/Rice Cooker ($3). new Fry Baby ($1) with no cord (one from another appliance fit!)

Δ See Appliance Repair in the *Yellow Pages* for repair service stores. They have cords, parts, manuals for appliances.

Arts & Crafts

Δ Michael's, 60l Mission Valley Center West, 297–2826; 816 Jackson, El Cajon, 442–6666; Other stores located in Escondido, Oceanside Carlsbad, La Mesa, Chula Vista, Clairemont Mesa (Lee Wards), El Cajon, Poway, Carmel Mountain. **Floral, craft and party goods** at savings of 20% to 50% off retail prices. Specials are featured weekly, and there is usually a 40–50% off coupon in the Sunday *Union–Trib*. Senior discount, 10%.

Δ Value Craft, 3825 Plaza, Oceanside, 758–9233; 342 W. El Norte, Escondido, 747–9222. Lots of craft supplies, specials, good prices.

Δ Check "Arts & Crafts" and "Floral Supply Houses" in the *Yellow Pages* for discounted ribbons, vases, pots, artificial trees and assorted craft supplies.

Δ Paint and Decorate Your T–Shirt with paints from the swapmeet. Or, If you don't like the colors on ready made T–shirts, paint over T–shirts with ready made designs. in a coloring book. Use their design for starters and go from there. Also, you can paint over spots on clothing rather than throwing it in the recycle bin, a great idea for children's wear.

△ KPBS TV have lots of has sewing, painting, watercolors, quilting, and lap quilting classes. Discovery Channel has lots, too. Check "TV Guide" for times.

△ Take a free and low cost sewing and craft classes at West City Center Adult School, 221-6973, Sports Arena area. Learn how to applique, quilt and decorate clothing. Enroll any time.

△ To receive a free 60-page catalog of crafts kits, write to: Better Homes & Gardens, P. O. Box 374, Des Moines, IA 50336

△ Send for Beads, Stones and Jewelry wholesale supply catalog, free, P. O. Box 1421, 150A Church Street, Burlington, VT 05402.

△ Triarco Arts & Crafts Catalog, discounts on quantities, 300 pages, everything your imagination needs and more, established in 1946, (800) 328-3360.

△ For a 70-page sewing craft kit catalog, write to Herrwschners, Inc., Hoover Road, Stevens Point, WI 54492

△ Free catalog of over 600 crafts and hobbies. Write to Dover Publications Inc., Complete Crafts & Hobbies Catalog, 31 East 2nd Street, Mineola, NY 11501.

△ Several community colleges extended studies programs offer 3-hour seminars on how to market your arts and crafts.

△ Check "Art Supply Stores" in the *Yellow Pages*. Get on the mailing list of H.G. Daniels, Aaron's Art Mart and The Art Store and be notified of future sales.

Auctions (Don't Miss Out!)

Not for everyone because you have to have a little "know how," but you can buy automobiles and other vehicles, bicycles, jewels, watches, furniture, appliances, crystal, oriental rugs, antiques, office supplies, tools, fixtures, equipment, furniture, building supplies, and store equipment.

Auctions feature a variety of merchandise that is surplus, no longer needed, has been left unclaimed, is being liquidated by heirs or creditors or being sold for other reasons. When hotels, restaurants and office buildings remodel, the old fixtures, furniture, and equipment are frequently liquidated at auction. U.S. Customs auctions have merchandise that people attempted to import at the border who didn't have the proper documentation or the money to pay import duties, or failed to claim the goods within the one–year limitation. Auctions are attended by the general public, dabblers, novices, semi–professionals and professionals who buy goods to resell (a *very good way to raise extra money in your spare time*). Viewing is prior to sale and items are sold to the highest bidder.

There are three methods of bidding: 1) At traditional–type auctions, oral bids are taken from the audience item by item. 2) At "spot–bid" sales, written bids are accepted item by item. 3) A "sealed–bid" sales consist of offering bids by mail, with bids opened in public. Winning bidders cannot remove property without first paying for it in full by cash, money order, traveler's checks, cashier's checks, credit union checks or U.S. Treasury checks. Novices should educate themselves by attending several times to get acquainted with the auction procedure. A word of warning: you can get caught up in the frenzy and pay too much for an item, and end up with buyer's remorse. Get educated quick: pick up a book on auctions at the library or book store.

Here's an example of a real surprise at an auction: a couple bid $100 on a box that they thought contained tools, only to find it contained several pieces of valuable turn–of–the–century sculpture by a San Francisco artist worth boo–coodles of money.

Most people don't know where or how to find out about auctions. Here's how: auctions are publicized in the display and classified ads (Section #700) in the *Union–Trib*. You can also call and get on the mailing list (free or for a subscription fee) of auction houses listed in the *Yellow Pages*. Others are listed below.

Following are hard–to–find auctions that are not listed in the *Yellow Pages* that sell confiscated goods, bicycles and vehicles, unclaimed articles and court evidence, surplus items, patrol cars, articles from drug busts and much more:

San Diego Police Department Auction; general property (stolen and unclaimed merchandise and bicycles), 531–2767 (recording of next date of sale)

General Services Administration (GSA), Federal and local government vehicles, (619) 754–3600

Department of Defense (DOD); hundreds of items each sale including televisions, computers, restaurant, equipment, navy motor boats, 437–9440

U.S. Customs Auctions (vehicles), 279–5450

County Public Administrator, personal property and real estate, 694–3500. Auction every third Saturday at 5201–A Ruffin Road. General estate and conservator property including furniture, autos, toys, miscellaneous. Call for brochure of real estate.

McCormack Auctions (handles government auctions) for Southern California, (310) 787–0080

U. S. Marshal Auctions (vehicles), 557–620

Champion Auctioneers, personal items, Corona (909) 735–0486.

Police and sheriff auctions (autos), 661–1022.

Auction Productions, Ltd. 598–9922

L. A. Police Department Auction, (213) 485-9515. Similar to the SDPD auction, only bigger.

Goodwill Industries Auctions, 453 4th Ave., downtown, 696-6705. Daily auctions, M–F, 8:30–11:15 a.m., 1–2:30 p.m.

Salvation Army Auctions, 1335 Broadway. Call 239–4037 for more information.

Not the most exciting event I've ever been to, but an auction at the Otay Mesa border facility began at 10 a.m. with an hour before hand for inspecting the merchandise. The sale included a computer which sold for $125, several industrial machines, an ocean meter for $260, four boxes of used stereo receivers and tape decks for $140, 96 hot water heaters for a $2,300, a ceiling fan for $25, two cartons of cups and mugs for $30. The real buy of the day was a $5000 bamboo bedroom set that sold for $275!

∆ Auction Buyers News, (800) 917–9997

Automobiles

To save money on a car, keep yours longer than five years, choose a small car, don't trade in your old car (sell it privately), opt for manual shift, limit number of options, reject extra services, pay cash or check finance charges in advance and have a sizeable down payment. Then, wait til the end of the month to make an offer. Salesmen have quotas to meet to get a bonus, and you can negotiate a better deal.

New Cars: Before you make this major purchase, pick up a copy of one of the annual new–car buying guides: *"Car Book,"* *"Car Driver,"* *"Edmund's New Car Prices,"* or other title. There are many on the market. They report how a car ranks in performance and what defects appear. They give the dealer's invoice price, and tell you how much you should/should not pay over the invoice price. These manuals are available at libraries, supermarkets, drugstores, newsstands, bookstores, credit unions and banks.

∆ For a printout guide to dealer's cost for a specific new car, write to: Consumer Guide Printout, POB 570, Lathrup Village, MI 48076 or Consumer Reports Auto Price Service, Box 8005, Novi, MI 48050. Include make, model and style.

∆ **New Cars Inc.**, 7304 El Cajon Blvd., San Diego, 697–2886, is San Diego's largest non–franchised **auto buying service** specializing in acquiring your car for as little as possible, and, with 14 other offices, has the buying clout to do it. They take the hassle out of negotiating with the dealer. New Cars Inc. customers say they save an average of $1,100 on new cars, not to mention countless hours of comparison–shopping hassle. They enable you to buy a new car, truck, van or recreational vehicle, domestic and foreign, at a price below what you can get the same vehicle for at a dealer. Price quotes include all dealer and broker fees. Contact them after you have shopped and decided on the exact vehicle you want including make, model, colors, finishes and optional equipment. They then locate the vehicle to your specifications, frequently in another city, and bring it to San Diego for you. They also have a large inventory of used cars.

∆ **Autoland**, an auto broker, 6705 Mira Mesa Blvd., 457–1898, similar to New Cars Inc. is another source for new autos at a discount. Save the hassle of negotiating.

∆ Luxury cars with a manufacturer's rebate are sometimes cheaper than economy models!

∆ When the new models of cars come out, the unsold last year's models can be negotiated at very good prices. These are brand new cars with brand new warranties that are considered to be "a year old" because a newer model is out. You can really get a deal here, so take your time and do your best negotiating.

∆ Car manufacturers lure customers in by offering interest rates as low as 3.9%, depending on the car and model. This can save you more than a cash rebate.

∆ Every Sunday, the Sunday *Union–Trib* publishes the auto loan rates for local banks in the Business Section. Credit unions have good rates. The *Pennysaver* is a good source for locating auto loans for those with credit problems. Several companies advertise there. Every week, they have display ads for auto dealers who specialize in financing problem loans. You will pay more interest.

∆ Buying factory–direct in Europe: Volvo advertised that you could get your car direct from the factory including a ticket to Sweden, and still save money. People go to Europe and bring back their own Mercedes, Porsches, BMW's, etc., complete with California specifications, save money, and get a vacation thrown in, too! You can travel in your new car all over Europe, saving car rental fees which can be $400 a week, then have your new car shipped home! Call Volvo, (800) 631–1667; BMW, (800) 932–0831; Mercedes–Benz, (800) 222–0100. For other autos, contact the dealer and ask if they have a plan for buying factory–direct.

∆ A money–saving alternative to the Dealer's Extended Service Warranty is available through GEICO, (800) 841–3000. The next time I buy a new car, I will definitely get the longest extended warranty available and I'll check out sources other than the dealer. And, you can negotiate the cost of a service agreement at the dealer.

∆ If you feel you have bought a **"lemon,"** take your complaint to CALPIRG, (California Public Interest Group), (310) 397–5270.

△ **Used Vehicles**: Before purchasing a used vehicle, ask if it has been in an accident and take it to a garage that will do a diagnostic evaluation of the condition of the motor, transmission and other parts.

△ The Auto Club of Southern California (AAA) has a **diagnostic service** for members *and* non-members. For around $50, you can have a car tested for various ailments which could save you a bundle of money and headaches. AAA also publishes a free directory of AAA-approved mechanics for members and non-members.

△ *Consumer Reports* devotes an issue every year to auto **repair records** for 288 late model used cars up to five years old, indicating which cars cost the least to maintain. Check here before buying a known loser. Available at newsstands, bookstores and libraries.

△ To find out if a used car has been **"recalled"** due to manufacturer defects, call (800) 424-9393, or any dealership.

△ Budget Rent-a-Car's rental fleet is sold at Budget Car & Truck Sales, 400 N. Johnson, 593-3611. Buicks, Oldsmobiles, Pontiacs, Hondas, Cadillacs, Chevrolets, Fords, Lincoln's, etc. 30 day warranty. Lots of cars.

△ The Federal Government sells over 40,000 **government used vehicles** each year including sedans, station wagons, trucks, vans, motorcycles and buses to the public for nearly $70 million through the General Services Administration (GSA). Information on how to buy **seized vehicles** is sold for $10 and up through the classified ads of local and national newspapers. Do not succumb to advertisements offering to sell you information on "how to purchase government property at insider auctions for ridiculously low bids." What you get for your 10 bucks is a list of addresses and phone numbers of GSA offices around the country, which you can get yourself, free. If you are interested in buying a well-maintained used government car at a fair price, the information on GSA sales is FREE, FREE, FREE. Do not expect to purchase a luxury vehicle for $250 or a jeep for $50, as you may have been led to believe. GSA offers **three methods of purchase**: the basic auction sale, in which the auctioneer asks for and accepts a voice bid on each vehicle; the spot-bid sale, in which a written bid is submitted as each vehicle is offered; the sealed-bid sale, in which offers are mailed in and the highest bidder is the winner. See "Auctions," above.

Δ **Automobile Insurance:** According to one of the Big Time Financial Gurus, you have to call at least six insurance agencies and compare rates to get the best price. So, dial on, my friends, and you will be able to save some substantial bucks on this, usually several hundreds of dollars. Three companies who have been consistently lower are Wawanesea (285-6000); 20th Century, (800) 443-3100; GEICO, (800) 382-9436. If you carry more than one type of policy with a broker (such as homeowners *and* health), you usually get a 10% discount. Insurance Express, 576-3200, has a large computerized base and they can locate the best price for you.

Δ For advice and information on various insurance coverages, call (800) 942-4242.

Δ **Auto Repairs/Paint/Upholstery:** Experts advise that you get at least three estimates before making your decision. The dealer will usually have the highest bid. You can save money on paint jobs and upholstery in Tijuana. Buy the paint from the dealer and take it down. Get three estimates in San Diego before you go and get three down there. Your car may have to be left overnight for painting. Some people get the dents knocked out down there and have the painting done up here, if returning to Tijuana to pick up the car is inconvenient. There are dozens of auto body and upholstery shops between the border and Revolucion. I had a car painted down there and I have a friend who restores cars and has had many, many painted and upholstered there. Many people get radiator and muffler work done there, too. Go early, drop off your car, go shopping and have lunch at Sanborne's on Revolucion just a couple blocks past the Jai Lai Palace, then pick up your car.

△ Just got wind of a good place to get your car repaired: Thao's Auto Repair, 3752 Park Boulevard and Robinson, Hillcrest, 692–1065. It's owned and run by an oriental woman! This came highly recommended to me, and I intend to go there for any future work.

△ Aamco Transmission offers free towing in for free estimate.

△ Get an estimate from the companies that advertise themselves as offering "Discount" services: Discount Transmission Repair, Discount Auto Parts, Discount Auto Supply, Discount Battery Co., Discount Auto Electric, Discount Radiator & Muffler, and Discount Tire Co., listed in the telephone directory. However, some discount companies aren't always "discount," so do your comparison shopping.

△ **Charge your auto repairs** on a major credit card and if there is any problem that you are not happy with and cannot resolve, your credit card will back the charges off your account! Keep copies of all bills, correspondence, calls, etc.

△ **Auto Complaints**: If you feel you got stung in an auto repair, call the consumer's complaint and protection agency at 560–0114 or (800) 952–5210; or CALPIRG Consumer Assistance, 297–5512. They love to help in these matters.

△ If you *really* need to save the money, and you have the time to go this route, check into auto mechanic classes offered through community colleges, adult schools, vocational schools, ROP, and high schools to see if they can take your car as a class project (the teacher oversees everything). It isn't always possible to get your car fixed when you want it, but if you have the time and can coordinate it with a school, you can have the work done for just the cost of parts.

Δ Look for discount **coupons** for a smog check every week in the *Pennysaver* and in your neighborhood newspaper. Buy "How To Pass Your California Smog Check and What To Do If You Don't," by Brentwood Communications in Vista. Unfortunately, you can really get "taken" on a smog check if you aren't informed. Thao (above) charges about $17 for a smog check, including the certificate, depending on the car, etc.

Δ Discount coupons are always in the above newspapers for an oil change, $10 off. If you use them, you can get your car washed with the money not spent and still have $$ left over!

Δ For used auto parts, call Ecology Auto Wrecking or check "Auto Parts Wholesale" and "Junk Dealers" in the *Yellow Pages*. A great place to get mirrors, doors, seats, axles, hubcaps, etc.

Δ Price/Costo has good prices on tires, and tire sales are in the newspapers *every* week.

Other auto info:
Δ **Emergency road service policies** are available from the Automobile Club of Southern California (AAA), 233-1000, Signature, (800) 323-2002, and Sears. I've had an AAA card for almost 20 years and consider it one of the most important life-savers around. It pays for itself if you have car trouble only once, and I wouldn't want to be without the peace of mind it affords me. It's the best friend you could have if you have a car problem. For a fee of $58 the first year (and $38 thereafter), if your car needs to be towed, they tow it for you; if you have a flat tire, they fix it for you; if you lock yourself out of the car, they come to the rescue; if your car won't start, they try to start it. Membership includes their Travel Club, which provides you with local maps including Tijuana, maps for your trips, a quarterly magazine with

international travel opportunities and more. They have a huge Travel Show in San Diego every three years, and I won an American–Hawaii Cruise for two at the last show. AAA membership is a great gift, too. I received my membership as a gift the first year. I love it! Exxon Travel Club & Emergency Road Service, (800) 833-9966, $39, rated highest by *Money Magazine*.

Δ Discount coupons for a nearby car wash are on the back of your supermarket receipts. (Car washes have gotten expensive, but they save you lots of time!!)

Δ Pay parking tickets promptly. Failure to do so may result in an automatic warrant for your arrest. Then, if you are stopped for any reason, you'll go to jail.

Δ If you get a ticket, ask the officer about going to traffic school, or call SDPD and inquire. Your ticket won't show on your DMV record and your insurance company won't be informed. (For certain violations only.)

Babysitting

This is a tough one, but I was asked to come up with something for people who have sitter needs. So here goes:

Δ When I went back to college, I had two young kids and there was no way I could be at home with them and at school at the same time, so I looked in the classified ads of the newspaper under "Services Offered Housekeepers" and found someone who lived in for three years. She was very young, and didn't speak English at first, but I bought audio tapes and she learned! The only reason she eventually left was because my kids each needed their own rooms. Here are some other suggestions:

△ Get a college student to live in or out.

△ Call churches to see if you can post a notice for someone to live in or out.

△ Many seniors would love to help with your children. Call any Senior Center. They may be lonely, have a need to feel useful or could use the extra money. Strong friendships can evolve from these mutual needs.

△ I found another mother who was also a student the day we registered our sons for kindergarten. We arranged our class schedules the next semester so that she picked up my kids on Mondays and Wednesdays, and I picked up her kids on Tuesdays and Thursdays. This way we were both able to continue our college courses and our kids were well cared for. Incidentally, this is how I managed to complete my degree and teaching credential, and how the other mother went on to get her degree and a law degree. We are the best of friends to this date (and so are our kids), and this is many years later! To think we all met on the steps of kindergarten!

△ Form a **Neighborhood Babysitting Coop**, where mothers babysit for one another and earn hours of credit toward having someone babysit for their children. The more participants, the merrier. Make allowances for one child versus three children, etc.

△ Most community colleges have a **Child Development Center** with a job board. Call your local community college to post a "Help Wanted" position and hire a child development student. They are receiving training and want to work with kids as a profession. Or, if you enroll at the college, you can take your kid(s) to the Child Development Center while you attend classes. The requirement is that you take one two-unit child development course per semester with your child, which is great, because you'll spend quality time interacting with your child during enrichment and developmental activities. This can make study-time easier for you when you get home because you've had this quality time together. You will also learn good parenting skills, which makes your job easier. To place a job listing at Mesa College Child Development Center, call 627-2812; Regional Occupational Center (Metro), 292-3760; (East County), 579-4709; (South County), 691-5611; (North County), 741-5558.

Bartering

If you own your own business or have something to trade, you will want to consider this one. Join a barter club which functions as a clearinghouse with a bank of goods and services for its members to trade. For a membership fee, you get a list of members, and you can trade your "whatever" in exchange for something else. The barter club takes a broker's fee for the match-up, frequently in the form of your goods or services, so there may be no money exchanged! However, some barter clubs charge a membership fee. Businesses from Mom 'n Pop operations to major corporations trade goods and services including optometry, podiatry, ski equipment, broadcast commercials, accounting, massage, trips, hotel rooms, office supplies, restaurants, display advertising, and anything else you can think of. See the *Yellow Pages* for listings of "Barter & Trade Exchanges." And, you can, of course, make your own private deals, too. It's worth asking! A consultation client of mine who lives in Santee said she would drop by my house after going to the chiropractor in Pacific Beach. I inquired why, if she lived in Santee, she used a PB chiropractor. She said her husband is a carpenter, so they exchange services with her chiropractor who needed some cabinets installed! If anyone wants to trade something with me for copies of my book, or to speak to your organization, or a consultation on how to self-publish, let's talk! Call me at 222-0772 and leave a message.

Beauty Supplies & Services

Here are a few suggestions that can put more beauty products and services into your life, and you'll save money, too!

△ Look under "Beauty Colleges" in the *Yellow Pages* for savings on all beauty services including **shampoo and set, perms, coloring, facials, manicures, pedicures**. You will be worked on by a student, one who is well along in her course work, and all the work is overseen by an instructor. It takes a little more time, so go on a weekday...early in the week is best. Good savings.

△ City College Department of Cosmetology, 230-2574, offers beauty services performed by a students, at a savings.

△ Many beauty salons need "models" for their stylists to try new products and methods. For a **free haircut**, maybe even a perm or other service, check "Notices" in the *Reader* classifieds.

△ For discounted cosmetics and **bulk hair care products**, look under "Beauty Supplies" in the *Yellow Pages*. You can pick up gallon jugs of shampoo and rinses at big savings. Price/Costco, Fedco and Costco sell bulk hair products at great savings, too.

△ Most swap meets have a stall with **discounted cosmetics and hair care products**, too, with some well known brands including Paul Mitchell.

△ Hair+, 5027 Newport, Ocean Beach, 223-8847. They carry 29 top brands of hair products at discount prices including Paul Mitchell, Sorbie, Tresa, and Image and you can bring in your empty bottles for a refill and save! A $10 product refills for $6.

△ The coupon supplement section of the Sunday newspaper has **discount coupons for beauty products**, hair coloring, cleansers, shampoos, hand creams, etc. I used a $1 off coupon at Von's recently for a $1.79 bottle of Vaseline Intensive Care hand lotion, which I got *free*, since Von's gives double coupon value!

△ Target Stores, Kmart, Mervyn's, Long's, SavOn and Thrifty frequently have **25–50% off name brand cosmetics**. A good time to pick up a few things. See their advertising supplements every Sunday in the *Union–Tribune*.

△ **Perfumania**, North County Factory Outlet Mall, 1050 Los Vallecitos Blvd., San Marcos, 591–0320, has real fragrances at real savings from 10% to 60% off related items. Fragrances include Georgio, Passion, Nini Ricci, Opium, Poison. Call and ask to be placed on their mailing list to receive list of monthly specials.

△ **PFC Fragrance & Cosmetics Factory Store**, San Diego Factory Outlet Mall, 4498 Camino de la Plaza, San Ysidro, 428–4400; cosmetics, skin care, fragrances, sun tan products, men's fragrances, nail care and other beauty items that were discontinued, mispackaged or leftover promotional items, at deep discounts, 30–70% off.

△ **Perfume "fakes,"** copies of designer scents, don't last as long on the skin because they are made from a lower percentage of perfume oils, but they are extremely affordable, and are in some cases, very much like the finer perfumes. "Fakes" are available at Long's, SavOn and Thrifty Drugs, Mervyn's, Target, Kmart, and swap meets. (When you buy your ticket as you enter the swapmeet, ask where the perfume stall is.)

△ Tijuana is a freeport, meaning you can save 10% on import taxes. Designer perfumes are available at a number of places including **Sara's** on Revolucion at 5th, **Le Drug Store** at Revolucion and 4th, telephone 0115266–85–0374. Both are nice places to shop and English is spoken at these boutiques.

△ Better name brand cosmetics and fragrances offer special **"gifts with purchase"** as a promotion at department stores. That's the time to buy them! You can ask to be placed on the mailing list and you'll be notified of the next promotion. There's always something coming up: Valentine's Day, Mother's Day, etc. For example, during the past several Christmases, Bullock's gave away crystal earrings, and a bracelet or necklace with a minimum fragrance purchase.

△ Don't forget to ask for your **free samples** of fragrances before you leave department stores!

△ Major department stores have **free fashion shows**, some with complimentary wine, hors d'oeuvres and a 10–15% discount coupon for anything in the store purchased that day! *San Diego Magazine* has a fashion column with show dates, and there's a fashion column in the *Union–Trib* every Saturday morning with show dates. A great way to see the latest fashions and get a discount coupon, too.

△ Discover your best colors. Carol Revelli is the frontrunner of color experts. Call (800) 738-3554 for a free catalog of books (some under $10) and kits they offer with complete color and style analysis for your wardrobe and for a color coordinated home! Carol is the foremost runner in the color field, with hundreds of thousands of her books in distribution.

Bicycles

Police auctions are held several times a year during which hundreds of unclaimed bicycles are sold. As you can imagine, all kinds of bicycles are there, from beat-up to brand new. My electrician said he took me up on this and went to see what they had, and scored a $2000 custom super-deluxe bike for a few hundred bucks. Was he thrilled or what! Viewing is one hour before the sale and is usually held at a major hotel. Cash or personal check, no credit cards. Call 531-2767 for a recording of sale dates. If you can't wait for the next auction, try the "Thrifties 780" classifieds in the *Union–Trib*, or the classifieds in the *Reader*. People buy and sell bikes all the time.

Books

If a book store doesn't have a book you're looking for, fret not, for behold! They can get it for you if the title appears on their computer (usually within less than a week), and they'll call you when it's in. They usually order books weekly to replenish what's been sold, so it's not like it's as "special" as it sounds. There is no charge for special ordering, and you'll save a lot of time running around town looking for a title you can't live without. Most discount book stores do not special order, however, in order to keep pricing low.

Δ For wonderful books on San Diego, see chapter on "Things to Do." Titles include *San Diego Trivia, Cycling San Diego, American Institute of Architects Guide to San Diego, Afoot and Afield in San Diego,* something for every interest. There are over 100 books with a San Diego orientation. Ask your bookstore manager for a list of San Diego titles from Sunbelt Distributors. Will you be surprised! Unfortunately, no store carries all 100+ titles.

Δ If your question is: "Where can I find the answer to ....?," call your local librarian, who *loves* to help you find information. I call them all the time. The downtown library is the largest in the County and has more books and services than the branch libraries, but I always check with the nearest branch first. Other services available at libraries include audio tapes, typewriter rentals, and more. You can also call the Mayor's office and ask questions about San Diego and its services. They have a large staff of volunteers for callers.

Used Books:

△ Friends of the San Diego Public Library, a California tax exempt corporation, is an organization dedicated to the support and future of the public libraries. FSDPL sells the libraries' **surplus books** at prices you won't believe: hardbacks, mostly $1; paperbacks 25¢ to $1. Great reference books, oversized books, children's books, fiction, etc. The San Diego downtown library has a sale every Friday, Saturday and Sunday. Your branch library has ongoing off–the–cart sales and an occasional big sale. City and County libraries are listed in the Government section of the white pages telephone directory.

△ A number of used book stores are listed in the *Yellow Pages*. These stores are thriving. You can sell your surplus books (not for much, but make them an offer: so much for a bag full of paperbacks, etc. Also, I pick up a lot of great books, not only for myself but others at yard sales, usually 25¢ to $1 or so.

△ Friends of the San Diego Public Libraries has an annual book appraisal clinic at the central library every April. Bring in your rare books for an official written appraisal by an authentic appraiser. One book, $5, three books, $10. Call 542–1724 for exact date.

△ The San Diego Booksellers Association has an annual used book fair every June with about 50 booths between the 3200 and 3300 block of Adams Avenue. At that time, they offer free book appraisals, up to four books.

Carpets

You're crazy if you pay full price for carpets. There are carpet sales advertised *every* weekend in newspapers. I kept a diligent watch over this for several months and the same companies have sales every month or so, especially around holiday weekends when people have extra time to fix up their homes. If you can use carpet remnants, you'll really be able to save. Carpet remnants are roll ends, usually small room size, but I've seen them up to 25–30 feet long. If you put tile, either ceramic or vinyl, in your hallways or just across your door jams, you might be able to use a remnant for each room! It works best if you use only one color carpet, like all beige with beige tile. Department stores, even when they have carpet sales, are usually, but not always, higher priced. However, if you open an account at Broadway the day you purchase your carpet, you get an additional 10% off, and that can be significant. Broadway also usually offers deferred billing on purchases over a few hundred dollars with no payment and no interest for 90 days.

Here are some carpeting stores to check out:

△ **Cole's Carpets**, 1170 W. Morena, 276–5140 and 850 Los Vallecitos in San Marcos, 741–1001. Cole's has great sales, and a Remnant Outlet Shop with hundreds of very nice quality remnants, many top of the line, that are half price or less. Frequent free padding offers, so don't forget to ask about that.

△ **The Carpet Factory**, 1202 Knoxville, 275–1250, has lots of roll ends, many large sizes, and good prices on large rolls. I bought Queens carpeting there for over $10 less than it was at other stores. My girlfriend bought it, too!

△ **Sid's Carpet Barn**, 132 W 8th Street, National City, 264–3000, has a lot of lower–priced, thrift quality carpets. Ask about warranties against holes. Better quality carpets last longer.

△ I have also heard good things from happy clients about carpet from Talbert's and San Diego Carpets, and West Coast Carpet Outlets (with locations on Miramar Road and San Marcos). Their sales are advertised every weekend in the *Union–Trib*. There are really good sales before holidays, particularly before Thanksgiving and Christmas.

△ Home Depot Expo Design Center, 7811 Othello near Balboa & Convoy, has a good carpeting department.

△ You can buy your carpeting wholesale, **factory–direct** from the mills in Georgia, have it shipped out, and still save money. Here's how: shop around, find what you want in the department or carpet stores, write down the exact brand name, number, color, and all other information and call some of the following 800 toll–free numbers to see if they can beat local prices. You can save sales tax, too, depending on where it is shipped from. Shipping costs are about 70 cents a yard, so 100 yards would ship for only $70, and you save more than that in sales tax. For installation, look under "Services Offered" in the *Union–Tribune* or *Reader* classified ads, or call a local carpet company and ask if they have any installers who moonlight.

△ Here are carpet wholesalers to call. Some carry over 50 brands. Most will send you samples upon request. S&S Mills, (800) 363–4036; Factory Direct Carpet Outlet, $1 square yard over dealer cost, (276–4053; Carpet America, (800) 491–0677; Quality Discount Carpet, (800) 233–0993; Warehouse Carpets of Georgia, (800) 526–2229; Johnson's Carpet, (800) 235–1079.

△ Consider buying a steam carpet cleaner ($150–$300), when they are on sale. (Wards and Penney's have 25% off sales a few times a year.) Your own shampooer can save you lots in cleaning bills and you'll probably do it more often.

Catalogs Sales (Mail Order)

Over 80 million shoppers buy from catalogs and mail order firms. Half spend less than $100 per year, but one in 10 spends $400 or more. Catalog sales are on an upward trend, as busy people are finding it convenient to browse through catalogs at home and phone in an order. We'll all be doing more of this in the future. Shopping and buying directly from computers shopping services is the new wave.

Tips for catalog shopping: consider shipping fees; pay with a credit card to minimize return problems; understand the company's return policy and save your paperwork.

Here are some of the top rated mail order companies:

L. L. Bean, (800) 221–4221
Patagonia, (800) 638–6464
Land's End (800) 356–4444
REI, (800) 426–4840
Cabela, 900–237–4444
Road Runner Sports, (800) 551–5558
Talbots, (800) 882–5268
Eddie Bauer, (800) 426–8020
Brooks Brothers, (800) 274–1815

Neiman Marcus, (800) 825–8000
J. C. Penney, (800) 222–6161
J. Crew, (800) 562–0258
Sears, (800) 366–3000
Bloomingdale's by Mail, (800) 777–0000
Lerner Direct, (800) 288–4009
Chadwick's of Boston, (800) 525–6650

∆ **Nordstrom Catalog**. Fine quality fashions with unconditional guarantee. Fast delivery (FedEx, two–day) with maximum freight charge of $12.95 no matter how much you buy, free returns (they send a mailing label to you already made out and FedEx picks it up), free gift boxes. Catalog personal shoppers have the exact measurements and specifications of every item at their fingertips. Great selections. You can order in more than one size and return the one that doesn't fit, or both. Charge to your Nordstrom's credit card. (The merchandise is not in Nordstrom Stores), but it's great stuff, and so convenient. Get on the mailing list, (800) 285–5800.

△ **Catalog Service Center**: Obtain a catalog of dozens of unique catalogs from them by writing 144 S. lst Street, P. O. Box 4507, Burbank, CA 91503.

△ **Best Products Co.**, 7938 El Cajon Blvd., 698–7244, is a large catalog showroom with giftware, housewares, cookware, cameras, electronics, luggage, sporting goods, toys, jewelry, silver, crystal. Sample items are displayed with both prices, retail and 20% discount. An Emerson AT1100 Microwave oven was $149 (retail $199), a rattan high–back swivel rocker $89.95 (retail $199.99). After selecting an item and paying for it, your purchase is brought to you from the warehouse. A hefty catalog is available for a nominal charge, (800) 950–2378.

△ **Wholesale by** *Mail Catalog*: A phone–book thick catalog with more than 600 entries featuring clothing, crafts, sports and recreation, artwork, accordians, clothing, computers, furniture, foodstuffs, vacuums, vitamins, tools, silverware, sheets, all at extraordinary discounts. Selected by *Book of the Month Club, Playboy* and *Better Homes and Gardens* book clubs. Contains information on how to purchase brand names from suppliers. Available in book stores for $19.95.

△ **Products for a Healthy Planet**, (800) 456–1177. Green cottons, organically grown, recycled paper products, environmentally safe cleaners, and other healthy products. Call for free catalog.

△ **The Ultimate Outlet** catalog **(free),** features big designer names in 50 states, such as Calvin Klein, Misty Harbor and Alexander Julian with savings from 20–80% off regular retail. Clothing, shoes, jewelry, accessories for both men and women, call toll free, (800) 345–4500.

△ Here's one for you: The Neiman–Marcus By Mail catalog, P. O. Box 2968, Dallas, Texas 75221–2968. Nice to have around so you know what's the latest in top of the line stuff; then shop for copies.

Classified Advertising

△ The *Reader* still gives free classified ads to private parties and nonprofit organizations that do not charge for their services. Each ad must be typed on a 3x5 card (mailed inside an envelope) or on a postcard. Free ads are limited to 25 words. Send to: Reader Classifieds, POB 80803, San Diego, CA 92138. Must be received by 7 a.m. Monday, three days in advance of issue. Phone Matches (personal ads) are limited to 25 free words. You can pay for additional.

Clearance Centers

Clearance centers are filled with wall–to–wall bargains. Unsold merchandise is "cleared out" from stores and sold at bargain prices in special "clearance centers." Some stores own and operate their own clearance centers. Other stores return their unsold merchandise to the manufacturer, who re–sells the merchandise by the truckload to stores that specialize in buying overstocks and cancellations. Here are some interesting ones.

△ The entire basement of the **Broadway** in Chula Vista, 555 Broadway Avenue at H Street, 427–1161, is the Clearance Center for all 47 California Broadway Stores! They carry all the fine Broadway merchandise at clearance prices. Items that have "remained on the floor for 90 days" are shipped to this center to be marked down for clearance! Most were marked down before they arrived. Most is regular merchandise, but there are some display samples, discontinued and damaged items. Mainly women's and children's clothing; handbags; some housewares; domestics; linens;

a lot of comforters. When I was last there, they had a ton of comforters being cleared out at the end of the season at prices you wouldn't believe. A semi-truck load of new merchandise arrives every few days, so there is a constant turnover of merchandise; however, if the place is loaded with inventory, no trucks arrive for a while. You can hit this place after a sale and it looks empty! So, call first to find out if they are loaded. All articles are half off the original prices when they arrive at the Clearance Center. For example, let's say a $100 dress is marked down to $50 in the regular store before it comes to the clearance center. In the Clearance Center, ticketed prices are reduced from time to time, by colors, as follows: Orange, 25%; purple, 50%; blue, 75%; yellow 90%. You can get some truly incredible bargains here.

△ **Nordstrom Rack**, 824 Camino del Rio N., in Mission Valley West Shopping Center, 296-0143, is the place to find unbelievable bargains in better clothing for men, women and children, accessories and shoes, with 30-70% savings and more on everything. You'll need to spend some time here digging through the racks and racks of clothing, but you'll be happy with the price you pay for goodies from Nordstrom, even if the ambiance is a bit frantic. Suits, dresses, separates, sportswear, evening wear, petites, lingerie and more for women. Sportcoats, suits and sportswear for men. Children's clothing, too. Periodic 35%-off Red Tag Sales every couple months with further markdowns to please the avid bargain hunter. I know people who take annual leave to hit these sales. Ask to be placed on the mailing list. Go during the week if you can because this place gets busy. Another Nordstrom Rack is located in Santa Ana at 3900 S. Bristol Street, (714) 751-5901.

△ **Charlotte Russe Clearance Center**, Grossmont Center, 462-2060.   This is the clearance center for the 30 Charlotte Russe stores in Southern California and Arizona, and is about the same size as their regular stores. Final reductions; drastically reduced prices, everyday. New arrivals on Tuesdays, Thursdays and Fridays. Big store. Lots of separates. Skirts on sale for $6.99-

$9.99. Blouses, blazers, very few dresses. Earrings, 2/$6 and $2/8, some 99¢. Sale racks with 50% off.

∆ **Sears Outlet Store**, Marketplace at the Grove, Hwy. 94 and College, 583-9802; Encinitas, 942-6021. An entire store that carries only furniture (and major appliances) which are overstock, surplus, discontinued, returned or damaged.

∆ The **J. C. Penney Furniture Outlet Store** is located at 741 Broadway, Chula Vista, 422-4486. Frequent 30% off sales on recliners, sofas, dining tables, already marked down merchandise. Example: Regular price, $399, sales price $239, additional 30%: $71, and you pay $167!

∆ **GTM Discount General Store**, 716 16th Street, 234-7122; 8967 Carlton Hills Boulevard, Santee, 449-4953; 7551 Broadway, Lemon Grove, 460-2990; this is your basic "no frills" clearance store with over 20,000 items. Much of the merchandise is from Price/Costco (slightly damaged goods or perfectly good items in damaged cartons, etc.) GTM buys overstocks, distressed and discounted merchandise from over 130 vendors. Toys, food items, paper plates, odds and ends, clothes, TV's, stereos, cameras, drinks, household items, hardware items, stationary, pet food, you name it. Ask the manager for what you want: you may not see a computer in the store, but the manager can get you one! Good prices. Rice: bulk or bag, 15¢ pound; 16 oz. cans of Snapple, 47¢; Colgate toothpaste, 8.2 oz., $1.76; Olympus SuperZoom 3000, $207.99 (over $300 value); 27" Sony, $499 (value over $600.)

∆ **La Costa Resort Products**, 2875 Loker Ave., Carlsbad, 438-2181, (800) 522-6782. Overstock from their boutique and items from the catalog, some returned, are sold at their warehouse, Monday-Friday, 8:30-5 p.m. All very good quality leisure wear including shorts, T-shirts, swimsuits, sandals, etc. at a fraction of the original cost. Some really incredible buys here. $65 sandals, $5; Semi-annual sale. Call for dates. This is a great find!

△ **Pic 'N Sav**, with 15 locations including 3705 Rosecrans, 260-0109; 1085 East Main Street, El Cajon, 442-2870; 1625 E. Valley Parkway, Escondido, 747-7467; 1210 Broadway, Chula Vista, 420-4716; 1655 Euclid, San Diego, 264-6644; 6145 Lake Murray Boulevard, La Mesa; 2017 Mission Avenue, Oceanside; 1410 Plaza Boulevard, National City; 9340 Mira Mesa Boulevard, Mira Mesa, Clairemont and North Park. Pic 'N Save, a national chain, is a paradise for bargain hunters with tons of designer ends and closeouts. People go there for "therapy" whenever they have the urge to spend but don't want to blow a lot of dinero. It's open Friday nights til 10:00 p.m. (and all nights) and is a fun place to hit after a quick happy hour. The shelves are stocked with giftware, household items, sheets, towels and comforters, cosmetics and sunglasses, candles, wine, books and cookbooks, clothing for men, women and children, food products, tools, artificial flowers, lots of wicker accent furniture, more! Although about 60% of the merchandise is often "thrift" quality, which may or may not interest you, the rest is name brand goods at 40-70% off or more. Sanyo CD players, Sharp radios, Uniden cordless phones, Wamsutta comforters, Danskin, Oscar de al Renta, Diane Von Furstenberg, Evan Picone hosiery and other name brand "finds" will delight you at prices you won't believe. Boys' corduroy shorts, $3.98, (value $9), Lily of France Bikini panties, $1.69, (value $6), Danskin bras, $2.98, (value $9), Limited Express slacks, $10.95, (value $38), men's Gitano pants, $10.95, (value $24), silk neckties, $2.98, Cannon potholders, 50¢ (value $1.29), children's activity books, 39 cents, (value 99 cents), and more! This is one of my favorite bargain hunting places, and one of my earliest "bargain discoveries," too. Some of the stores are nicer than others to shop in -- *mine*, the one on Rosecrans, is *great!* Ask the manager when new truckloads arrive (it's Wednesdays and Fridays in Pt. Loma.)

△ **Bargain Center Inc.**, 3015 North Park Way, 295-1181. This is a large store with lots of surplus military items, funky pants, hats, camping bags, flannel shirt, T-shirts, boots, shoes, jeans, pants, wearables and outdoor equipment. Some great buys; unique stuff.

Δ **"99¢ Stores"** are a new arrival this decade and an interesting concept, since nothing in the store is priced over 99¢! In fact, some things are 3/99¢! These stores buy large inventories of clearance items, overstocks, unclaimed merchandise, returned merchandise, bankruptcies, close-outs from wholesalers. Merchandise includes health and beauty aids, tools, toys, children's party favors, housewares, food, hair accessories, picture frames, light bulbs, phone cords, cleaning supplies, candles, food, hardware, hair decorations, cosmetics, earrings, candy bars and more, all 99¢. There are several in San Diego including:

Maxim's 99¢ Store . .   223-6634
4991 Newport Ave., Ocean Beach

Maxims 99¢ 582-1999
5079 El Cajon Blvd., San Diego

Maxims 99¢ 272-7751
1701 Garnet, Pacific Beach

Maxims 99¢ 476-1999
362 F Street, Chula Vista

99¢ City   460-3949
6525 Bisby Lake, La Mesa

99¢ Superstore   695-0243
8190 Mira Mesa Boulevard

One Dollar Store . . .   235-9012
2121 Imperial Avenue

99¢ Bargains   527-4549
6251 Imperial

99¢ Great Store 679-0175
12354 Poway Road, Poway

Out of the area (but let's face it, you do get around):
Δ Bullock's closed its great Gran Finale clearance center in Grossmont Center, but if you love Bullock's, there is a Bullock's Clearance Center in Panorama City, (818) 509-4575. The Bullock's store in Costa Mesa is wonderful -- much larger than any store in San Diego.

Δ J. C. Penney Clearance Store, Garden Grove Mall, 9741 Chapman Avenue, Garden Grove, is the last Southern California one of its kind, with regular and catalog merchandise at clearance prices, including family clothing, housewares, linens, and furniture, at 15% to 75% savings. No appliances or hardware. (Penney's furniture clearance store is in Chula Vista.)

∆ If you get to New York, you won't want to miss this one. Gabays, 225 lst Avenue between 13th & 14th, 212-254-3180, receives clearance items from Bloomingdale's, Bergdorf, Saks, and Neiman Marcus and sells them at a steal. Gorgeous quality designer men's and women's fashions, leather jackets, towels, housewares, some furniture, etc. The best time to shop is after the holidays, when Gabay's receives all the unsold and returned deluxe gift items.

Computers & Software

∆ Price/Costco carries a limited number of top of the line, discount priced computers. Also, check deals at Office Depot, CompUSA, Computer City, Wards;

∆ IBM Factory Outlet store, Morrisville, NC (919) 380-1442. Mail order.

∆ For discount mail order catalogs, see "Appliances & Electronics" this chapter.

∆ Students and educators can buy Macs, IBM's and compatibles at the best discounts available at SDSU Aztec Shops. Get your kid to check on this one for you.

∆ For a used computer, check the classified ads of the *Union–Trib* (Computers #723 & Thrifties #780), *Reader* and *Computer Edge* (a free publication available at computer stores, or call them at 573-0315 for nearest drop-off point.) If you need advice, *Computer Edge* lists computer consultants and software user's groups for support. Also, check "Auctions #700).

∆ Anyone can use the computers at Midcity West Center, 221-6973, free. Ask about other locations. Enroll in a class or work on your own project.

∆ Hire a "whiz kid" to hook up your computer, load the hard disc and set up your files. Call the SDSU Student Employment Office (or other colleges, community colleges or high schools). You might want to negotiate a flat fee for specific services, or offer an hourly rate. The Student Employment Office can tell you what the going rate is for students.

Copy Shops

∆ Office Depot and Staples have prices for copying that I have not been able to beat in San Diego (two cents a page with 100 copies or more, and it goes down from there!) Full service, production, and extended hours.

Dinnerware, Pottery, China & Crystal

∆ The department stores have sales on name brand china and crystal, with 20-35% off every month or so. It would be crazy to pay full price if you can wait until a sale, always just around the corner. Their sale prices are very competitive with factory outlets. Ask a sales associate in the department stores to notify you of the next sale. They're happy to do it. Also, you can buy a whole set of china, crystal or silver on the club plan and make payments. You get 10% additional off if you open an account at Broadway or Bullocks.

∆ **Bohannan's**, 1231 Camino del Rio S., Mission Valley, 294-9894, has 650 china patterns, casual dinnerware, crystal, flatware, acrylics, wall decor, home accessories, silk plants, patio, bath, etc.

Sales every week, $4–5 million dollar inventory in 18,000 square feet.

△ **Tuesday Morning**, a big national housewares discounter and growing, Garnet and Jewel, Pacific Beach, 274-3880; 13179-2 Black Mountain Road, Rancho Penasquitos, 538-8534; 7740K El Camino Real, Carlsbad, 634-1790; 4242 Camino del Rio, Ste 7, Mission Gorge, 283-7203. Nice selection of housewares including cookware, half price; bakeware, gadgets, cutlery, ceramics, crystal, and glass serveware and gifts, bed and bath linens, stationary, more. Typical examples are: crystal stemware, $49 (value $108–120); brass frames $4.99 (retail $12– to $20); towels, $4.99, value $16. Down comforters, $49 (value $125). Fabulous closeout prices. You'll love this place.

△ **Mikasa Factory Outlet Store**, 4410 Camino de la Plaza, San Ysidro, 428-2022, carries a large collection of the Mikasa line from closeouts to current popular patterns at discounts of 30%–60%. Stoneware (Garden Harvest, $29.99; retail $60 a place setting), fine china, bone china (Rememberance, $150 place setting for $79.99), flatware, crystal frames, placemats, tea kettles, crystal stemware ($16.99, value $32–37), silk flowers, bakeware, linens, kitchen and bathroom goods. Most goods are first quality; closeouts; discontinued; some seconds. Special order, too, from their over 300 patterns. Other Mikasa outlets are located at 20633 S. Fordyce Ave., Carson, (213) 537-2060; 2500 North Palm Springs, (619) 778-1080; and at the Lake Elsinore Factory Outlet Mall, (909) 674-7130.

△ **Corning/Revere** at North County Factory Outlet Center, 1050 Los Vallecitos Boulevard, #108, San Marcos, 471-6240. Visions cookware, Corelle dishes, Pyrex measuing cups, bowls, bakeware at 20–60% off retail. Many discontinued styles, plus overstock of new designs; some seconds. Kitchen utensils, cookbooks and other items from outside suppliers.

△ **Famous Brands Housewares Outlet**, San Diego factory Outlet Mall, 4498 Camino de la Plaza, San Ysidro, 690-5420; also at North County Factory Outlet Center, 1050 Los Vallecitos Boulevard, San Marcos, 744-8844. A complete kitchen store featuring Libby, Nordic Ware, Anchor Hocking, Rubbermaid, Ecko, Intercraft, Mirro, and other houseware brands at 20-50% off.

△ **Canyon Pottery**, 3621 Bandini St., Old Town, 298-5400. Previously selling only to dealers, Canyon Pottery is now open to the public offering 40% off retail prices. Exotic planters, urns, glazed pots from all over the world.

△ **Price/Costco**, listed under Wholesale Warehouses in this chapter, has great buys on fine china, pottery, dinnerware and Waterford crystal, and you can special order on their computerized catalog, Quest.

△ If you're really into cookware, check out restaurant supply houses listed in the *Yellow Pages* under "Restaurant Equipment & Supplies." There are several on both sides of Market Street between Pacific Highway and 20th Street that have large soup pots, tons of dishes, cups, bowls, utensils, pots and pans. Clearance tables, too.

△ Good ole **Pic N Sav**, mentioned under Clearance Centers, this chapter, has wonderful buyouts of overstock, bankruptcy, and discontinued inventories....some very nice quality dinnerware, utensils, cookware, glasses and more mixed in with thrift quality items. You have to know your stuff.

△ Professional Cutlery Direct, (800) 859-6994. Discounted.

△ **The China Warehouse**, Gorham, Towle, Royal Copenhagen, Wallace, Yamazaki, china, crystal and flatware direct from warehouse to you by mail, save 25-50%, (800)-321-3212.

△ Here are a few **800 numbers** to check out prices of silver, china and crystal, advertised at "spectacular savings." Some carry jewelry and other lines as well. Catalogs available. Nat Schwartz & Co., 800-526-1440; Amos Silver Flatware, 800-22SILVER; Ross Simon (800) 556-7376; Sterling Silver Savers, 800-525-7319; Thurbers Discounted Major Brands, (800) 848-7237; Buschmeyer Exchange, (800) 626-4555.

△ China Finders, (800) 255-6868. All brands and patterns, current and discontinued, (800) 255-6868.

△ **Pottery Shack** in Laguna Beach, 1212 S. Coast Highway, Laguna Beach, (714) 494-1141. Take I-5 to Laguna Beach sign, about 75 miles up the road. Savings are enormous at this delightful seaside location, a landmark since 1936, a "must" if you're into dinnerware. Set the perfect table from the large selection of placemats, china, dinnerware, serving bowls, vases, silk flowers, sets of dishes and china, both fine and pottery. A four-quart giant clam-shaped ceramic serving bowl was $6.98 ($35 at gourmet shops), Oscar de la Renta lead crystal stemware was $9 for large water glass ($12.50 at Bullocks), and fantastic savings up to 50% on most name brand items, with a table or two of items marked down even more. A wonderful place to browse, then have lunch along the coast. Really loaded with inventory. Ask about their clearance section. I fell in love with this place years ago, and have returned many, many times.

△ I find some of my greatest treasures for the kitchen at yard sales including copper molds, unique serving dishes, cookbooks and decorator items. My kitchen looks like I'm a gourmet cook (which I am, in my *fantasy* life!) I bought a fabulous Wedgewood plate for $1 (seriously!) which is great for serving cookies or entertaining, punch bowls, a crystal champagne bucket I've wanted for years ($3), a white wrought iron stand to put it in (25¢!), a Cuisinart mini-grinder for $1 (value $35!), all sorts of things like rice cookers, deep fat fryers, hot trays, wine glasses, all at one tenth or less the original cost.

Discount Shopping Services

Δ Versatel Advantage Shopper offers the ultimate of convenience to its members: You can call for today's discount prices on more than 250,000 top quality, name brand items. Shopping consultants answer questions over their toll-free line, (800) 526-4848, seven days a week. Call to compare their prices to those you see advertised in newspapers or listed in catalogs. Prices quoted include sales tax and delivery charges directly to your home, from the supplier, with the lowest available discount price from their network of vendors throughout the U.S. Products include everything from audio/video to other electronics, appliances, dinnerware, computers, home furnishings, cars, cameras and accessories, sports equipment, luggage, power tools, gift items and more, all at a savings of 10–50% or more off manufacturers' suggested prices. Brand names from Amana to Zenith. The cost of the service is $49.95 per year, and you receive a free gift with your free 30-day trial period. You get a full refund if not completely satisfied.

Δ Prodigy, the new software "the PC was invented for" has a service that turns your computer into a personal shopper. Check airline schedules to find the lowest fares on over 300 airlines, order the latest music and videos from Sam Goodie delivered to your door, an online discount brokerage, discount travel club and more. Available at software stores, about $35, plus $12.95 monthly.

Discount & Off-Price Stores

Some of the nation's largest discount and off-price chain stores are here in San Diego, offering merchandise at lower prices than full-service retail stores. The discount chains are: Walmart, Kmart and Target and are priced competitively. A discount store is a no-frills, no service version of the old department store, with more merchandise. They buy in huge quantities from manufacturers, offering both name brands and their own brands of merchandise. Usually short on trendy clothing, but long on underwear, sportswear and casual apparel. Their loss leader ads in the Sunday *Union-Trib* are worth jumping out of bed for on Sunday mornings. Then, suit up and show up when the store opens because the advertised specials can go fast. If what you raced in for isn't on the shelf, ask the department manager for a "rain check," so you can pick it up later when it is restocked, at the *sale* price. See "rain checks" in chapter on Shopping Tips.

△ **Kmart**, 7655 Clairemont Mesa Boulevard, 279-26823; 5405 University Avenue, 286-9733; Spring Valley, Poway, Ramona, Chula Vista, El Cajon, San Ysidro, Escondido and Vista. Kmart, the nation's second largest retailer in the world, is a general merchandise discount superstore, selling quality goods at bargain prices, 20%-50% below regular retail. The stores are filled with name-brand goods in all departments. Name brand apparel includes Jacklyn Smith, Kathy Ireland, Maidenform, Diane Von Furstenberg, Sasson, Bill Blass, Gitano, Candies, Botany 500, Wrangler, Nike, Gloria Vanderbilt, Sunbeam, Black & Decker, GE, RCA, first quality merchandise at below retail prices. If you haven't been there in a while, you might be surprised. Blue Light special sales for limited periods of time.

△ **Target Stores**, a leading discounter, with several locations in San Diego including 3245 Sports Arena, 223-2491, Escondido, Oceanside, Encinitas, Kearny Mesa, Clairemont, a new 2-story building in Grossmont, El Cajon and Poway, National City and Chula Vista. Target has great advertised specials every Sunday in their supplement in the *Union-Trib* that are worth giving up your afternoon for. Housewares, great organizers, domestics, curtain rods that don't cost a fortune. Their garden department has good sales on house plants and flowers. Great place to buy a watch on sale (Timex, Casio, Gittano, Brittania, Gloria Vanderbuilt). Inexpensive telephone answering machines ($29). Many quality labels (Sanyo, Zenith, Sony, Panasonic, Hanes, Fruit of the Loom) and many made expressly for Target stores including Honors, Stanza. Every Wednesday, items are placed on end caps for clearance. Target offers credit, with 10% off when your card arrives.

Δ **Walmart**, the largest retailer in the world, guarantees they won't be undersold and is known for good customer service. Stores are in Poway, Santee, Aero Drive & I15, Otay, Oceanside and Vista, and more to come. There is an optical department, pharmacy, appliances, hardware (drawer pulls, too), footwear, bicycles, jewelry, and men's (McGregor, Manhattan, Wrestler, Wrangler,), women's (Brittania, Jordache, Bonjour, Beverly Hills, Vassarette) and children's clothing, and their own private store brands. Name brand electronics. Their loafers look like they are a much more expensive brand. There is only have one price marked on tags, so you don't know what things sell for at other stores, but they guarantee they won't be undersold. Leather purses, $15 (a great buy); T-shirts, $6.94; cotton slacks, $15; Bill Blass beautiful bras, $5.94; Playtex bras, $12.

The **off-price chains** in San Diego are: Marshall's, Mervyn's, Ross and T. J. Maxx. These stores buy overruns from factories and department store overstock. With sales down in department stores, more goods are being picked up by the off-price chains. You see current season fashions that are simultaneously in department stores, plus last season's fashions. The difference is: the department stores carry a wide selection of sizes and coordinates. We consumers benefit from the intense competition that exists between these off-price stores, which are particularly good resources for fashions, housewares, small electronics, appliances and 14 karat gold jewelry.

△ **Marshall's Department Stores**, Mission Valley, Mission Valley West, 260-0981; Solana Beach, 755-0791; Fletcher Pkwy, in El Cajon, 462-1530; Carmel Mountain Plaza, 451-2883; Marshall's on Nobil Dr. & I5, 587-3984; Chula Vista, 425-6006; Balboa & Genessee, 467-9330; Escondido, 480-1534; Carlsbad, 434-8900; Mira Mesa, 549-9060, Marshall's is the #1 off-price nationwide chain store (over 500 locations) offering mostly first-quality closeouts and leftovers plus special purchase merchandise. About 90% of their stock is "overbuys" (goods that are returned to the vendors by the stores because they over ordered). Marshall's motto is: "Name brands for less." They carry Evan-Picone, J.H. Collectibles, Carole Little, Chaps and more. Suits and sportswear for men, women and children. Silk-blend sweaters, fleece separates, men's dress slacks. Cookware, leather portfolios, leather bags, shoes and boots (9 West and Bandolino reduced 50%!). Overall savings throughout the store are 20% to 60%. Men's, women's and children's clothing, shoes, housewares, linens, gifts, lingerie and perfumes. They had a sale on down comforters for $49, a real steal (mine cost lots more!)

△ **Mervyn's**, with several stores throughout the county including 3345 Sports Arena Boulevard. Call (800) MERVYNS for store nearest you. Over 300 stores nationally, which means they buy in huge lots at discount prices, and pass the savings on to you. This is a great place to shop for advertised specials on name brands, including the same items that are sold in Express, Victoria Secret and the Limited. L. A. Gear, Reebok, Nike, Jockey. Excellent for children's clothing, name brand sports wear, linens, bedding and housewares. When you open an account at Mervyn's, you get a 10% discount on all your purchases that day.

△ **T. J. Maxx**, the number one major off-price retailer with 574 stores nationally and 5 stores in San Diego including Clairemont, 483-1286; Escondido, 746-9528; San Carlos, 460-4150; Pt. Loma, 224-2754; Encinitas, 942-1275. Save 20-60% off retail; name brands including separates of Jones New York, Guess, Calvin

Klein, Ralph Lauren, Liz Claiborne, DKNY, Ralph Lauren Polo. Men's, women's and children's clothing, home accessories, luggage, shoes, fragrance, jewelry, lingerie, hosiery, hair accessories. Two truckloads of merchandise arrive a week. Casual wear year round; cocktail wear arrives in the fall.

∆ **Ross** (Dress For Less) is one of the big top three off–price store with 275 stores nationally and 14 in San Diego: Sports Arena, 223-2453; Chula Vista, 420-1245; La Jolla Village Square, 450-1233; Oceanside, 439-4040; Clairemont, 292-7515; Escondido, 480-0307; La Mesa, 698-9222; Santee, 258-0301; Solana Beach, 259-2208; Carmel Mountain 451-9716; Rancho San Diego, 670-9869; Vista, 758-6992; and Mission Valley. Fashions for the men, women, and children, businesswear to active wear to clothes for going anywhere. Ross buy overruns and sells at 30-50% off. Many buyers, previously employed by Lord & Taylor and other major east coast stores, have great contacts, and they are able to get many current season things. High end fashions including Adrienne Vittidini coordinates, Jones of New York, Bali, Lizbeth, Liz Claiborne and their own labels. Five truckloads arrive each week. Markdowns every week. Bed and bath, home accents, luggage, shoes, fragrances. Seniors day every Tuesday, 10%, age 55.

Dry Cleaners

A friend called snorting mad because she put a few things in the cleaners and found out it would cost her $62. She insisted I find something for this book on dry cleaners. OK, so here it is. Check your *Penny Saver* (see chapter on *Resources)* for discount coupons good for all garments, no limit, no pre-pay (there is *usually* a coupon in every other week for your area). Wait a week if there isn't, or try Discount Cleaners & Laundry, 5237 El Cajon Boulevard, 582-3390, where every item of clothing is 99¢! Also, there are usually discount coupons for dry cleaning on the back of your supermarket receipts! Another suggestion is to take your clothes to Tijuana. Limpiaduras (cleaners) are everywhere. I took a suede jacket to TJ that they wanted an arm and a leg to clean up here. I was pleased with the great job they did. Also had it redyed for about half what I could have had it done for in San Diego.

△ There are no more "do–it–yourself" dry cleaners in California because of the problems they had with the gases catching on fire.

△ Be sure you *know* the fabric is dry cleanable because if it isn't, cleaning fluids can ruin it. Check your label first.``

△ Try some of the commercial spot removers available at the supermarket. Heloise, the helpful household lady, has several products on the market that do the job. Home Depot has a killer grease remover that *works*. It even takes chewing gum out of delicate fabrics like silk and carpeting.

△ A student in one of my bargain hunting workshops told me the fabulous outfit I had complimented her on was an unclaimed garment from her dry cleaners and that her entire wardrobe when she was a teenager came from dry cleaners because her parents owned one! Ask your dry cleaners when they sell unclaimed clothing, usually once or twice a year, sometimes for just the cost of cleaning. If your little cleaners says they don't sell them, call one that has lots of stores.

Fabric Stores

△ **Cutting Corners**, 5150 Convoy near the 52 freeway; 560–5831. A fabric discount supermarket and mill outlet with decorator fabrics for upholstery, draperies and specialties. Current fabrics, colors, styles. They do custom draperies and bedspreads. Ask to be put on the mailing list to receive advance notification of sales.

△ Jane's Fabrique, 7547 Girard Ave., La Jolla, 459–5828. Fine fabrics. Call and ask about sales.

△ **Sew & Save**, 9760 Campo Road, Spring Valley, 463–9770; knits, cottons, cotton poly, spandex at a discount.

△ **Calico Corners**, 4619 Convoy Street, Kearny Mesa, 292–1500. Decorative fabrics for the home. With 90 stores nationwide, their buying power can offer you good prices. About three sales a year.

△ **B & B Laces**, 117 E. Park Avenue, El Cajon, 440–4569, is a factory outlet with laces, ribbons, elastic, fabrics, rhinestones, satin roses, fringes, sequins, velvets, velcro, baskets and more. Good prices.

△ **UFO**, 1918 Roosevelt Avenue, National City, 477–9341, and 1120 N. Melrose Drive, Vista, 941–2345. Open Mon–Sat, 9–5:30 p.m.. UFO stands for Upholstery Fabric Outlet, with everything you need in the line of upholstery fabrics for home and auto. Foam rubber, too. No seconds, no closeouts, all first quality. Very few sales, but there is always a clearance table with markdowns. This is a huge place!

△ **Discount Fabrics**, 3325 Adams Avenue, Normal Heights, 280– 1791; 6,000 square feet of fabrics of all types and varieties for apparel and upholstery. When manufacturers make clothes and furniture, there is always about 10–12% fabric left over. This store sells the left overs at good prices, in season, because the clothing or furniture was made 6 months ahead of season.

△ **Fabric Villa**, 6364 El Cajon Boulevard, College Area, 286–4364. Imported, hand woven fabrics, Guatemalan cottons, cottons from India, Dashiki panels, batiks, African prints, silks. For clothing, pillows and curtains. They haven't had a sale in 20 years because their prices are right.

△ **Fabriholics**, 3205 Midway, Sports Arena Area, 221-1203. Over 2000 bolts of only 100% cotton at a discount.

△ Get on the mailing list for sales at House of Fabrics/Fabric King, 224-2331 and Beverly's 460-9511. Ask about a location near you. Frequent sales, 30-40% off and more.

△ There are several wholesale fabric, notions and millinery supply stores in the Los Angeles Garment District, including B. Black & Sons, 548 S. Los Angeles Street, with imported fabrics for men's and women's clothing, trimmings, shoulder pads, dress forms and more at below retail prices for the general public. Discounts given to teachers and classes.

△ Locate the decorating fabric you want in stores. Write down specific information including mill, color, design, fabric number; then call the toll-free number to see if you can buy it for less by mail. No California sales tax. Fabric Outlet: up to 60% below retail, 35 major brands, Waverly and Robert Allen Fabrics, (800) 635-9715; Marlene's Decorator Fabrics, (800) 992-7325; not toll free, *but*: The Fabric Center (Massachusetts), 508-343-4402 (save 50%).

△ If you are looking for *special* hard to find luxury fabrics that are not wholesale, there are many fabric stores listed in the AT&T 800 Directory that you can call toll-free.

Factory Outlet Malls

If you are not familiar with the terminology, a factory outlet is a retail store that is usually owned and operated by the manufacturer;

therefore, there is no middle–man markup. If you're in to fashions created by some of the most famous high end designers in the country, you'll be thrilled with the large number of factory outlets that have opened in the last few years in Southern California. There are over 300, located in malls that are removed from the center of town where they would compete with department stores.

A manufacturer may make several lines: high end, middle and low end, all under different names. Some of the low end may be copies of their own high end, created in different fabrics and sold under different labels. You may see first quality and goods with slight defects; irregulars should be well marked. Ask if you aren't sure what you are looking at.

Be aware that there are different types of outlets. The majority of outlets sell only products that they manufacture and sell to department stores or chains. Some sell several other designer's lines. Then there are stores that rent space in outlet malls that sell apparel exclusively in outlets! These lines are never seen in department stores or elsewhere. For example, Aileen fashions are found only in their own "outlets" and are not sold elsewhere. (This hardly represents a savings from the regular price in they aren't even sold elsewhere!)

Factory outlet prices range from 20–30% or more off, with clearance racks up to 90% off the normal retail price. Although a fairly new concept in San Diego, on the East Coast there are dozens of factory outlet shopping malls. People spend their vacations going from one factory outlet center to another all over the East Coast! The factory outlet mall in Gurnee Mills, Illinois, has over 220 stores!

Some say you can do just as well at department store sales and this is often true....if you want to wait for the sale to come around! Some factory outlets won't have all the styles that a department store has. But many have more styles because they carry the whole line which department stores usually don't. Some outlets sell things that are currently seen in department stores. Others only have things that are a few months behind (sometimes more). You never know what you might find, so call first and find out if they have a lot of inventory. Maybe they just got in a new shipment and are loaded with stock. Or, if they just had a big sale, the store might be half empty. Ask when they expect a shipment in.

Tips for factory outlet shopping: Read the list of outlets and what they carry. Make a list of the stores you want to visit and what you are looking for. Call ahead to find out if what you want is available. (They don't quote prices over the phone.) Ask if the ticketed price is the retail price found in stores, or the discounted price. Ask about return policies. Find out if they are loaded with stock or just had a sale down to the bear walls. When you get there, ask if an item is 1st quality, this season. And by all means, wear comfortable shoes and clothing as you'll probably be doing a lot of walking around.

San Diego has two factory outlet shopping malls: one in San Ysidro that has been around a few years and one that opened in San Marcos in late 1992. There are several other factory outlet malls with top designer stores in Southern California within a few hours driving time from San Diego that are definitely worth going to (also listed below). Telephone numbers are provided so you can call and find out if that Ann Klein outfit you saw in Neiman-Marcus or Bullock's is available for less at the Ann Klein outlet!

Δ San Diego Factory Outlet Center ...... **(619) 690-2999**
Near the border at 4498 Camino de la Plaza, San Ysidro. Take Interstate 5 South or Interstate 805 South to the last exit before the Mexican border, which is Camino de la Plaza. Go right on Camino de la Plaza one block to the factory outlet mall. Here's what is in their 33 stores. Several have closed; lots of new stores:

Δ Ashworth: golfwear for men and women's, 690-5000

Δ Banister: shoes for men and women, dress, casual, Easy Spirit, Bandolino, Cobby, Reeboks, Capizio, 428-2215

Δ Bass Shoe Factory Outlet: fashion footwear for the family, 690-6029.

Δ Carter's Baby Clothes: infants to girls 14, boys 7; 690-1106

Δ Christine's: Sweaters sold at Nordstrom Town Center, more, 428-2209.

Δ Designer Brands Accessories: precious and costume jewelry, handbags for women, 690-6339.

Δ Designer Labels For Less: Carole Little, Jones of New York, more, 690-6016

Δ Docker's: pants for men and boys, 428-1180

Δ Eddie Bauer: outdoor clothing for men and women, 428-7611

Δ El Portal: luggage, wallets, handbags, briefcases, some irregulars, 428-1181

Δ Famous Brands Housewares: Rubbermaid, Mirro, kitchen goodies, 690-0420

Δ Georgiou: career and casual clothing in natural fibers for women, 690-3116

Δ Guess, junior sportswear, 428-2234

Δ Guess Footwear: sandals, boots, loafers, etc., 662-3570

Δ Jockey: sportswear for men and women, undergarments for family, pantyhose, 662-1135

Δ Leather Loft: luggage, belts, briefcases, wallets, 690-5100

△ Levi's Factory Outlet: family fashions and accessories, 662-1244

△ Maidenform Factory Outlet: intimate apparel for women, 662-1244

△ Mikasa: dinnerware, flatware, giftware, crystal, 428-2022

△ Nike: athletic, apparel and accessories, shoes, 428-8849

△ OshKosh B'Gosh: infants to age 7, some adult, 690-2255

△ PFC Fragrance & Cosmetics: fragrance, cosmetics, 428-4421

△ Rocky Mountain: chocolates, candy, 690-6024

△ Socks Galore: sox, tights, hosiery for the family, 662-9112

△ Spectacular Eyewear: sunglasses, Raybans ($39 up), Killer Loops, Sunclouds, 662-1544

△ Toy Liquidators: name brand toys, Hasbpro, Mattel, Fischer-Price, 428-4826

△ Van Heusen: men's and women's apparel, 690-6028

△ Van's Shoes: walking, skating, tennis shoes, canvas shoes, found at department stores, Footlocker, 690-2725

△ Welcome Home: gifts and home accessories, 690-2944

△ San Diego/No. County Factory Outlet Center ... 595-5222
1050 Los Vallecitos Boulevard, San Marcos. Open Monday thru Thursday: 10 a.m.–7 p.m., Friday & Saturday: 10–8 p.m., Sunday, 11–6 p.m. From Interstate 5, go East on Freeway 78 to the San Marcos Boulevard exit. Left on San Marcos, left on Los Vallecitos and continue for approximately one mile to the center. The 25 stores are:

△ Adolfo II: ladies apparel, but not related to THE exclusive designer Adolfo, Raphael, only sold in factory outlets, 591-4128

△ Arrow Factory: Arrow men's dress, sport and knit shirts, sox, sweaters, pants, ties, 744-2884

△ Black & Decker: power tools, small appliances, reconditioned with 2 year warranties, can openers, coffeemakers, 471-5285.

△ Bon Worth: ladies, missy and plus size sportswear, children's wear, coordinating accessories, 591-3459

△ Book Warehouse: overstocks, hardbacks, paperbacks, fiction, children's, non-fiction, and software, 471-8828

△ Bugle Boy: women's, men's and kids' casual wear. Sold at Mervyn's, 471-9347

△ California Luggage: Samsonite, American Tourister, 578-4337

△ Capezio: fashionable shoes from Capezio, Evan Picone, Liz Claiborne, Bellini, Calvin Klein, more, 744-3599

△ Corning/Revere: tabletop ware, Corning Ware, Revere, Pyrex, Corelle, Visions, accessories, 471-6240

△ Designer Labels For Less: Current designers fashions including Carole Little, Jones of New York, Adolfo and Christian Dior, 471-9550

△ Diane Freis: top of the line designer women's wear up to 50% off, moved to Sedona, (520) 284 9690.

△ Discount Watch: Timex, Casio, more, 744-5983

△ Famous Brands Housewares: Rubbermaid, Intercraft, Ecko,

Libby, Nordic, Anchor Hocking, 744-8844

△ Famous Footwear: family shoes, Nike, Reebok, Keds, Naturalizer, 471-2750

△ Leather Loft: jackets, handbags, luggage, wallets, belts, 752-1925

△ L'eggs/Hanes/Bali hosiery, lingerie, socks, activewear, 736-9212

△ Paper Outlet: party goods, decorations, balloons, gift wrap, cards, wedding supplies, bows, ribbons, 471-4811

△ Perfumania: designer brand names including Liz Claiborne, Passion, Opium, Poison, Georgio, Red, 591-0320

△ SDI: designer resort fleecewear, 471-1043

△ Socks Galore & More: sox for the family, pantyhose, tights, more, 471-6286

△ Sunglass Outlet: Rayban, Suncloud, more, 736-9942

△ Toy Liquidators: Nintendo, Mattel, Playskool, 752-1418

△ Trend Club: fashions for women, sportswear, 471-7804

△ Welcome Home: traditional accessories and gifts for the home, 591-4258

△ Westport Ltd.: Famous label women's suits, dresses, sportswear, 471-2750

△ Westport Woman: Women's size 12-20+, 471-2750

△ **Factory Merchant Outlet Plaza** (Barstow) .   (619) 253-7342 2837 Lenwood Road, Barstow. One of the best factory outlet malls for women's fashions. Over 95 manufacturer's outlets including:

ALL AREA CODES ARE **619**:
△ Adolfo II: women's fashions, , 253-5661
△ Aileen: sportswear for all size women, 253-5599
B American Eagle, 253-3131

△ Anne Klein Outlet: Accessories and perfumes, , 253-5690
△ Banister Shoe Outlet: shoes for men and women, , 253-2850
△ Barbizon Lingerie; 253-2850
△ Bass: shoes, 253-2850

△ Big Dogs Sportswear: family's active sportswear, 253-3808

△ Black & Decker: tools, 253-5024

△ Book Warehouse: books for 50% and 90% off publisher's retail price, 253-5024

△ Boot Factory: 253-4940

△ Bruce Alan Bags;

△ Brooks Brothers: 253-5750

△ Bugle Boy Factory Outlet: Men's, women's and children's, 253-3436

△ Capezio Factory Direct, 253-3007

△ Casual Corner, 253-2900

△ Chorus Line, 253-4648

△ Corning/Revere: 253-2772

△ Danskin, 253-4000

△ Designer Brands Accessories: "1928" Jewelry, 253-5586

△ Donna Karan, 253-2330

△ Etienne Aigner, 253-2141

△ Florsheim, 253-3791

△ Guess, 253-2800

△ Hush Puppies, 253=5818

△ Izod-Ship'n Shore-Monet: family apparel, 253-5608

△ J Crew, 253-3113

△ John Henry and Friends: Men's and women's fashions, 253-2229

△ Johnston & Murphy: dress and casual shoes, accessories, 253-5920

△ Jones New York: women's better dresses & suits, 253-2544

△ Kitchen Collection, 253-2185

△ L'eggs/Hanes/Bali: hosiery, 253-2119

△ Leather Loft: luggage and accessories, 253-2288

△ Lenox Factory: dinnerware, 253-7668

△ Levi's Outlets by Most: family Levi's including lingerie, activewear, 253-5502

△ London Fog: Rain wear for men and women, 253-2113

△ Maidenform, 253-5057

△ Naturalizers: shoes, 253-4730

△ Nautica, 253-2020

△ Oneida Factory Store: dinnerware, 253-5400

△ Oshkosh B'Gosh: family sportswear, 253-5230

△ Paper Outlet: party good and office supplies, 253-5584

△ Polo/Ralph Loren: 253-5333

△ Ribbon Outlet: varieties of ribbons and trims, 253-3422

△ Royal Doulton Direct: dinnerware and giftware, 253-2161

△ Sergio Tacchini: family designer clothes and shoes, 253-3499

△ Socks Galore & More: 60,000 pairs of socks, 253-2818

△ Stride Rite, 253-4096

△ Swank: accessories and leather products, 253-3031

△ Toys Unlimited, 253-3420

△ Van Heusen: Men's and women's, 253-2710

△ Wallet Works: men's and women's wallets, 253-3402

△ Welcome Home: Interior decorating accessories, 253-2117

△ **Lake Elsinore Factory Outlets**, 17600 Collier Avenue, Lake Elsinore, CA 92330, (909) 245-4989. Lake Elsinore is considered to be one of the best factory outlet malls for fashions. Less than two hours from San Diego!! Take Interstate 15 North to Nichols Road. Left on Collier. Open 7 days a week, Monday to Saturday, 10-9 p.m.; Sunday 11-6 p.m.

△ Adolfo II: women's fashion, 674-6674

△ Aileen: women's clothing, and plus sizes, 674-9444

△ American Tourister: luggage, 674-0799

△ Barbizon, 245-2463

△ Big Dog Sportswear, 674-8414

△ Bruce Allen Bags: handbags, wallets, leather, 674-1167

△ Cape Isle Knitters: mainly sweaters, 245-0588

△ Capezio: shoes, 245-0042

△ Carter's: children's and infants, 674-1496

△ Chicago Cutlery: knives, cooking, 245-0503

△ Cole Haan: mainly women's, expensive shoes, 674-7164

△ Colours & Scents: cosmetics and fragrance, 674-2854

△ Corning/Revere: kitchen wear, 245-1302

△ Elizabeth, plus sizes, 674-0062

△ Etienne Aigner: purses, belts, accessories, 245-0047

△ Famous Brands: housewares, kitchen gadgets, 245-4078

△ Geoffrey Beene: designer men's and women's mostly casual wear, 245-4779

△ Harry & David, gourmet foods, gifts, 245-1347

△ He-ro Group: beaded gowns, cocktail wear, 674-5665

△ JH Collectibles: women's designer clothes, 674-0578

△ Jockey, 245-7671

△ Jones NY: women's designer clothes, 245-4699

△ Jordache, 674-7371

△ Koret: designer women's clothing and plus sizes, 245-2222

△ L'eggs/Hanes/Bali: lingerie, 674-3291

△ Leather Loft: wallets, briefcases, office supplies, some purses, 245-0877

△ Leslie Fay: women's designer, 245-0255

△ Levi's: jean and casual wear, 674-2694

△ Liz Claiborne: designer women's clothing, 674-1401

△ London Fog: rainwear for men and women, 245-0450

△ Maidenform: lingerie, 674-7335

△ Marika: weekend exercise wear, for women and girls, 245-5545

△ Mikasa: china and crystal, 674-7130

△ Nike: athletic shoes, 245-5665

△ Nordic Track, 674-1947

△ Oshkosh B"Gosh, kids, 245-9900

△ Olga: lingerie, sweepwear, 674-2833

∆ Oneida: flatwear and silver hollowware, 245-5445
∆ Perfumania: fragrances for men and women, 674-9288
∆ Publisher's Outlet: books, 674-6263
∆ Royal Doulton: fine china, 674-5884
∆ Socks Galore: sox and more sox, 245-1236
Shoe Pavilion, 674-7607

∆ Swank: men's and women's accessories and gifts, 674-1590∆
Toys Unlimited: 674-6170
∆ Van Heusen: men's and women's apparel, 674-1190
∆ Wallet Works: men and women's wallets, 245-4838
∆ Welcome Home: gifts and home accessories, 245-8900
∆ Welcome Home: interior decorating.

∆ **The Citadel** . . . . (213) 888-1220
5675 E. Telegraph Road, Commerce, CA 90040.   The Citadel has 44 stores in one location. Take Interstate 5 North to Atlantic Blvd. North, right on off-ramp, see center on the left.

ALL AREA CODED ARE 213:
∆ Adolfo II: Women's mid-line apparel, 888-1220
∆ Anne Taylor Clearance: up-scale, 725-7033
∆ A&Y Leather: handbags, no shoes, 728-2690
∆ Benatton: men and women's sweaters, etc.,721-3676
∆ Blue Wave: beach wear, 724-9877
∆ Book Warehouse, 722-7210
∆ B.U.M., 728-6080
∆ Capezio: different brands casual and dress shoes, 724-7723
∆ Corning/Revere: kitchen ware, 725-3155
∆ Designer Labels for Less: men and women, 887-887-9280

∆ Desre' Exotic Imports: women's clothing,
∆ Eddie Bauer: men and women's outdoor clothing, 725-1858
∆ Francine Browner: women's casual, medium priced, 888-1400
∆ Geoffrey Beene: 728-2070
∆ Joan & David: upscale women's shoes, some men's, 722-5844
∆ Kitchen Collection: appliances, kitchenware, 722-3272
∆ L. Bates: contemporary women's, 887-0224
∆ Leather Loft: no shoes, 721-0609
∆ Max Studios: women's upscale, 721-2200
∆ L'eggs/Hanes/Bali: hose, lingerie, workout wear, 724-8391

△ Linen Club: domestics, 721–2444

△ Nathan J Children's Wear, 725–1781

△ Paul Jardin: men's suits, 721–6400

△ Politix: sportswear for men, 887–1140

△ Prestige Fragrance & Cosmetics, 887–1135

△ Prime Time: watches and sunglasses, 724–1550

△ Sbicca Shoes California: women's shoes, 722–1228

△ Toy Liquidators: Fischer–Price, Milton Bradley, Mattel, 722–1998

Van's Shoes, 887–7802

△ Welcome Home: home accessories, gifts

△ **Desert Hills Factory Stores (Cabazon)** . . . (909) 849–6641
48650 Seminole Road, Cabazon, CA 92230, about two hours
from San Diego. Take Interstate 15 North to 215 North to 60
East to 10 East. Exit Field Road to the factory stores, 20
minutes West of Palm Springs.

ALL AREA CODES ARE **909**

△ Adolfo II: women's fashion, 9222104

△ Adrienne Vittadini: designer women's fashions, 922–2241

△ Aileen: sportswear for women of all sizes, 922–2254

△ Albert Nipon/Leslie Fay: designer women's fashions, 922–9250.

△ American Tourister: luggage, 849–1177

△ Anne Klein: designer women's clothing, 849–1114

△ Ann Klein Petites, 922–0733

△ A/X Armani, 922–2333

△ Bass Shoe: family shoes, 849–3788

△ B.C.B.G., 922–2615

△ Big Dog Sportswear, 922–1960

△ Book Warehouse, 849–5661

△ Bose, call info operator

△ Brooks Bros., 849–0072

△ B.U.M. Equipment, 849–7788

△ Barberry's, 922–2222

△ Cape Isle Knitters, 922–0966

△ Capezio Shoes: women's shoes, 849–0247

△ Carter's Childrenswear, 849–2300

△ Coach: premium leather purses luggage, belts, 849–0277

△ Colours & Scents: fragrances, 922–9204; Spa, 849–5480

△ Corning/Revere: kitchenware, 849–3665

△ Crabtree & Evelyn, housewares, 922–0696

△ Designer Brands Accessories: 1928 and other designer jewelry, 849-0216

△ Dockers, 849-0874

△ Donna Karan: DKNY and Donna Karan, 922-9862

△ Eddie Bauer: men's and women's casual fashions, 922-9202

△ Ellen Tracy Fashions, coming

△ Esprit: casual clothing women and children, & shoes, 922-2171

△ Etienne Aigner shoes, 849-1459

△ Famous Footwear: shoes and boots for family , 849-8649

△ Founders Club, home furnishings, 922-2166

△ Four Seasons Sunglasses, 922-1948

△ Full Size Fashions:: women's plus clothing, 849-6845

△ Geoffrey Beene: men's & women fashions 922-0066

△ Geoffrey Beene Mens: 849-4490

△ Genuine Kids, 922-1998

△ Guess?: men's and women's designer jeans and casualwear; children's, too, 849-1585

△ Harry & David, home furnishings, 849-7272

△ He-ro Group: designer Bob Mackie, Oleg Cassini, Bill Blass, 922-9400

△ Izod, 849-4335

△ J. Crew, 849-1411

△ Joan & David Shoes: designer shoes for women, 922-2237

△ Jockey, for the family, 849-2003

△ John Henry, Perry Ellis, 849-3521

△ Jones New York, 849-2099

△ Kitchen Collections, 922-2194

△ Leather Loft: luggage, purses, wallets , 849-0669

△ L'eggs/Hanes/Bali, 922-9393

△ Le Gourmet Chef, kitchen things, 922-0049

△ Lenox Factory Outlet, 849-8775

△ Levi's, 849-0125

△ Liz Claiborne, 849-2247

△ Maidenform: lingerie, 922-2266

△ Maternity Works, 922-0600

△ Max Studio, 922-0077

△ MCM, 849-6006

△ Mikasa, dinnerware, 922-0662

△ Movado, 849-0515

△ Music for a Song, 849-3281

△ Nautica, 922-0798

△ Nike: sport shoe store, some clothing for the family, 849-0466

△ Nine West, 849-6922

△ Oneida Silver: flatwear and halloware, 922-2200

△ Oshkosh B'Gosh: children's clothing, 849-3883

△ Paper Outlet: wrapping paper, stationary, cards, 849-4771

△ Pfaltzraff: stoneware, dishes, gifts, 922-9038

△ Robert Scott/Brooks Harvey: women's apparel, 849-0666

△ Rockport, 849-6799

△ Ribbon Outlet: ribbons and craft items , 922-2131
△ Royal Doulton: china and giftware, 849-4222
△ Sharif Collections, purses, 922-2621
△ Socks Galore: only sox
△ Sideout Sport, 922-2611
△ Spa Gear: men and women's resort wear from La Costa, 922-9600
△ Timberland, 922-0082
△ Tommy Hilfiger, 849-5848
△ Toy Liquidators: name brand toys , 849-8155△ Unissa, shoes, 922-0576

△ Van Heusen: men's and women's casual designer, dress shirts, 849-1299
△ VF Factory Outlet, 922-9668
△ Viceroy & Roch, 849-0047
△ Wallet Works: wallets, purses , 849-3925
△ Welcome Home: gifts and household accessories, 849-9511
△ West Point Pepperell: linens and towels, 849-0644
△ West Port Ltd. 922-1968
△ Windsor Shirt, 849-0856

△ **Plaza Continental** . . . . (909) 980-6231
3700 E. Inland Empire Boulevard, Ontario, CA 91764. This is one of the manufacturer's newest outlet malls in Southern California 20-75% savings. Take 15 North to 10 West to Haven Avenue, North on Haven and Right on Inland Empire Boulevard. About 5 minutes from the Ontario Airport. About a 2+ hour drive. Black Angus, El Torito, Spoons, Bittersweet Caffe on site.

ALL AREA CODES ARE **909**:
△ Adolfo II: women's clothing and accessories, 989-7752
△ Aileen: Women's apparel and accessories, 948-2207
△ Book Warehouse, 944-7645
△ Cape Isle Knitter: all hand knitted sweater, men and women, 945-1917
△ Converse: athletic shoes and apparel, 941-0164
△ Corning/Revere: household, 466-7901

△ Designer Labels for Less, 980-4486
△ Designer Labels for Men, 980-4486
△ Kitchen Collection: Rubbermaid, Hamilton Beach, Proctor Silex, 941-4808
△ Leather Loft: luggage, purses, wallets, belts, 466-6901
△ Muscatel Collection, 941-1409
△ Prestige Fragrance, 944-5881
△ Ribbon Outlet, 989-3950
△ Shoe Pavilion, 944-5881

△ **Los Angeles Garment District** in downtown Los Angeles. A 20 square block area in downtown Los Angeles with endless clothing, accessories, shoes and jewelry stores arranged around the capital of it all: the Cooper Building, 860 So. Los Angeles Street at 9th, (213) 622–1139. This 11–story building has over 35 jobbers and outlets carrying designers including the 860 Club (213) 627–3059 (which carries Carole Little and Saint Tropez West, Liz Claiborne, Esprit, Organically Grown, J.H. Collectibles, Chaus, St. Germain and more at 50% off retail.) I bought an $82 black crepe top at 860 Club for $21, and they had an outfit there I had just paid double for at a local department store.   Other stores include International Designers (489–7601) which carries Bloomingdale's overstock (all the designers!); **Paul Stanley Ltd.,** (213) 627–4536); Tabari, (213) 689–9121; I.D. for Women (large) famous designers, (213) 614–0992. Other stores have cosmetics, accessories, men's, large sizes, children's, cashmere, linens, shoes, lots of sequined cocktail dresses, luggage, sports wear including Reebok and Nike, European imports, and lots of thrift quality items. You can drive up in about two hours, or take a tour bus for about $29, Cunningham Tours, 292–5522; or Tour du Jour, 560–6545.

△ **California Mar**t,110 E 9th Street in downtown L.A., (213) 239–9200 The headquarters of major clothing manufacturers with over 1500 showrooms, each carrying at least 5 lines of designer wear on display. This is where the wholesale buyers come to do their shopping and ordering for their department stores around the country. The last Friday of the month, however, the show rooms are open to the *public* for sale! Samples plus discontinued items. Twice a month, they have big sales on Saturday. Mainly women's apparel; men's and children's, too; brand name apparel, jewelry and leather accessories. It gets crowded, but the exceptional buys make it all very much worthwhile. You oughta see this place! Call (800) 979–0949 for sale dates.

Food & Beverage

OK, so let's get down to the *really* important things in life: FOOD!! Yes, food *is* a major item in many household budgets, but there are so many ways to save money if want to. And, it's all so *fun!* The secret is to shop at a variety of *types* of stores and the bottom line is, you will save money! No longer are people going only to the supermarkets. The competition is fierce from the warehouse clubs (Price/Costco) and other food warehouses (Food For Less, Save U Food); the specialty stores like Boney's, Trader Joe and Barron's; and the farmers markets. Take advantage of shopping opportunities.

△ The **weekly grocery ads** from the *Union–Trib* Food Section are posted on Thursdays in the supermarkets, usually near the entrance. "Loss leader items" are intended to entice you into their store to do your weekly shopping, so take advantage of these excellent buys. Shop for the advertised specials at two or more stores for better savings. If an advertised item is not on the shelf, ask for a "rain check," which will allow you to buy the item at a later date when they are restocked, at the lower advertised price. If the store runs out and the ad did not say quantities were limited, the Federal Trade Commission says the grocer will give you a "rain check," or offer a comparable item, or some other equal compensation, *if you ask for it.* (And, there is so much competition out there, every store is willing to try to make you happy in order to have your business!!) For more information on "rain checks," contact the Federal Trade Commission, Enforcement Division, Washington, DC 20580.

△ Shop at **Lucky Stores, the "low price leader"** for several years according to studies done by CALPIRG, the California Public Interest Group. Lucky has lowered their already low prices, and you can now charge your purchases at Lucky on a Mastercard, Visa or Discovery credit cards. (If you have a credit card through an airline, you will get your frequent flyer miles, one for every dollar you spend on your credit card!!)

▵ Buy bulk at the **wholesale warehouses** like Price/Costco, Fedco, Food For Less and Smart & Final. Repackage into smaller sizes if necessary or trade with friends.

▵ **Smart & Final** at Midway and Rosecrans, 223-5381; 720 15th Street, downtown, 239-3377; 5195 Clairemont Mesa, 541-2090; 5245 El Cajon Boulevard, 286-0688; Escondido, 746-5490; National City, 477-4126; Lemon Grove, 668-0220; Mira Mesa, 689-6242; and El Cajon, 562-4151; Carlsbad, 434-5036; Chula Vista, 427-0202; Smart & Final is a warehouse-type operation that deals in bulk for businesses, clubs, organizations, you and me. No membership fee. A five pound bag of shredded pizza cheese, $5.99, a 6 lb/14oz can of fancy pork and beans, $2.99. Great for paper plates and party supplies, giant cans of nacho cheese and chili, cleaning supplies, frozen meats, restaurant quality cheesecakes, baking goodies, gourmet foods in holiday wrappings, much more. Cash-and-carry since 1871 throughout California and Las Vegas.

▵ **Price/Costco Club** (see General Merchandise Warehouses, this chapter, for locations) is a warehouse with about one-third or more of the floor space devoted to food and beverage, mainly in bulk. There's a fresh bakery with muffins to die for. You know the fabulous muffins that sell for $1.50 in muffin shops? They're $4.49 for a *dozen!!* You heard me right, $4.49 a dozen. I thought I was misreading the price. Not so! and you can get a personalized sheet cake that serves 30-48 people, $11.99-$14.99), fresh and frozen restaurant quality gourmet meats, stuffed salmon, bulk cheeses, frozen French Gourmet cheesecakes (whadda deal!), Naked Salads (my favorite), gourmet restaurant quality fresh produce (huge strawberries, apples, huge avocados that are *not* prepackaged), sodas, booze, canned and packaged goods in large sizes, paper goods at real savings (their large paper napkins make me a happy camper), and I wouldn't dream of leaving without a one pound jar of fresh grated Parmesan for about $3.69, a huge can of clams and a few magnums of their Cook's champagne under $5!! True, there aren't dozens of different brand names for a single item like jelly, there isn't every kind of soda known to man, and there isn't a variety of an assortment of sizes, but Price/Costco Club only buys what they can get the best buy on, which translates into a low price to you. Yes, you can match the price at supermarkets on some things, so, know thy prices and plan what to buy at Price/Costco.

Δ Use your **grocery coupons** at a double coupon store. Coupon manufacturers produce over 7.7 billion "cents–off coupons," more than 1,100 for every man, woman and child in the country. Coupon conscious consumers redeem over $4.5 billion a year with 7 out of 10 households cashing in on them. (I wish they would just lower the price of the products instead of spending millions on printing the coupons, buying newspaper space, paying the stores to process them, etc.) There are more benefits to using coupons than just financial: University researchers found that more than 7 out of 10 users felt a happiness, a boost of ego, personal satisfaction, and a feeling they are smart and savvy shoppers! So, there!

You've probably heard stories of shoppers leaving a supermarket with over $67 in groceries without paying a cent for them; how a woman in New York bought $80 in groceries, paying only 32¢ for them; how another New Yorker bought over $130 worth of food and groceries, for only $7.07; how a New Jersey housewife purchased $32 worth of groceries for only $3.00. Couponing is definitely in with the new mentality for a new century. Smart shoppers are cashing in.

Ralph's, Von's and Big Bear will **double coupons** with a value up to $1. A coupon for $1.50 off will be worth $2.50. Many shoppers never pay full fare for soap powder, pain remedies, beauty supplies and other non–food products.

Coupons are available every Sunday in the *Union–Trib* in the form of two or three supplements, and Thursday's *Union–Trib* Food Sections have coupons, too. Clip, organize and carry them with you in a traveler's check holder, available free from banks, using 3x5 card dividers to create categories. According to a survey by Frankel & Co. marketing services, 81% of grocery shoppers are using coupons, and 54% are sending in for refunds or rebates.

NOW HEAR THIS: Some people who are really into this couponing deal get trapped into a life of being chained to the kitchen, eating too may prepackaged products and gaining tons of weight. I met a woman who was apparently addicted to couponing. She had about 10 bankers boxes of them (I was absolutely aghast!), was about 375 pounds and was clearly off in another world that revolved only around her stove. Fresh seasonal special buys can cost far less than frozen, canned or pre–packaged and are infinitely healthier. Be careful not to fall into that trap. There are too many other ways to save money that won't hurt your health. (Try garage sale–ing. Now there's a healthy addiction!! Ask me if I'm into that one!!)

∆ Coupon trading clubs are frequently listed in the classified ads in the *Reader* under "Notices" or "Personals." Or, organize and advertise your own club. *Reader* classified ads are free! Put one in. Here are two coupon trading clubs that I found. One has been meeting for 18 years at Cully's Restaurant on Poway Road in Poway, on the first Monday of the month at 9 a.m. Another group met for 12 years at the same location until the woman who ran it recently passed away. They now meet at 4180 Bonita Road in Bonita on the third Thursday of the month at 9 a.m. There used to be about 15 to 20 people attending, but with all the controversy going on about refunding, it has dropped down. For further information, call 423-5181.

△ A caller on a radio talk show said that although she doesn't have a lot of money to give to the needy during the holidays, she saves the coupons in Sunday's newspaper during the months of October and November, takes them to the store with her teen-aged children and uses them to buy groceries for the less fortunate. She said she can get around $100 worth of groceries for about $25-$30 at a double coupon store, not straining her Christmas budget. And what a nice thing to do for others!

△ The **Refund Express** is a refund bulletin with 350 to 500 new refund offers each month, company toll-free numbers, contests, credits, exchanges, tips. Single issue, $2.50; one year, $21; Send to Refund Express, P. O. B. 10, Allen Park, MI 48101. Say that you were referred by John N. Skuden, Acct. No. 1233. He will get credit (and he gave me this info and deserves credit!). You've probably read or heard about a few people who have recently been sent to jail for sending in refunds totalling $35,000 and more to a single company. There is usually a limit of 1-3 refunds allowed. Read the find print. Also, send for sample newsletter from the Refundle Bundle, P. O. Box 140, Yonkers, NY 10710, $2.

△ **Refunding Makes Cents**, $21 yearly subscription, Box R, Farmington, UT 84025.

△ **Von's** and **Ralph's** have their own private electronic coupon clubs. Apply at the manager's office for a free card that entitles you to automatic discounts at the cash register on certain items throughout the store, in addition to any coupons you might bring in. A list of specially discounted items is available in the front of the store. It's fun to get a little cash off when you hit the supermarket. It all adds up.

∆ **Lucky** gives electronic coupons at the cash register for products or related products that you just purchased, to be used on your next visit. For example, when I bought Entenmann's non-fat chocolate cake the other day, I received a coupon for 50¢ off another non-fat baked good. When I bought Contadina tomatoes, I received a coupon for another can of the same.

∆ Go for the **drug store advertised specials** at Long's, Thrifty and Sav·On Drugs. They have unreal prices on their "loss leader" items: cat food, booze, canned foods, at a real steal.

∆ Shop at **farmers markets**. They have fresh produce at its lowest price. I went to the Farmers' Bazaar downtown in January when the prices of veggies were at their highest for the year, and was I ever pleasantly surprised to find: broccoli, 3 lbs. for $1 (89¢ a lb. at supermarkets); tomatoes, beautiful ripe tomatoes in January, mind you, for 39¢ ($1.99–2.49 in supermarkets); red potatoes, 4 lbs./$1 (55¢ in supermarkets); bell peppers, 5 lbs./$1 (99¢ a lb. in supermarkets). Some produce was very old looking and unappetizing and not everything was a steal, but there was certainly enough beautiful produce at bargain prices to have me raving with delight and returning time and again. Here are some farmers markets for you to try:

Farmers Bazaar, 8th & K Streets, downtown, 233-0281 (rehoused, replacing the one that burned in 1989) with 20,000 square feet of produce, meat, fish, honey, flowers and gifts, good prices.

Coronado Farmers Market, Old Ferry Landing, lst and B Streets, Tuesdays, 2:30–6 p.m.

Farmers Market at the Promenade, Mission Bay Drive and Pacific Beach Drive, in Pacific Beach, Saturday, 8 a.m.–noon.

Hazard Center Farmers Market, Frazee Road at Friars Road, has fruits and vegetables from 3–6:30 p.m. Wednesdays.

△ Mission Valley Shopping Center Farmers Market, Thursdays, 9–12:30 p.m.

△ **Ocean Beach Farmers Market**, Newport between Bacon and Cable, fruits, baked goods, vegetables, plants, fresh flowers, fish, more, Wednesdays, 3–7:00 p.m..

Del Mar Farmers Market, Camino Del Mar, at 10th, 1–4 p.m. Saturdays.

San Marcos Farmers Market, 1020 San Marcos Boulevard, noon–4 p.m., Saturdays

Escondido Farmers Market 3660 Sunset Dr., (across from No. County Fair), Wednesdays, 9–noon.

Farmers Market, in Encinitas, just off Interstate 5 and at the Manchester East exit, produce.

North County Farmers Market, across from North County Fair, 3660 Sunset Drive, Wednesdays, 10–1 p.m.

Vista Farmers Market Eucalyptus & Escondido Avenue. Saturday mornings, 8–11 a.m. Also, on Vista Way between Santa Fe and Citrus, Thursdays, 6–9 p.m. closed winters.

La Mesa Farmers Market, Allison St. east of Spring St. Fridays, 306 p.m.

Poway Farmers Market, Old Poway Park, Temple & Midland, Saturdays, 8–11 a.m.

Chula Vista Farmers Market 3rd Ave between E & F, Thursdays, 3:30–6 p.m.

Kensington Farmers Market El Cajon Blvd, & Marlboro, Sundays, 10 a.m. –2 p.m.

Carlsbad Farmers Market, Roosevelt between Carlsbad Village Dr. & Grand, Wednesdays, 3–6 p.m.

△ All swap meets have great fresh produce stands.

△ Most shopping malls have fruit and vegetable carts with premium fresh, gourmet produce at reasonable prices.

∆ Food For Less, large warehouse, bulk and regular. The difference here is that Food For Less charges less because there are no baggers. Hazard Center, 683–7760; Clairemont Mesa, 278–0681; University, 287–6501.

∆ Sav–U–Food, 46th & University, 584–7721 about 10 stores in the county. All off–brand names. Regular supermarket with no brand names!

∆ Better Independent Grocers (B.I.G.) has stores all over the county that go by independent store names. They buy together as a group and offer savings to you. They offer three triple coupons every week in their ads which are delivered to your home. Perfect for those who don't use a lot because it you save triple! Great produce sections, just like farmers market prices. Stumps (B.I.G.) on Voltaire in Ocean Beach is great.

∆ **Bakery thrift stores**, also known as *Day–Old Bakeries*, are a great find. When a bakery makes its daily delivery to a supermarket, they remove any bread that remains from the previous delivery plus certain cookies and cakes (which can stay on the shelf several days longer than bread because they contain sugar) and return it to their own "thrift" outlets to be sold at bargain prices. Items include bread, rolls, bagels, buns, cookies, pastries, croissants, and specialty and seasonal items including fruit cakes. Most stores also carry *"today's"* fresh–baked goods at a discount plus items with sugar that are going to expire soon. Day old bread and rolls are wonderful if you pop them in the microwave. Items are usually color coded for different discounts. Quantity purchases further discounted. Usually there is a special day when you get two–for–one or some other fun gimmick.

Try these thrift bakeries:
∆ **Weber Cake Co.**, 3355 Sandrock Road, of Aero Drive, Kearny Mesa/Serra Mesa, 571–0423; El Cajon, 448–0214; Lemon Grove,

460-1830; Chula Vista, 425-6800; Escondido, 745-6773. Breads and pastries including Roman Meal, Weber, Mrs. Cubbison's stuffing, croutons, Millbrook. Millbrook, better way, roman meal, $1.04 ($2.35 in store), Weber 1 lb. white, 38¢; Specials include three loaves of white or wheat bread for $1.34. Fresh and day old. Senior discounts; every Tuesday, 10% off.

△ **Entenmann-Orowheat Thrift Stores**, discounts of 30-45% off breads and pastries. Fresh products: 20% discount. Orowheat and Entenmann's pastries, muffins, chips, croutons, breadsticks, cookies, whole grain cereals. Day old Bohemian, 79¢; fresh Bohemian, 99¢. Senior discount: 10%. When they have extra stock, they give free bread with minimum purchase. Wednesday special: 1/2 off pies and cookies. Saturday is bread discount day with extra discount. There is always a 1/2 price table. Open 9-5:30 p.m. Monday-Friday; 9-5 p.m. Sat; closed Sundays. Seasonal goodies and other specials are available at 7051 Clairemont Mesa Blvd., San Diego, 277-6886, 465 C Street, Chula Vista, 427-5030; 1090 E. Washington Avenue, El Cajon, 442-3404; and 800 W. Grand Avenue, Escondido, 741-3773; 2023 Mission Blvd., Oceanside, 439-1765.

△ **Fornaca Bread Thrift Store** carries Bohemian Hearth breads, cookies, sweetrolls, donuts, and various store specials. Located at 2828 National Avenue, Logan Heights, 233-5908; 8926 Carlton Hills Boulevard, Santee, 449-2500;

△ **Royal Pie Thrift Store**, 937 E Street, San Diego, 233-6704, carries pies, donuts, breads, cookies, Oreos, peanut butter cookies, donuts. Day-old products are sold at a discount, and fresh products are wholesale. Lemon pies, $3.65 wholesale (sell for $6 at supermarkets). With a purchase of $3, you get a free 1/2 dozen donuts free; purchase of $5, you get a dozen free.

△ **Wonder–Hostess**, 3510 College Blvd,, Oceanside, 631–0866; 1626 Sweetwater Rd., 477–8230; 2400 8th Avenue, National City, 267–8343. Hostess cupcake, Twinkies, muffins, snowballs, cakes, cookies, Swiss ice cream, Frito Lay Chips, cokes, cereals. Fresh and day old at a reduced price!

△ **See's Candies** has a retail *quantity* shop at 3751 Rosecrans Street in Point Loma, 291–6086. There are substantial savings on the purchase of one or more pounds of pre–packaged candy (a $9.90 pound box goes for $6.80) *if* you are an employee of a government agency, corporations, school district, bank or hospital or a member of any group that has purchased a minimum of 50 pounds per year. You can call to see if your employer or organization has qualified). Or, if you or an organization you belong to buys 50 pounds, you will qualify for the reduced price. Sees candy is never marked down. Still a deal: 3 candy sticks for 10¢ (great for Halloween).

△ **Thrifty Drugs** still has the biggest (and best) ice cream cone for the price: 69¢ a scoop, and the chocolate brownie is do die for. One–half gallons range from $1.99–$2.99 and there are 75¢ discount coupons in their flyer every few weeks. Smart and Final (above) has bulk ice cream for parties in three gallon drums, $14. Also, Baskin Robbins has "2 for 1" coupons in the *Entertainment* coupon book.

△ Most **Mrs. Field's** and **Blue Chip cookie stores** mark down their remaining cookies about an hour before closing, sometimes "two for one," sometimes less. Also, check at any bakery to see if they reduce prices on leftovers at the end of the day, usually an hour before closing.

△ **Bageliscious** donates their leftovers at the end of the day to Love's Gifts, who takes them downtown to the homeless. (If you know of an establishment that disposes of food at the end of the day, ask them to donate it instead to Love's Gifts, 581–3663.

Love's Gifts is a non–profit organization that picks up food for the homeless, for hospices, senior centers and the needy. They have an annual Mardi Gras fundraiser in February to help continue their effort and to purchase more trucks.)

△ I was at **Soup Plantation** one night about an hour before closing. A waiter approached us, gave us plastic bags and said we could go back to the fresh bread bar and help ourselves all the muffins, pizza, etc. that was left!   If they have a lot left over, they offer it to their patrons. Check about this policy at other soup bars, all–you–can–eat restaurants, etc. The way you ask may be the secret!!

△ Ask the meat manager of your supermarket if and when they usually mark down what's left. I have found by asking several employees at the same store that I get different answers, so bear with this one. :Wee don't have any left over. Beef is turned into hamburger." etc.   A woman told me she buys all her steaks 1/2 price when they mark them down at **Ralph's**. Check with the meat manager on this.

△ **Trader Joe's**, La Jolla Village Square Shopping Center, 546–8629; 1211 Garnet Avenue, Pacific Beach, 272–7235; Oceanside, 433–9994; Carmel Mountain, 673–0526; La Mesa 466–5998; Encinitas, 634–2114; Hillcrest (1/96); (over 20 locations in Southern California). Trader Joe's is a food and spirits store for the gourmet bargain hunter, with an emphasis on cheese, nuts, chocolates, imported items and gourmet foods at amazingly low prices. If you're not on the mailing list, give them a call, and you will be. The wine and beer list is superb, with their own brand as well as others. Walnuts $1.99 (value $2.99 up), Jack cheese $1.99 lb, Gouda $2.59 (value $4.99), Kahlua's Black Russian Cocktail 99¢ (value $2.49), Culbertson's Champagne $8.99 (value $14).

△ **Boney's Marketplace** specializes in lots of great bargain priced fresh vegetables, plus vitamins, nuts, tofu, bulk fruits and nuts in barrels, sunflower and other specialty breads and natural foods at great prices. Their 12 locations include 1260 Garnet, Pacific Beach, 270-8200; 6091 University, College area, 582-4343; 734 University, Hillcrest, 295-4569; 3332 Sandrock, Serra Mesa, 565-1714; 152 N. Second, El Cajon, 579-8251; Chula Vista, 476-1032; and Vista, 758-7175; 4630 Palm Avenue, La Mesa, 460-7722; UTC, 3358 Governor, 457-5006; Poway, 13536 Poway Rd., 486-7851; Escondido, 510 W. 13th Avenue, 745-2141; North Park, 4175 Park Blvd., 291-8287. Wednesday they honor both this week's ads and next week's (great day to shop).

Δ **Barron's Marketplace**, a specialty food store with good prices on eggs, fresh deli, wines, cheeses, nuts, coffees. Pt. Loma, 223-4397; La Mesa, 697-7063; Del Mar 481-2323; Encinitas, 942-9881.

Δ **Grocery Store**, located at 316 N. Horne, Oceanside, 722-5552; and 660 L at Broadway, Chula Vista, 422-2995; discontinued items, overstocked inventory, generic and name brand, small appliances, pots, pans, picture frames, household, beauty goods, paper goods, frozen foods, juices, pre-packaged deli products, dog food, garbage bags, condiments, cereal, pet food, household cleaners, wines, beers, spices and candy at 25-40% discount. Avoid cans that are damaged on the seams as they can make you ill.

Δ **S.H.A.R.E. (Self-Help-And-Resource-Exchange) Program** is a nationwide grass-roots community building organization begun in San Diego in 1983. It fit distributes $30-35 worth of grocery store food for$14 per package because SHARE buys in huge volume. There is a small paid staff and a large corps of volunteers who package and distribute approximately 20,000 packages of food throughout Southern California every month. The food package varies in content depending on seasonal buys, but a package typically contains about 30 pounds of wholesome food, including

6–10 lbs of meats, 7–10 fresh fruits and vegetables and 3–5 staple items such as rice, beans, pasta or cereal. (Meat free packages, same price.) There are no qualifications to receive the food, but you must complete two hours of volunteer service in addition to paying the $14, which can be completed by helping on distribution day. No limit to the number of packages you can buy. Distributed one day a month at 325 locations. Call 525-2210 for a location near you; register and pay, usually by the second Monday of the month.

△ You can bring back most groceries and food products from **Tijuana** with these restrictions: only beef (no other meat), lobster (four per person), most vegetables, some fruits (bananas, blackberries, dates, grapes, melons, pineapples, strawberries), nuts. (No potatoes, no avocados, no meat other than beef, no eggs, no citrus fruit.)

△ **Gevalia Kaffe** offers a free 4–cup ($29) value coffee pot when you join. For $10 you get a pound of gourmet coffee and the coffee pot. You can cancel your membership any time. Their gourmet coffee is one of the very best on the market. Many flavors. If you get someone else to join, you get two free mugs, so please say Sally Gary, Member #558-235-941 and tell them where you saw this listing. Say I told you to join, 'cause I love their mugs (coffee pot, and other stuff). They always send you lots of free samples, coffee filters, etc. as a bonus. Call (800) 438-2542.

△ Free cooking classes (See Classes).

Liquor and Wine
△ Here's how to get the best prices on booze for your next party. Compare prices at the following: Long's, Thrifty and SavOn Drugs liquor departments; supermarket specials; Price/Costco; Trader Joe's; and you can bring back one liter from Tijuana every 30 days.

The best prices are offered the last couple months of the year during the holidays, with lots of rebates. Cases are usually 10% off.

Drinking Water

△ **Bottled water** costs almost as much as gasoline! Pick up a few good quality two-gallon jugs at Von's and fill them for 25¢ a gallon at the water vending machines at supermarkets, usually located outside the entrance. What a *find!* Refill station of Pure Flo Water, 7737 Mission Gorge, 448-5120, sells five gallons for $1.

Flowers & Plants

The region's fresh cut flowers, flowers to plant, house and outdoor plants are so fabulous to have at home and the prices are very low compared to other areas of the country. North County has the most equable climate in the nation and is a prolific producer of flowers that are sold locally and shipped to the East. In addition to the many roadside flower stands, here are some places to pick up a good buy:

△ **Swap meets** are a great place to pick up fresh flowers for just a few dollars. Go early for the best selection as they'll be pretty well picked over later in the day. Negotiate a discount on quantities. If you have a special occasion coming up, you can place an order to be delivered, picked up at the vendor's or arrange to have them brought to the swap meet the following week. People special order tons of flowers for weddings, parties, etc. Gather a few vendor's business cards when you go to the swap meet and keep them on file for your special occasions.

△ Mixed bouquets and roses are available at the **Price/Costco**. Big bouquets for little bucks. Prices vary with season.

∆ **Wilson's Wedding Flowers,** 698–2863. Kathy Wilson does wedding and party flowers from her home. She purchases, designs and delivers customized floral arrangements throughout the county for less than many floral shops. She guarantees personal service because she books only one wedding per day.

∆ Hire a horticulture student to do a landscaping project for you. Call Cuyamaca College and ask for the horticulture department, and tell them what you want.

∆ You can bring back cut flowers from **Tijuana** but *no* plants with *soil*; many people buy flowers for parties and weddings there. You can get small bud roses for $2 per dozen at street stands. Remember, you can negotiate the price for quantities and arrange for large orders, too.

∆ **Evergreen Nursery** has great prices on indoor and outdoor plants. I like Home Depot and Target for potting flowers and houseplants.

∆ **Floral supply stores** have an incredible array of vases, baskets, ribbons, florist paper and seasonal decorations to put in floral arrangements. They sell retail to the public, wholesale to dealers. I was amazed at all the things they had at Growers Wholesale Florist, 1228 Knoxville, near Tecolote and Morena Boulevard, 278–4872. Check the *Yellow Pages* under "Florists' Supplies."

∆ I get some of my "best" pots and plants at yard sales. People who move out of state don't want to pay for moving them! Also, check the *Union–Trib* "Thrifties #780" classified ads for plants for sale. You frequently find both large outdoor varieties and small houseplants. I have seen all kinds of things advertised here. And, I advertised four huge Bird of Paradise plants and a large King palm for one dollar that I wanted removed from my yard. There were a lot of "takers." I waited til the rainy season when the ground is soft and easier to dig. The "taker" dug them out! Otherwise, I would have donated them to Balboa Park.

Formal Wear

Men have always been able to rent their tuxedos and formal wear, and now, women can **rent gala ball gowns** and short beaded and sequined cocktail wear, too. Here are a few places to check out:

△ **A Nite on the Town**, 8650 Genesee Avenue, UTC, 457–1233, rentals $65–$275;

△ **Dress To Impress**, 4242 Camino del Rio North, Suite 6, 528–9797, rental fee $35–$150 includes beaded bags, shoes and jewelry.

△ **My Magnin**, 4976 Cass Street, Pacific Beach, 483–2244, rental fee: $40–$125+

△ Men can purchase **tuxedos** at *real* good prices from tuxedo rental shops when they clear out their old models and buy new ones. Call around and ask when they plan a sale.

△ Men's tuxedos ($15) at the **Rancho Santa Fe Garden Club Rummage Sale**, 756–1554.

△ For formal bridal wear, see "Weddings," this chapter.

Frames

I like unique, old frames that I get at yard sales, estate sales, antique stores and second hand furniture stores. Matting and framing can be shockingly expensive, so get several price quotes by phone before you commit. Some framers charge an arm and a leg; some do only the finest and most expensive framing. Sales are worth waiting for.

△ **Aaron Brothers Art Mart**, 2790 Midway, San Diego; 4150 Convoy, Kearny Mesa, 8827 Villa La Jolla Dr.; 8396 Alvarado Road, La Mesa; 2550 Vista Way, Oceanside; 16771 Bernardo Center Drive. Several sales a year, some 1¢ sales with purchase, clearance sales.   If you need inexpensive plain frames, you can do better pricewise, elsewhere. Read on.

△ **Picture Frame Factory Outlet**, 1375 N. Cuyamaca, El Cajon, 449-6098; ready-made and custom. Wide selection; warehouse.

△ **Frame Gallery**, 305 3rd Avenue, Chula Vista, 422-1700.

△ You can do very well on inexpensive plastic, wood and metal frames at Pic'n'Sav, Everything's $1, the 99¢ Store on Newport in Ocean Beach, Target, Canned Food Stores, and when they are on sale at Thrifty, Long's and SavOn drugstores.

△ Michael's craft stores have sales every couple months on custom frames, up to 50% off. Ready-made frames, too. Ask when the next one is coming up.

△ **Tijuana** is a great place to get frames. Look in shops along the *tourista* area on Revolucion. A friend had frames made for $11 including glass, stretching and backing at Bernardo's on 5th (towards San Diego) at Revolucion. They would have cost her $25 each for the frame alone in San Diego. I've bought several frames at a nice, large frame shop on the side street across from the Jai Lai Palace.

Furniture

If you're in the market for new furniture, pick up a copy of a newspaper on weekends to see who's having *big* sales. Every Saturday and Sunday, stores like Jerome's, the Sofa Factory, Krause's, The Leather Factory, Lawrence, Levitz, Plummer's, V. J. Lloyd, Wards, Broadway, V. J. Lloyd's and others advertise their sales. Furniture stores advertise on weekends to lure in the shoppers, they hold semi–annual, annual, anniversary and clearance sales. There's always a sale, so shop around for a few weeks for that major purchase and you'll see how much you can save. There is a 200–300% or more markup on furniture suggested retail prices, so you can see why there are so many "sales." See if this works for you: ask if there are any floor models, returns, discontinued, clearance or damaged items. Don't forget that department stores are competitive, and some offer an 10% additional discount if you open an account (Broadway does, and if you buy/open an account on a weekend when there is a 10% discount coupon in the newspaper, you will get 20% off!), and some stores offer 90 day deferred billing. Check out the following:

△ **Arnold's Clearance Center**, 163 & Balboa, 277–9788, has discontinued lines and floor samples, the same quality furniture they have in their three other regular showrooms, including Thomasville. Lots of inventory, with $99 bar stools going for $19, $199 up queen sized headboards marked at $49, lamps and accessories marked up to 70% off, Italian leather sofas starting at $499. Many of the things in the store I had just seen priced higher at their other two locations. There is a–once–a–year sale with half-off the reduced prices every March. Mark your calendar for this one.

△ **V. J. Lloyd Clearance Center**, 4275 El Cajon Blvd., 281–6661. Above the Drexel/Heritage building. Quality furniture at 50%–

80% off mfg. sug. retail; $6000 bedroom set, $1700; Hancock & Moore leather sofas, retail $4500, $1499. In business since 1947.

△ **Sears Outlet Store**, Marketplace at the Grove, Hwy. 94 and College, 583–9802; Encinitas, 942–6021. An entire store that carries only furniture (and major appliances) which are overstock, surplus, discontinued, returned or damaged.

△ The **J. C. Penney Furniture Outlet Store** is located at 741 Broadway, Chula Vista, 422–4486. Frequent 30% off sales on recliners, sofas, dining tables, already marked down merchandise. Example: Regular price, $399, sales price $239, additional 30%: $71, and you pay $167!

△ Wacky Wicker, 4411 Mercury St., 541–2242. Name brand wicker furniture. Good deals on **wicker** can be found at Cost Plus, 4th & J, downtown, 236–1737; La Jolla, 455–8210. Also at Pier One. In you're really into wicker, try these catalogs: Bielecky Brothers, 306 East 61st Street, NY, NY 10021, (212) 753–2355; The Ralph Lauren Home Collection, 1185 Avenue of the Americas, NY, NY; Hickory Chair Company, (Division of Lane Co.), P. O. Box 2147, Hickory, NC 28603 (704) 328–1801.

△ There are a lot of vendors at the **swap meets** that sell new furniture, futons, sofas, lamps, etc., every weekend.

△ **The Broadway** has a Furniture Clearance Department in Panorama Mall in Panorama City, (818)–893–7811, with discontinued, damaged, customer cancellations, sofas, TV cabinets, library unit, china cabinets, etc. The whole third floor is clearance: electronics, furniture, clothing, everything.

△ e' klek tik, 7450 la Jolla Blvd., 454–1770, hand carved chairs, 30 styles, exquisite finishes, custom iron tables, lighting, mirrors, 50% below retail, 6 days a week, closed Mondays.

△ **Price/Costco** has a limited amount of brand name furniture at great prices. They also have a catalog service called "Quest." You can view and order a limited amount of discount furniture from their computerized catalogs in the store.

△ Inexpensive stylish furniture (mainly formica over pressboard, but some real wood, too) is available at Target, Kmart, Pier One, Cost Plus, Home Depot.

△ **Model home furniture** from condominiums and new home tracts is advertised in the "Furniture & Accessories #815" section of the *Union–Trib* classified ads. Also, check out Model Home Furniture, Morena Boulevard, 274–4090.

△ **Catalog furnishings stores** are usually fairly small because they carry very few pieces of furniture; however, they have hundreds of catalog sources for you to select your furniture from, sample of fabrics, plus sample displays of Levelors, drapes, shutters, carpeting, wallpaper and items for the whole house and patio. Major brands, 10–70% off. Occasional floor sample sales. Check out: Shand Home Furnishings Showroom, 525–3071; Al Davis, 1601 University, Hillcrest, 296–1221.

△ **Wholesale–by–mail furniture**: Here's how to buy furniture by mail. First, locate the item you want at a department or furniture store and **write down** the make, style, model number, color, fabric, and other identifying characteristics. Then call **one of the following toll free lines to see if you can get a better deal from the manufacturer or a broker who handles several manufacturers.** They will give you a price quote, an estimated freight charge base d on weight, and approximate delivery date. There is no sales tax, which and offset some if not all of the freight. It may take 10–12 week for delivery (but it can took that long when I ordered a sofa in Mission Valley!):. Here are some of the bigger furniture manufacturer's brokers: Cherry Hill Interiors offers savings up to

50% off the usual showroom prices. Name brands like Martinsville, Brown Jordan, Classic Leather, Design Institute of America, Leathercraft, Sealy, Simmonds, Lane. Office furniture, too. Stiffel, Wildwood and other lamps and accessories. Call (800) 328-0933 for quotes or free brochure. **Loftin Black,** since 1948, offers a free color brochure of major name brands, over 200 lines of furniture, phone quotes, (800) 334-7398. Barnes & Barnes Fine Furniture offers formal pieces, patio furniture, office furniture, clocks, mirrors, lamps, price quotes by phone, (800) 334-8174.

△ **EdgarB**, the largest discount mail-order furniture operation in the country, has sales totaling $16 million a year. Their catalog, filled with pricey furniture aimed at the upscale market, has furniture discounted 40-45% by manufacturers such as Broyhill, Henredon, Century, Drexel, Heritage and Baker. "I wanted to sell furniture to the same people buying Porsches and Jaguars," said Broyhill. An average shipment takes about 15 days from North Carolina. Inquire about their $25 catalog with 300+ pages of color photographs and prices (over 200,000 have been ordered). Call (800) 225-6589.

△ High Point, North Carolina, is the furniture manufacturing capital of the world! Within a 20 mile radius, over 300 brands are manufactured which can be shipped back. For further information, contact the High Point Convention & Visitors Bureau, POBox 2773, High Point, NC 27261.

△ European Furniture Importers, (800) 283-1955.

△ **IKEA Scandinavian furniture warehouse**, Tustin, (714) 838-4000

Used Furniture:
When you walk out the door of a new furniture store, half the value walks out with you. Used furniture is a good investment.

△ Check the "Thrifties #780" and "Garage Sales #707" in the classified ad column in the *Union–Trib* for used furniture. Check the *Reader* classifieds, too. You'll be surprised what is there! Call and ask about the condition, how old it is, etc. You can negotiate the price, too, as it is sometimes difficult to sell things through the classified ads since not everyone is aware of this marketplace.

△ Your best deals on furniture will be found at yard sales. People are moving, getting divorced, getting remarried and have two sets of everything, and you can pick up things for a song. Better neighborhoods often have better quality and aren't trying to raise money; they are just getting rid of stuff, cheap.

△ **Karen's Consignment Gallery**, 4051 Voltaire, Ocean Beach, 225–8585, is a 3300 square foot store with a variety of used furniture and household items ranging from antique to contemporary and simple to exquisite. All furniture is there on consignment which translates to good prices because Karen doesn't have to pay for her inventory until it sells. There is a lot of stock to buy from, and new items arrive daily. You can take your excess furniture, mirrors, lamps and do–dads in and sell them. Karen advertises a lot and gets good traffic in the store, so things move fast. You'll receive 60% of the agreed upon selling price and the shop gets 40%. Prices are reduced 10% if the item doesn't sell in 30 days. I buy and sell lots of things at Karen's. Say hello to Karen for me!

△ **Two Sisters Consignment Home Furnishing**, 616 Stevens Avenue, Solana Beach, 755–4558. Large store of home furnishings in near–perfect condition at comfortable prices. Consignments arriving daily.

△ **Marianne's Consignment Shop**, 1130 Camino Del Mar, Del Mar, 792–8550. Great things for the home: antiques, quality used furniture, unusual and unique decorator items. Charming store.

⌂ **Hunter's Consignment**, 2602 Adams Ave., San Diego, 295–1994. Classic furniture, new and used furnishings.

⌂ **Coastal Consignment**, Hwy. 101 between lst & H, Encinitas, 943–1199.

⌂ Cruise thrift stores like Salvation Army, Goodwill, etc. Everyone has a good story to tell about the big score they made on a valuable piece of furniture for a song at a thrift store!!

⌂ **Hotel & Motel Furniture Liquidators**, 3310 Via de la Valle, Oceanside, 433–1954. They buy and sell hotel furnishings from remodels and sell at good prices. A friend bought several down and feather pillows (4 for $10) and made a huge, puffy quilt like Maria Von Trapp had in the "Sound of Music."

⌂ **Fashion Furniture Rental** Clearance Center, 8990 Miramar Road, 549–0100, for the sales of their used rental furniture.

⌂ **32nd Street Flea Market**, 3803–9 32nd Street, North Park, 280–3444. Over 22 years, reasonably priced, new shipments every week. No consignment. Used furniture, collectibles, half antiques. Some new. Large selection. Closed Mondays.

⌂ For more used furniture, check the *Yellow Pages* under "Furniture, Used."

⌂ You can take **upholstery and refinishing classes** through adult education. *See Chapter on Classes.*

⌂ Here's a good one: **free furniture** on trash day (now we'll see who the snobs are!) A student from one of my bargain hunting classes who lives in Ocean Beach said that she has gotten a number of items for her apartment (great things, too) that people are getting rid of. O.B. is a very transient area with many people moving in and out. People either don't want to take things with them or don't have room for something they brought with them. Not everything you find is going to be in great condition, but I am saying keep looking because you'll find items that *are* in good condition. They're out there. If you don't see them, it's because someone else already saw them (and took them!) So, if you want free furniture, drive around beach areas or high density apartment areas (like in U.T.C. and Friar's Village where yuppies are on the move) the evening before trash collection when people are home and putting things out to dispose of them. Anything that is placed at a curb is being disposed of. If you don't feel comfortable with taking something that isn't yours, then go knock on the door and ask if they are getting rid of whatever it is and would they mind if you took it. My brother who lived in New York for several years had a magnificent old mahogany fireplace mantel in his apartment. When I asked him where he got this beautiful item, he said it was *in the street*, being thrown away by someone who lived in the same apartments! He said people are always carrying off things from the street, that it is a way of life in New York, and that you could furnish the world with all the furniture that you find there! A flight attendant in San Francisco says the thing she likes best about living there is trash day! She sets her alarm for 4 a.m. to see what's been put out in the trash. She raves about antiques and odds and ends she has picked up this way!

Δ There are some terrific books at **Home Depot** on the magic of paint, and the abracadabra you can perform on furniture to create faux finishes, glazing, graining, stenciling, marbling, lacquering, etc. Videos, too.

Garage/Moving/Estate Sales

San Diego is really a hot area for garage and estate sales. Let's face it, if you go to enough of them, you'll eventually find everything. Literally everything. I've been to sales in the most prestigious areas of the county. It's amazing how many well off people will put out that sign. Maybe not so many older people (it can be a lot of work!), but the aging baby boomers are right out there every weekend, selling off their excess. It's not enough to just drive around and stop at a sale here and there. The people who are totally into this (and it is addictive!) check "Garage Sales #707" in the classified ads of the *Union–Trib (or* the *Reader*, the Pennysaver and in your neighborhood newspaper). I've been converted from a night person to a morning person because of "weekend boutiquing" as we call it! Go to the better areas of town (La Jolla!) where people are just getting rid of things rather than trying to raise money. You'll find quality items in good condition. At a home that was in the $800,000 price range, I saw a brand new looking beige mohair sofa for $50; two king–sized bedroom sets with several pieces of furniture for $125; a fabulous antique bar for $20 that I wanted so badly but don't have a place for; a huge curved screen TV for $100; enormous framed prints for $10; rattan chair for $4, rattan end table, $1; old wooden wall clock $7 which I bought; a junior bed, $25 including mattress, etc. Get organized and go early because there is a regular crowd of garage sale prowlers plus professionals who resell who are sitting in cars waiting outside long before the sales begin at 7 or 8 a.m. every Saturday.   They know what they are doing.   I buy things at "weekend boutiques" for the home, my kids and friends and their kids and friends, everybody. This is a good place to try to negotiate the price if there isn't a lot of competition. Sometimes a person needs to get rid of something *today* and is in a position to make you a fantastic deal. You can have absolutely everything if you do this long enough. I wish I had known about this when my kids were young because I've seen every toy, every sporting good, every–everything. It's great entertainment.

If you're going to have a yard sale, here's some advice: advertise it, post signs at major cross streets, get everything out of boxes and price all your items (unmarked items don't sell as fast as marked ones; prices should be 10%–50% of retail value), begin early on a Saturday (Sunday sales get less people), start when you say you're starting (not before), holiday weekends don't get as many people as regular weekends, and get your neighbors to join in with you. The more, the merrier.

General Merchandise Warehouses

Sales at general merchandise warehouses in the U.S. are booming. We don't have Sam's Warehouse on the west coast. **Price/Costco** is the giant in California. Some people think it is "dangerous" to shop at a membership warehouse because you spend too much when you go. These people are in their own way when it comes to being practical. Trust me, you will save many times over the membership cost: ($35 a year), and even though my family has shrunk, it is very much to my advantage to belong. The key here, of course, is self-control. If you tend to over-indulge, make your list up and stick to it. Then only take a certain amount of cash. *There* is your self-control! Easy! A membership warehouse is one of the best money savers there is in San Diego, so don't fool yourself into thinking you're saving money by not shopping at one. You would be spending more elsewhere and you would be missing out on too much.

Δ **Price/Costco**, the largest in terms of sales (nearly $14 billion), has several locations including 4605 Morena Boulevard, 270–7601; 5651 Copley Dr., San Diego, 292–3232; 650 Gateway Dr., 266–1031; 1755 Hacienda, Vista, 631–7255; 725 Center Dr, San Marcos, 480–6611; 101 Town Center Pkwy, Santee, 491–1728; 951 Palomar Airport Road, Carlsbad; 429–0963; 1144 Broadway, Chula Vista, 427–6614; 895 East H St. Chula Vista, 656–0826; 12350 Carmel Mountain Road, Carmel Mountain, 675–0379 plus stores in Temecula, El Centro, Tijuana and Mexicali. This is a membership club warehouse ($35 for 2 cards), but you will save the price of your membership on your first shopping spree. Even if you're single, or if you shop only once or twice there during the year, you will more than make up for your membership fee, especially if you make a major purchase of a TV or other appliance. The average price is wholesale plus less than 10%, compared with regular retailers who average about a 100% markup, and discounters who mark up between 30–60%. Price/Costco carries only first line top name brands. To qualify for membership, you must own a business, be a member of a credit union (you can join most credit unions with a $5 deposit!), a Federal, State or local government employee, teacher, plus several other categories. You can shop at the store without a membership card, pick up a one-day pass and pay an additional 5% fee. Drop by and see if it's for you. I find fantastic savings here. It's a warehouse with over one-third groceries, many items in bulk packages or with several taped together, or in restaurant sizes, so you have to know how to deal with quantities. Some people arrange to share with a neighbor on a regular basis, or repackage things to your needs. There is a fresh bakery with a dozen muffins for $4.49(!) and personalized sheet cakes can be ordered from $11.99–$14.99 that feed 30–48 people! There are fresh and frozen gourmet meats, giant gourmet fruits and vegetables. Price/Costco has a limited selection of major appliances. Other departments include: small appliances, T.V.s, stereos, automotive, optical, pharmacy, photo, outdoor furniture, barbecues, housewares, garden, office supplies, computers, phones and a tire center some real savings here. Name brand apparel include (not always, of course, because they purchase only the *best* buys available) Jones of New York, Jordache, Leslie Fay, Evan Picone, Diane Von Furstenburg, Gloria Vanderbilt, Ashley Morgan, Palmetto, Ralph Lauren, Ideas, Guess. Men's labels include Pierre Cardin, Pacific Beach, Christian Dior and Members Only with ultra suede and raw silk sportcoats. You can even buy cars through their discount car-buying program. Quest is their computerized catalog from which you can order furniture, china, jewelry, silver, fragrances, etc. Know your prices; not every item is a steal. I wouldn't dream of leaving without a magnum of champagne in a very attractive bottle for under $5 and a trip through the sportswear department for a new sweatshirt.

Green Resources

Δ The **Green Store**, 4827-A Voltaire, Ocean Beach, 225-1083. Recycled paper, T-shirts, bumper stickers and information on local, national and global environmental and peace issues and organizations, alternative press magazines, catalogs for environmentally safe products.

Δ **Seventh Generation**, products for a healthy planet. Free catalog, (800) 456-1177.

Home Improvement, Tools & Hardware

Δ **Home Depot**, 3555 Sports Arena Blvd, 224-9200 (and several other locations throughout San Diego) has become one of my favorite haunts. It's a fantastic warehouse of everything you need for the home from hardware, tools and paint, to kitchen cabinets, lighting, furniture, carpets, plants and flowers. Their everyday prices are excellent, and they have their own credit card. I ask my kids for gift certificates from Home Depot for Christmas! (My, how my priorities have changed! This is definitely one of those things Mother *didn't* tell me about!) Home Depot's Expo Design Center, 7803 Othello near Balboa & Convoy, 569-9600 is the Rolls Royce of home improvement stores. They've got it all. Home Base has good prices, too. San Diego Hardware, 840 5th, in downtown San Diego, 232-7123. is over 100 years old, has all the things you can't find at Home Depot or Home Base and will order anything for you from thousands of sources. It's a great place to get that missing widget, gadget or unusual brass hardware.

△ **Black & Decker**, North County Factory Outlet Center, 1050 Los Vallecitos Boulevard, San Marcos, 471-5285. Discontinued, blemished and reconditioned power tools, coffee makers, table saws, kitchen gadgets, irons, housewares and accessories, all with 2 year new warranties. Some new appliances in damaged boxes.

△ Check the classified ads in the *Union–Trib* under **"#780 Thrifties" and "#780 Tools, Lumber & Building Supplies"** and you'll find great bargains. You can pick up doors, bricks, shutters, cabinets and everything else that's left over from projects completed. Also check "#707 Garage Sales" and "#700 Auctions." Don't pass up the *Reader* classifieds, too.

△ Great buys on building supplies are available at the El Cajon swap meet where you can pick up everything: **surplus bricks, lumber, fixtures, etc.** at the very best prices in town. I have a friend who goes there almost every Sunday who bought a $2,000 bronze chandelier for $35, all the windows for his home, etc., etc. Eat your heart out.

△ **Used Building Materials**: Building Materials Recycling, 8467 Datson Rd, Otay Mesa, 661-8155; Escondido Sakes Yard, 1428 W. Mission, Escondido, 747-3332; K Surplus, 1403 Cleveland Ave., National City, 474-6177; Ralph's Used Building Materials, 1444 Island Ave., downtown, 232-2633; Roger's Supply Co., 8714 Cuyamaca, Santee, 448-1200.

△ **Antique Building Materials**, 2266 San Diego Avenue, Old Town, 233-1144. Mantels, beveled glass, light fixtures, doors. Auctions.

△ Before you have home repairs or improvements done, call the local office of the State Contractor License Board, (619) 455-0237, for a copy of their 32-page publication, *What You Should Know Before You Hire a Contractor*. Get three to ten bids, asking for references. Be sure to ask if your contractor is licensed. Unlicensed contractors may not have the skills necessary to do the job if they have not passed state tests. (However, if a repair is under $300, then the contractor doesn't need a license, according the call I just finished making to the above number.) In any case, check with the Better Business Bureau, 496–2131, to see if there have been any complaints against the contractor. California law limits down payments on repairs to 10% or $1,000, whichever is lower, so don't be fooled into paying more up front! For real savings, think in terms of specialization: hire individual contractors to get the job done (someone who specializes in wall board, wiring, plumbing, etc.), and save by not hiring a general contractor, who will always cost more. Of course, the whole thing requires nerves of steel, and everyone has their nightmares to report, so the best advice I can toss your way is to get references from satisfied customers. You can't beat that.

△ If problems arise, the job does not get done, or it doesn't get done satisfactorily or timely, contact the local State Contractor's License Board and the Better Business Bureau at the numbers above. Also, you can sue in Small Claims Court for amounts up to $5,000, 687–2180. Information is available at the Court to assist you in filing your claim.

△ *How To Get It Built (Better–Faster–For Less)*, by La Jolla architect Werner R. Hashagen, 6th printing, 240 pages, everyone's guide through the construction process and a frank inside report from the files of an architect, $22. Call 459–0122 for ordering information.

△ *How to Hire A Home Improvement Contractor Without Getting Chiseled* by Tom Philbin (can be ordered at book stores if not in stock) says you should make no down payment, pay only for completed work, and hold out 10 to 20% of the fee until 30 days after the job is completed to ensure the contractor will return to fix any problems. According to Tom, if the contractor doesn't pay the supplier, the supplier can get a lien against your property, even though you paid the contractor, so make out a two-party check or make separate checks.

△ For inexpensive yard work and some home repairs, use college and high school kids. Call the student placement office of a school near you. Or, call a senior center.

△ **Free classes** are offered at the San Diego Community Colleges Continuing Education on plumbing, heating, air conditioning, landscape construction, and more. Call 221-6973 for information on the nearest class to you.

△ Household Repair/Maintenance, **free class**, lots of women in this one, Clairemont Adult School, over 15 years, 627-2405.

△ **Mexican tiles:** good prices at the factory in Tecate, about an hour from here. The factory is near Rancho La Puerta Spa, a few minutes down the road that goes from Tecate to Tijuana. You'll see the tiles stacked in piles on the right side of the road. Be sure you know your prices in the U.S., and prepare to bargain to get a good price down there. There are loads of ceramic and unglazed tile stores in Tijuana, too.

△ *San Diego Home & Garden Magazine* is filled with ideas: unique hardware, contractors, how-to's, etc. *Sunset Magazine* is great for ideas but *San Diego Home & Garden* has specific local resources for getting the job done.

△ *Sunset Magazine*'s free catalog of publications: "how-to" books on carpentry, fireplaces, children's projects, bookshelves, bathrooms, gardens, lighting and dozens more titles for Southern California living at its best, (800) 321-0372.

Information for Sale

You've seen those ads telling you to send $10+ to receive information on how to get a government loan to start up a business, how to buy VA foreclosures, how to buy seized government property. Don't do it! Don't be a sucker. What you will get is a page of information retyped from a government publication or just a government address to write to for the information. You can get that information *free* in any library. Ask for government publications.

Insurance

ᐃ **Direct Insurance Services**, (800) 622–3699, will give three free price comparisons from the country's most financially sound life insurance companies; long term health care. For auto insurance, see "Automobiles," this chapter. To get the best deals on any insurance, always check six to 10 sources. They won't all be the same. Many companies offer a 10% discount if you carry more than one type of policy with them (auto + household, etc.)

Jewelry

Never–never–never–never–never pay full price for jewelry. Since the markup on jewelry is often from 200–500%, you can understand why there are so many 50% off sales!! If you fall in love with a piece that isn't on sale, you can certainly negotiate the price. Otherwise, wait for sales or buy from a wholesaler, like Sid Allen's diamond wholesale downtown.

ᐃ **Sid Allen Jeweler**, 501 W. Broadway, Suite 250 in the Koll Center downtown, 232-8666. Gold, diamonds, pearls, onyx and others. Specializing in ideal cuts and premium cut diamonds, large selection of wedding bands and engagement rings for about 50% off retail price with documented appraisal.

▵ Jewelry sales at major department stores feature diamonds, gold and other fine jewelry, 25–50%–70% off. Anniversary and holiday sales can be anticipated, so if you can put off your purchase til then, you're better off. Ask a sales associate when the next sale is. Ask to be placed on the mailing list and you will receive advance sales information. Saks Fifth Avenue has a once a year fine jewelry sale the first two weeks of August, 25% off. Some other department stores offer 10% off on first day purchases. Worth looking into.

▵ **Mervyn's** has a 50% sale about once every month or so, and a 60% off sale a few times a year on Super Weekends. A New York professional jeweler told me Mervyn's carries quality jewelry.

▵ If you're going to buy diamonds, you need to know a little bit about quality, points, and color, which any jeweler can provide you, or check with your librarian or local book store.

▵ **Imposters**, 110 Horton Plaza, 233–6733, and 5500 Grossmont Center, 464–1800. With 100 stores through the U.S., Imposters specializes in copies of Cartier and Tiffany and other fine jewelry. Some gold, mainly gold vermeil. They have a look–alike of a Cartier ring ($8,500) for $65; a Cartier necklace ($10,500) for $75. A Tiffany–lookalike diamond bracelet made in X's, $95. Lots of large, fashionable fake jewels, etc.

▵ **Pawn Shops** have interesting one–of–a–kind jewelry, and judging from what I've seen, some very wealthy ladies sell their very expensive jewelry to pawn brokers! This could be lucky for you. Ask for the manager and negotiate the price. You're dealing with a pro but with perseverance and a little luck, you can do some very good negotiating here. See *Yellow Pages* for listings.

∆ **Jewelry Center**, 861 6th, downtown. A whole building with lots of jewelers. This should keep you busy for a while.

∆ There are over 300 fine jewelers in the **International Jewelry District** (near the Garment District) in Los Angeles that sell to the public at below retail costs (some say the best prices on the West Coast). Not all sell to the public, buy many do in the St. Vincent Jewelry Center, 650 S. Hill Street, (213) 629–2124. Jewelry to fit any budget from shoestring to plush bucks. Ready made, custom design, restoration, repair. For information on the California Jewelry Mart, 607 S. Hill Street, (213) 627–2831, 200 showrooms, some exclusively wholesale.

∆ **Treasures**, 9550 Waples Street, Suite 120, (Mira Mesa), 458–0871. A factory outlet, all work done on the premises. Earrings from $5.90–$25 up that retail at major department stores around the country from $50. Huge selection.

∆ If you're into natural or ethnic jewelry, there are wonderful buys at the swap meets, Cost Plus and Pier One. I like the natural jewelry at the gift shops at the Museum of Man and the Museum of Natural History in Balboa Park, and at The Galleria (very pricey) at Bazaar Del Mundo in Old Town. I pick up a lot of interesting pieces at garage and estate sales, too.

∆ I go to the gem, jewelry and mineral shows at the Scottish Rites, Del Mar Fairgrounds and the convention centers when they are in town. I'm on the mailing list now for several shows a year. For more information call the Scottish Rites, Fairgrounds, convention centers or contact the **San Diego Lapidary Society**, 295–6905.

Leather & Luggage

△ **California Luggage Exchange**, 9242 Miramar Road, Miramar, 578-4337. Major brand–name luggage and business cases (Samsonite, Tumi, Hartman, Andiamo, Travel Pro, Lark), on board, rollers, at discounts. Good selection. Guarantee lowest prices.

△ I have bought **briefcases** at great prices at Office Depot, department store 1/2 price sales, the swap meet, and at yard/moving sales (which have, of course, the best prices!)

△ **Leather Loft**, San Diego Factory Outlet Center, 4498 Camino de la Plaza San Ysidro, 690–5100, San Marcos Factory Outlet Mall, 752–1925. Luggage, briefcases, wallets, organizers, portfolios, belts, jackets. Jackets, bombers, utility jackets. Long dusters were 50% off (clearance). Some items on clearance table. Most items are 10–50% off retail price; Private labels. Kenneth Cole carried in Nordstrom.

△ People pick up a lot of leather goods in Tijuana. If you know your prices and quality, you're better off.

For more luggage, see "Factory Outlets," this chapter (American Tourister and Coach).

Linens

I do very well at department store sales on linens, sheets, down comforters and towels. I like quality linens but never pay full price for them! Here are a few stores where you don't have to wait for sales:

△ **Stroud's Linens**, Midway and Rosecrans; 8867 Villa La Jolla Drive, La Jolla 457-0525; 8410 Center Drive, Grossmont Center, 697-2678; 2570 Vista Way, Oceanside, 967-0303; Escondido 745-2468. Stroud's Linen Warehouse has stacks of linens, imported and domestic for every room in your house at savings of 10%-60%. Included are sheets, towels, tablecloths, and comforters in a rainbow of colors. They stock first quality products at terrific savings. White goose down comforter, Cal King, $99 (retail $300); Springmaid bedspread, Cal King $39.99 (originally $110); 60x120 oblong tablecloth $23.99 (was $64); Martex 100% pima cotton towels, $9.99 (value $20). Custom window treatments.

△ **Pic'n'Sav** has some fine quality name brand linens mixed in with thrift quality. Very good prices, $50 comforters for $19.

△ **Domestications**, a free 90+ page catalog of linens for the home, beautiful bedding, good decorating ideas, (800) 782-7722.

Membership Department Store

△ **Fedco**, membership department store, 1100 National Avenue, National City, 474-9111; 1475 East Valley Parkway, Escondido, 740-0100. Fedco is located only in Southern California, with two local stores. They have an optical, pharmacy, bakery, major appliances (Maytag washer, $499), furniture, small appliances, housewares, jewelry and watches, food and mid-priced and inexpensive but stylish fashions for the family (great for teenagers: T-shirts with shoulder pads, $5.99), plus a few high-end items like leather pants and suede jackets. There is also a new car buying service. "The Fedco Reporter" is their publication of sale items in effect for two weeks. Bay scallops, $3.98/lb., 1/4 pan of corn bread, 99¢; 3 lobsters for $9 (1/2 lb. each). Conair cordless telephone, $29.97; 10 pk. of plastic hangers, 79¢. Of course, not everything is a bargain, but their sales items were good to excellent. Know thy prices! The general public can join for $10 for 5 years. There is a $10 lifetime membership available for: Federal, state and local employees, certain credit union members, social security and disability recipients, military, veterans, school employees, full time students, alumni members, hospital employees, banks and other company employees.

Men's Clothing

△ **American Fashion Inc. Factory Outlet**, 642 Arizona Street, Chula Vista, 426–1212. Call first because they are only open a few days a week. Save 40–70% off regular retail on thousands of pairs of slacks, $39.95 (were $75), 100% cashmere, camel hair and ultra–suede sport coats, $125–150 (were $350–450). Wholesale plus 10% to the public. Two big sales a year with greater savings. Get on the mailing list.

△ The **Men's Wearhouse**, Loma Square, 222–6301 and locations in Mira Mesa Mall, Escondido, Clairemont, 569–9896, and El Cajon, carries top quality designer fashions at 20–30% less than department stores; every day. Big and tall sizes, also. Big sale after Christmas with many mark down, including tuxes.

△ **Men's Fashion Depot**, 3730 Sports Arena Blvd, (Sports Arena area), 222–9570; The Men's Fashion Depot buys designer suits that are sold in major department stores directly from the manufacturer. They are discounted about 40%, with suits priced from $69–$240 and sport coats from $59–$109; silk ties, $3 for $25/value $15+. Tuxedos, $109; tux shirts, 2/$30 ($27 elsewhere). Name brands; some labels have been removed because the manufacturer doesn't want the identity known to protect the department stores. Suits that sell here for $230 are $400 at department stores.

△ **Nordstrom Rack** in Fashion Valley West, 824 Camino Del Rio N., 296–0143, has a good selection of marked down men's clothing from the Nordstrom main stores, including pure wool suits ($169–

289), sport shirts ($14–19), special purchase silk ties, $9.97, sweaters, slacks, sport coats, shoes, etc. And, the Rack has frequent sales with further markdowns.

∆ There is a General Store at the **Veteran's Hospital** in the back of the first floor that anyone can use. Men's jean, dress pants, $15.

∆ San Diego Factory Outlet Shopping Mall, 4498 Camino del la Plaza, San Ysidro, has a **Van Heusen Factory Store**, 690–6028, with quality current season men's apparel at 30–60% discounts; **Eddie Bauer**, 428–7611, outdoor outfitters for men and women with down jackets, quality casual clothing at prices reduced to 40–70%. To order a free catalog, call (800) 426–6253. **Levi's Factory Outlet**, 662–1244, with jeans, jackets, shirts for men (women and children, too). **Dockers Outlet**: Dockers labels pants, shorts, shirts, 428–1180. **Ashworth Outlet**: discount golf wear, 690–5000. **Jockey Outlet**: sportswear, undergarments, 662–1135.

∆ San Marcos Factory Outlets, 1050 Los Vallecitos, San Marcos, has **Arrow Factory Store**, 744–2884, with Arrow dress shirts, sport and knit shirts, socks, sweaters, pants, ties and more;

∆ **Price/Costco** carries a limited number of great buys. Designers have included Jack Nicklaus short sleeve knit shirts, $10.50; Bill Blass knits, $14, Options 100% silk sport coat, $60; J.G. Chappel wool blazer, $99. You won't find these regularly, but you will find the best quality designer they are able to get a good deal from.

∆ **Polo Ralph Lauren**, 7th Street and Madero, (Tijuana), 011–52–66–85–13–89. Within walking distance to the border is a Ralph Lauren store which carries a number of polo shirts, turtlenecks, Oxford shirts, sweaters, pants, suits, sport coats at 20–50% off. Everything is made in Mexico City but they have the license from Ralph Lauren in New York. Also, there is a Polo factory outlet in the Barstow Factory Outlet Mall. See"FactoryOutlets," this chapter.

△ **Men's Christian Dior shoes**, $29, Lapiel, Avenida Revolucion 728, Tijuana, 011-52-66-85-8526.

△ **Leather Loft**, San Diego Factory Outlet Center, 4498 Camino de la Plaza San Ysidro, 690-5100, San Marcos Factory Outlet Mall, 752-1925. Belts, jackets, bombers, utility jackets. Some items on clearance table. Most items are 10-50% off retail price; Private labels. Kenneth Cole carried in Nordstrom.

△ Watch for the big sales at Bullock's (Pre-Season sale in August), Nordstrom (half yearly sale in June) and other department stores, and you can call to get on the mailing list to be notified of forth-coming sales. Open an account and you are automatically advised of future sales. Broadway and some other stores give 10% off on everything you purchase the first day you open an account. So, go to your closet and make separate lists (include colors) of each of the following: all your sport coats, all your suits, all your slacks, all your shirts and all your ties. Make a list of what you need to complete and/or update your wardrobe. Then, wait for Broadway's next big men's sale (or call and ask about it). Take in any items you don't have coordinating clothing to wear with and a sales associate will match them up for you. You'll get 10% off everything you buy (even if on sale) for opening your account and they frequently have a 10% off coupon in the newspaper. You can use that, too!! Even if you go over the limit they give you on the first day, they still give you the 10% off.

△ The **Four Season's International Tailors of Hong Kong** visit San Diego on a regular basis. They measure you, then send you your custom suits selected from an array of wools, silks, cash-meres, blends, tweeds, camel hair, etc. To find out when their next visit is, write to Four Seasons International, TST, P.O.Box 96166, Kowloon, Hong Kong. Recommend a friend and you get a free shirt. Mention my name when you write and I'll get a free ladies' shirt/blouse!!

∆ For more men's clothing, including spa and workout gear, see:

"Gen. Merch. Warehouses"   "Formal Wear"
"Clearance Stores"   "Resale/Consignment"
"Discount/Off–PriceStores"   "Factory Outlets" this chapter.

Office Equipment/Supplies/Furniture/Stationery

∆ The **Office Depot**, 909 Morena Boulevard, 297–2582; 8255 Camino Santa Fe, Miramar, 558–2222; 8481 Fletcher Parkway, La Mesa, 464–2900; Chula Vista, 427–2582 and 476–9101; downtown, 238–4991; Escondido, 739–5555; Kearny Mesa, 569–9971; Oceanside, 439–0712; Santee, 596–2582; Vista, 631–2870.; With 480 stores nationally, Office Depot has big buying power. Bought Eastman stationer. A complete line of discount office supplies, good selection of computers, software, all kinds of equipment, furniture and printing (business cards, stationary, forms, and copying). Free delivery on orders over $50. Red Tag mark downs on floor models, discontinued items, bangs and dings. Will install computers, software. Anyone can fill out form to join the VIP Club and receive catalogs in the mail with coupons for $10 off a $50 purchase; $20 off a $100 purchase. Great place. Guarantees "We'll beat their price."

∆ Staples, 3337 Rosecrans, Sports Arena; 4240 Kearny Mesa Rd., Kearny Mesa; Escondido, 1256 Auto Plus Park Way. Very similar to Office Depot. Everything you need under one roof. Copying: 100 copies of one original, 2¢ each.

∆ **Price/Costco** has great buys on computers, typewriters, office supplies and equipment (see General Merchandise Warehouses).

∆ Check the "Used Office Furniture and Equipment" classified ads in the *Union–Trib*." A lot of offices have closed so you have a lots to choose from. I picked up a great wrap–around desk and chair for a song. Also, see "Auctions" in the classified ads for used office equipment sold by the government and by liquidators.

△ **Shore Office Furniture**, 241 National City Boulevard, National City, 474–6488; 5670 El Camino Boulevard, Carlsbad, 431–0898; large supply of new and used desks, etc.

△ **PS Business Interiors** has used office furniture in a large warehouse at 2233 Pacific Highway, Ste. D, (800) 870–4772.

△ **Gypsy Office Supply**, 3409 30th Street, North Park, 295–1553 and 8828 Cuyamaca, Santee, 562–2220. This place has purchased a lot of crates of partially damaged goods and sells them for a fraction of the retail price. You can't get everything here, but almost. Lots of paper, pens, staplers, files, stickers and the gamut of office supplies, new, used, some slightly damaged boxes, some not. The Santee store has used office furniture, too.

△ **Currents Factory Outlet**, 173 Fletcher Parkway, El Cajon, 440–4292; 1054 W. Valley Parkway, Escondido, 738–7181; stationery (& gifts), greeting cards are always 49¢; first quality paper items at factory outlet prices.

△ Look under "Paper Supply" in the *Yellow Pages* for good prices on stationery, envelopes, color paper, invitations. I like Kelly's Paper.

△ A lot of the department stores including Nordstrom, Charlotte Russe, and more, have occasional sales of mannequins, fixtures, etc. Fun for unique decorating. Call and ask when their next sale is.

Paint

Δ If you can use them, you can't beat the price on "OOPS" paints at Home Depot. "Oops" paints have been custom-blended for a customer and for whatever reason, the customer didn't want the paint, so they marked it down to about 1/2 price or less. If the color is right, you can cash in on the savings. There's everything from pints and quarts of gloss to five-gallon drums of interior and exterior paints. Their regular paints are at good prices, too. Prices are even better for larger cans.

Δ There is a paint sale at all paint stores just before every major holiday when people have time off to paint. Why pay $22 a gallon for paint if you can get it on sale for $14? There is a holiday in almost every calendar month, so keep a look out for the sales.

Δ Better paints are usually a better buy because cheaper paints drip, fade, don't cover as well, require more coats, don't last as long and don't wash up well. And, remember Murphy's Law: Any paint will adhere permanently to any surface if applied accidentally! (Unfortunately.)

Party Supplies

Δ **Party Savers**, 3609 Midway Drive, San Diego, 224-7300 and 5120 Baltimore Drive, La Mesa, 589-6767 Carmel Mountain, 592-9878. Open Sunday 11-5 p.m., Mon-Fri 10-9, Sat 10-6. Party supplies galore. Gift wrap, personalized cards. Also, Michael's and Lee Wards have lots of good buys on party supplies. Price/Costco and Smart and Final are great for paper plates, napkins, plastic glasses, etc. in bulk.

∆ Great children's party favors are at **Max's 99¢ Store** on Newport in Ocean Beach and other 99¢ stores (see "Clearance Centers," this chapter. Some party favors are 3/$1.

∆ **Paper Outlet**, North County Factory Outlet Mall #147, 1050 Los Vallecitos Boulevard, San Marcos, 471–4811, invitations, party goods, decorations, balloons, gift wrap, bags, bows, cards, wedding supplies at outlet prices.

∆ Check **"Florists Supplies"** in the *Yellow Pages*. I had a fabulous time at Dave's Displays downtown and the San Diego Florist Supply on El Cajon Boulevard. They have an incredible array of decorations.

∆ Buy special occasion party supplies and cards (St. Patty's Day, Valentine's Day, 4th of July, Christmas, etc.) *on sale* at real savings the day *after* the holiday for next year. Check this out at gift shops, party supply stores, supermarkets, drug stores and department stores. Robinsons–May etc. have 50% or more off the seasonal items the day after holidays, sometimes on the day of the holiday.

∆ Grossmont Nutrition & Gifts in the Grossmont Shopping center has greeting cards, 4/$1, always, 465–5225.

∆ **Parties For Children by Liz**, a professional party planner who hosted her own TV cooking program for children in L.A. Now Liz specializes in planning and organizing unique children's birthday parties in San Diego. She also teaches cooking for children in San Diego. For information, call 929–0939.

∆ The Old Globe and Junior Theater sell great adult costumes around Halloween. Call them for further information.

Pawn Shops

Pawn shops have been around since ancient times, and it was during the Middle Ages that the three golden balls became a symbol for them. They resell unclaimed items including mainly very nice gold jewelry, gemstones and watches. They have a number of other things like TV's, typewriters, silver, china, cameras, stereos, etc. They are usually Mom 'n Pop operations, so you can try to negotiate the price here. All goods are held for police clearance to see if they are stolen prior to selling them. They will lend about 25% of the value of an item for 30 days with a 60–day grace period which means an item can't be sold for 90 days. The interest charges are set by local laws and are steep, but you can get small loans of a few hundred dollars or so that banks aren't willing to bother with. See *Yellow Pages* for listings.

Pets

△ Dogs and cats including purebreds can be adopted at a nominal cost from the **San Diego County Humane Society**, 887 Sherman Street, 299–7012. SDCHS pays for medical exam within the first week. If the pet needs anything, the Humane Society will take care of it. There is a return policy if the pet doesn't work out. You also get a $60 coupon book good at Pet Co.

△ Pet People has a mailing list. Get on it. They send you coupons for 10% or more off your next purchase.

△ **F.O.C.A.S. (Friends of County Animal Shelter)**, 685–3536. You can adopt a pet, Afghan to Siamese, mixed and purebred, cats and dogs.

△ Cats can be donated or adopted at the **Cat Protection Society**, 9031 Birch in Spring Valley, 469–8771. This is a good place to take baby kitties. They go fast. I adopted the most beautiful three–year old calico cat here who is a real "love bug."

△ Birds, purebred cats and pedigreed dogs, guinea pigs, bats, mice, fish, goats, ponies, horses and you–name–it are advertised in the "Thrifties #780" classified ads in the *Union–Trib*. Good prices, too, and often free to good homes. Also, check the "Pet Adoptions #835" classifieds. Check the *Reader*, too.

△ **Mobile veterinary clinic**, (800) 564–6459 and (800) 336–4228, comes to your neighborhood for three hours for vaccinations, shots, tape worms, spay and neuter, good prices. Call for schedule, serving the County. Ask the manager of a pet store where to get the best prices on shots, too. Sometimes they post this information.

△ For information on low cost **spaying and neutering**, call 544–1222; **Pet Assistance Foundation**, 697–PETS; North County, 745–7986; Oceanside, (800) 284–4661. I had my cat neutered for $20! Whaddadeal!

△ **Fleas**: it takes a three–pronged attack to control them: lawn, carpet and pet. Experts say spray malathion, Dursban or Vapona on lawn. On the carpet, use Dursban or Precor. Treat the pet with Petcor, which has Precor in it. Precor has an insect growth regulator in it that tampers with the bug's hormones so it can't reproduce.

△ **Pet sitting** can save you some bucks over using a kennel. Call Pet–Tenders with a staff of 24. Licensed and bonded, 298–3033. Good Buddies Home Pet Care, 453–6857.

△ **Project Wildlife**, 692–9453, is a good place to call if you find an injured bird or wild animal; call Seaworld for water life.

△ Free dog run on Dog Beach in Ocean Beach. No leash required.

Photography & Video

△ **Olan Mills**, 419 Mission Valley Center West, and several other locations in San Diego, El Cajon, Santee, National City, Poway, Escondido, Vista, Oceanside. For an appointment, call 299–7310. Olan Mills Studios are throughout the U.S. and they have a club plan for professional portraits that you can't beat: you get three sittings within a year, with three 8x10's, for about $20 (less when there is a promotion) including tax. They advertise only by direct telephone call and if you want to join, they send a vehicle to your house to pick up your payment. Babies, children, adults, families and groups.   Your first sitting must be within four weeks of joining. Call for further information.

△ **Glamour Shots**, Fashion Valley, 299–5665; Parkway Plaza, 593–1655; No. County Fair, 739–5665; Frequent advertised specials, $19.95 includes makeover and 16 pose session. Many people who need business photos go here because they make you look good.

△ To save money on photo developing, watch for discount coupons in the newspapers for SavOn, Thrifty, Longs, Von's and Lucky super markets.   You get real savings on free duplicate sets, enlargements, reprints and discounts on video transfer service. (Put your home movies and slides on video tape for TV viewing!) And, there are additional coupons in with your newly developed photos!

△ Giant color enlargements, 20"x28", $12.95 at SavOn Drugs. They also put photos on mugs, etc., very inexpensively.

△ Get a color xerox blow up your color photo to 11"x17" on bond paper about $3.50 at copy shops. Lamination available.

△ **Buck's Video Productions**, 565–7010, guarantees to video your seminar, home, personal property or convert your movies and slides for about 40–50% less than the going rate.

Plumbing

△ **Budget Heating and Plumbing**, 563-1400, charges $45 for the first hour, plus $5.50-$25 for drain equipment used. Try to get an estimate by phone.

△ Don't call a plumber for stopped up drains, call **Baird's Drain Service** at 462-8229. They clear drains for $20, main sewer lines for $40. I've had them out several times, find them very timely (come when they say they will), very friendly and work fast. All work is guaranteed.

△ You can get plumbing (and electrical) work done by a licensed *handyman* for considerably less per hour, probably $15-25. They are qualified to do jobs up to $300 without having a specific plumber's or electrician's license. It's best to use someone you know is reliable, but if you don't have a source, check the "Services Offered" classified ads in the *Union-Trib* or your neighborhood newspaper. Home Depot will show you how to do it yourself! They also recommend contractors.

Records, Tapes & Videos

△ **Public libraries** have records, tapes and videos that can be checked out. A current movie or an educational or travel video rents for about 50¢ a day. Some libraries are better stocked than others (Carlsbad and Chula Vista libraries have lots. Some libraries have free rentals.

△ **Long's Drugs** has video rentals for 99¢ and coupons for 2 for 1 rentals about every two weeks in their advertisements (Ads are in stacks in the store.)

△ **Time Warner's Viewer's Edge**, (800) 854–7200, a video club, where all videos are $9.95 or less which normally sell for $19.95, $29.95 even $39.95. Find a better price and they refund the difference. Satisfaction guaranteed. No tapes sent unless you order them. Columbia Video costs more with more commitment.

Resale/Consignment Shops

There all different kinds of consignment shops: clothing, furniture, appliances, sporting equipment, etc.

Clothing consignment shops carry "previously owned" apparel that is in perfectly good, next-to-new condition. A resale shop may or may not buy from customers; but a consignment shop always buys from customers (but may have other inventory also).

Recycling has been popular for many years, and the "used" market is thriving. Today people clean out their closets and find things they simply don't wear any more, things that never fit in the first place, things that simply don't flatter, things they can no longer squeeze into and things they have dieted out of. They may donate some of the things to a charity thrift store and take the better items to a privately owned consignment shop where they can retrieve some of their original outlay. A price is established by the consignor and the consignee. You will earn about 60% of the selling price, and the store gets 40%. Consignment is usually for a 90 day period, with the selling price reduced 10% every 30 days until it is sold. (A pitfall here is that some women say they never get paid, so be sure to keep your receipt and check back before 90 days to see if your garments have sold.) There are shops that specialize: women, men, children, big women, vintage, maternity You see upscale fashions for women, bargains in designer clothing. casual wear, formal wear and things for the household. You'll see women drive up in their big Mercedes to add to their wardrobes or sell their excess. Consignment shops carry everything: casual, formal, suits, lingerie, you–name–it. They are a great place to pick up belts, purses, jewelry and outfits for costume parties. If you haven't been shopping at a resale or consignment shop, now is the time to investigate them. We have lots of new shops, and shopping resale is definitely the trend of the future.

Here's a success story: a friend was invited to a very yuppie wedding in Chicago and she didn't want to pay for a designer dress she'd never wear again. I suggested she try one of the better resale shops that carries designer clothing, Your Favorite Things, in La Jolla (rich ladies live there, right?) not thinking she'd ever do it. Well, she did, and she called to report she had found THE PERFECT DRESS to take to Chicago. She went to the wedding and had a fabulous time because she knew she was wearing something spectacularly competitive (when you have *that* feeling–– it really makes a world of difference in the fun you can have). When she got home, she sold the dress right back to the store! So, it only cost her a few dollars to have a *fabulous* outfit to wear for a special occasion! You can do it, too. Some of today's resale shops specialize in a specific type of clothing: designer fashions, maternity wear, children's clothing, wedding gowns, men's wear, large apparel or vintage clothing. Browse through some of the following:

△ **A–1 Consignment Shoppe,**
  341 W. Felicita, Von's
Center
  Escondido, 740–2420
△ **Act II**(Women's)
  6195 Lake Murray Blvd.
  698–8636
△ **Act II**(Women's)
  6195 Lake Murray Blvd,
  La Mesa, 698–2392
△ **A to Zebra**
  4224 Adams

  Kensington, 280–6776
△ **Attic** (CLOTHING)
  6402 University
  College area, 286–0581
△ **Big City Woman**, (size 16+)
  4185 Adams Avenue
  Kensington, 521–0121
△ **Buffalo Exchange** (Women's
  & Men's Casual)
  1007 Garnet
  Pacific Beach, 273–6227
  Used, plus some new

clothing. nearly new, natural fibers. Sell your clothes for 40% of ticket price and receive cash, or receive 55% in store credit.

Δ **Carolyn's I & II** (Women's)
6033J Paseo
Delicias
Rancho Santa Fe, 756-2765

Δ **Carolyn's Such a Deal**
920 1st Street (Ladies)
Encinitas, 943-1556

Δ **Carolyn's Grand Affair**
(women's)
565 Grand Ave, Carlsbad
720-2075

Δ **Consigner's Closet**
(Women's)
121-C University, Hillcrest
298-5527

Δ **Coronado Classics**
1017 C Avenue (Women's)
Coronado, 437-8927

Δ **Cream of the Crop**
(Women's)
5005 Cass Street
Pacific Beach, 272-6466

Δ **Cream of the Crop II**
(Women/Men/Interiors)
4683 Cass Street
Pacific Beach, 272-6601

Δ **Country Cousins**
2889 Adams Ave.
San Diego, 284-3039

Δ **Daily Exchange**
628 First Ave.
Encinitas, 753-2211

Δ **Deborah's Next To New**

(Everything)
1624 E. Valley Parkway,
Escondido, 743-8980

Δ **Designer Consigner**
(Women's designer)
834 Kline St.
La Jolla, 459-1737

Δ **Designer Resale Boutique**
690 University (women's)
Hillcrest, 692-3343

Δ **Designer Savvy**
1650 N. 2nd Street
El Cajon, 440-4504

Δ **Diabolik**
3827 Park Blvd.
Hillcrest, 688-3075

Δ **Discovery Shop** (everything)
3651-B Midway Drive
Point Loma, 224-4336

Δ **Discovery Shop**
Avocado & Hwy. 94
Rancho San Diego, 660-1760

Δ **Discovery Shop**
800 Escondido Ave., Suite E, Vista, 724-9222

Δ Diva's 1539 Garnet
Pacific Beach, 581-9258

Δ **Donna's Resale Boutique**
Clothes/miscellaneous
913 E. Valley Parkway
Escondido, 743-7433

Δ **Down on the Corner**
(women's casual)
3572 Mount Acadia Blvd.
Clairemont, 279-9649

Δ **Dress to Impress**
4242 Camino del Rio North

(women's rentals & resale)
Mission Valley, 528-9797
△ **Double Take** (ladies)
144 E. Vista Way
Vista, 758-4840
△ **Echoes Boutique**
7705 Fay Ave (ladies)
La Jolla, 459-6588
△ **Encore** (women's designer)
7850 Herschel
La Jolla, 454-7540
△ **Fair Mairs** (men's/women's)
4879 Newport Avenue
Ocean Beach, 222-0220
△ **Fantastic Finds**
2180 Chatsworth
Pt. Loma/OB, 222-1158
△ **Fashion Occasions Bridal**
8341 La Mesa Blvd (women)
La Mesa, 697-9219
△ **Garment Gourmet**
(women's clothing & bridal)
831 Williamston
Vista, 630-6630
△ **Gentlemen Resale Clothier**
1530 Jamacha Rd.,Ste. W,
El Cajon, 442-6701
△ **Gillespie Thrift**
7631 Girard Ave
La Jolla, 454-4124
△ **Goodwill Boutique**
444 5th Avenue
Downtown, 696-6710
△ **Gown Pavilion**
(wedding &
cocktail)
277 S. Rancho Santa Fe Rd.
San Marcos, 471-4500

△ **Gypsy Treasure**
(vintage & costumes)
8127 La Mesa Blvd
La Mesa, 466-2251
△ **London Underground**
23807 5th,
Downtown, 298-6821
△ **Melrose Exchange Boutique**
4508 Cass, #D
Pacific Beach, 270-ROSE
△ **Mr. C's** (men's clothing)
4242 #10 Camino del Rio N.
Mission Valley, 528-8738
△ **My Magnin** (resale & rental)
4976 Cass St.
Pacific Beach, 483-2244
△ **One of a Kind** (Vintage)
1026 Garnet
Pacific Beach, 581-1406
△ **Pia's Vintage**
(men's & women's)
1570 Garnet
Pacific Beach, 483-6175
△ **R.A.G.S. Fashion Exchange**
5957 El Cajon Blvd
College area, 229-1350
△ **Refinery**
3028 Canon
Pt. Loma, 222-2760
△ **Reincarnation** (women's)
7709 Fay
La Jolla, 459-9007
△ **Rodeo Drive**
(women's designer)
2920 Jamacha Road,
El Cajon, 660-7787
△ **Sack's Thrift Ave.** (women)
1819 Adams, Univ. Hgts),

297-3023
△ **Second Act** (women's)
7449 Girard Avenue
La Jolla, 454-6096
△ **Second Chance-His &
Hers** (women's & men's)
1482 Garnet
Pacific Beach, 270-6930
△ **Second Nature**
4652 Mission Blvd.
Pacific Beach, 272-7399
△ **Second Time Around**
688 Broadway
Chula Vista, 425-1232
△ **Sentimental Values**
(juniors, women)
1077 Broadway
El Cajon, 442-3231
△ **Sparkle Plenty Boutique**
(women's)
1919 Apple
Oceanside, 757-8804

△ **Stork Club**
4838 Rolando Boulevard
San Diego, 287-9449
△ **Stork Club II**
(maternity & baby
331 W. Felicita
Escondido, 747-3667
△ **Your Favorite Things**
(women's + designer)
5645 La Jolla Boulevard
La Jolla, 459-0311
△ **Wear It Again Sam**
(vintage men's & women's),
3922 Park Boulevard
North Park, 299-0185

For more stores that sell slightly used clothing, check "Thrift Stores," this chapter. Also, for more consignment stores, see "Furniture" and "Children's Clothing & Furniture," this chapter.

△ For consignment stores for furniture and decorator items, appliances and electronics. sporting equipment, see other sections of this book.

△ There are 43 consignment shops in Palm Springs (rich folk's used goodies). Should make for a day of fun. Also, there are many resale shops in Laguna Beach. (Ah, yes! With lunch above the Pacific! Are we having fun yet?!)

Rummage Sales

There is nothing like the news of a *good* rummage sale coming up to get the blood rushing.! I hadn't been to one in years, so when I was dragged off to one, I didn't expect much. Ho! HO! Was I ever pleasantly surprised! Now I wouldn't miss a good one for the world. Tips: Come prepared. Bring tote bags, plastic grocery bags, boxes or crates with you to put things in and carry around with you. Come early (the very best buys are always scooped up within the first hour).

Here are some of the best annual rummage sales. Put them on your calendar.

∆ **Junior League Rummage Sale**, the first weekend in October or November. For exact date of the sale and admission price, call 234–2253. If you're a bargain hunter, you won't want to miss this one! San Diego's largest rummage sale, held at the Del Mar Fairgrounds Exhibit Hall, in 56,000 square feet of space. This annual spectacular event has been held by the Junior League since 1944, netting over $150,000 *yearly* for children's benefits and community service projects. It is reported to be the largest rummage sale in California, with only one larger in the country, and that's in Utah. Besides working 13 hours during sale week and at the sale, each of the League's 500 active members must contribute at least $200 worth of rummage to the sale which they collect throughout the year. Some customers begin lining up for the sale up to 24 hours ahead of time! They pitch their tents and actually sleep right there in the parking lot. The media shows up for this one! There are 20 fully stocked departments with furniture, TV & stereo equipment, hardware, plants, books, toys, linens, appliances, kitchen supplies, novelties, sporting equipment, antiques, clothing (men's, women's, and children's) and a boutique with the "best." Over 15,000 attend. Half price, second day.

People who go to this sale take big 33–gallon trash bags and buy everything with abandon. Everything is very cheap: all little girls' dresses, $2; all men's suits $5; all ladies' sweaters, $2; all ladies' belts, 50¢; etc.). Some people buy their entire wardrobes and all their kids' clothes and toys. I met a young woman at the Junior League Rummage Sale who said she had been to every Junior League Rummage Sale since she was five years old. She's now in her thirties. One year, she bought a snake skin purse for $4 and when she got home, she found out it was brand new and still had the tissue and tags in it. It was worth $300! She said she buys all her children's toys there, once bought a huge triple dresser for $25, etc., etc., and that she shows up every year, sick or well.

∆ **Rancho Santa Fe Garden Club Rummage Sale**, corner of La Granada & Avenida de Accacoa, Rancho Santa Fe, 756–1554. Held every May, this is another two–day major "event." All items are reduced half price the second day. Call in the spring to find out the exact date, 756–4101. Also, all year long you can buy large items like stereos, typewriters, refrigerators and furniture on Wednesday mornings, 9–11:30 a.m.

∆ **St. James By The Sea Episcopal Church**, 743 Prospect, 459–3421. There is an annual two–day rummage sale every September. Call for exact date. A woman told me she buys all of her clothes at this rummage sale because there is such good quality clothing (designer labels) hardly worn!! (Rich La Jolla ladies get rid of clothing that is perfectly new or in great condition!) She said that by purchasing her wardrobe at rummage sales, she can save her money for travel!

∆ **Thursday Club Annual Rummage Sale** (in its 60+ year), held every March at the Balboa Park Club near the Aerospace Museum. In the spring, call the Thursday club 224–5264 for exact date.

∆ **La Jolla Lutheran Church**, 7111 La Jolla Blvd., 459–342, every

September. Call for date.

△ **Berkeley Ferryboat Auxiliary**, since 1967, 1306 N. Harbor, 234–9153. Every April. Call for date.

△ **La Jolla United Methodist Church**, 6063 La Jolla Blvd., 459–5264. Every March. Call for date.

△ **United Methodist Church**, 1702 South Ditmar, Oceanside, has their annual rummage sale every October.

Wanna know how to get the best deals at a rummage sale? Volunteer to help in the organizing of it!! Sometimes helpers are allowed to make early purchases.

△ Not a rummage sale, but here's another big spectacular event. The Junior League of Orange County has a Christmas bazaar at the Orange County Fair Grounds every October with fabulous gifts, etc. People take bus loads up for this one. For info, call (714) 660–5118.

Shoes

Major department stores including Nordstrom, Neiman's, Bullock's, Broadway and others regularly schedule their anniversary sales, semi–annual and end–of–season shoe sales. Scoop up designer labels at discounts up to 50% (sometimes more). If you and Imelda Marcos have something in common and you're really on a roll with shoes, ask the shoe department manager to put your name on their mailing list and you'll be notified by mail (or called) about their future sales. Call your favorite stores now! You can have quality designer shoes in every color at a fraction of the original cost.

Δ **Capezio Factory Outlet**, 1050 Los Vallecitos Boulevard, #115, San Marcos, 744-3599. Fashionable shoes from Capezio, Evan Picone, Bellini, Calvin Klein and more. Other stores are at the factory outlets at Barstow, Lake Elsinore, Desert Hills, Plaza Continental Factory (See "Factory Outlets," this chapter.)

Δ **Famous Footwear Factory Outlet**, 1050 Los Vallecitos #114, 591-9240, North County Factory Outlet Mall, Carries shoes and boots for the whole family: L.A. Gear, Reebok, Keds, Naturalizer, Florsheim, Nunn Bush, Cherokee, K-Swiss, Ipanema. Not their latest styles, but all on sale. Some clearance prices.

Δ **La Sandale**, 3761 Mission Boulevard, Mission Beach, 488-1134, has Birkenstock "look alikes" for nearly half what the real thing costs. They are outrageously comfortable and good for the legs.

Δ **Wall To Wall Shoes**, 3007 Highland, National City, 474-2760. Major name brand shoes which have been previously purchased and returned to upscale department stores all over the country are sold here. Name brands include 9 West, Amanda Smith, John & David, Via Efpiga and high end, Ferragamos. Over 3,000 pairs arrive every Monday (sometimes there are lines waiting for the store to open!) and are usually sold by the following Sunday. All shoes are $17.99 a pair; boots arrive in mid-September 18th, same price!

Δ **Shoe Obsession**, 3350 Sports Arena, 224-9830. Returned shoes, from department stores, Italian shoes, Ferragamos, ($40), Bally, ($35) great prices. Boots, $25, etc. Shoes arrive on Saturday.

Δ **Banister Factory Outlet**, 4498 Camino de la Plaza, San Ysidro, 428-2115 (San Diego Factory Outlet Mall, with over 40 famous brands of shoes for men and women including dress, casual and athletic shoes (San Diego Factory Outlets Mall)

Δ **Guess Footwear Outlet**, 4498 Camino de la Plaza, San Ysidro, 662–3570, San Diego Factory Outlet Mall, shoes, boots, sandals for men and women.

Δ **Bass Outlet**, 4498 Camino de la Plaza, San Ysidro, 690–6029, San Diego Factory Outlet Mall, with fashion footwear for men and women including casual, boots, dress shoes. All are Bass labels, sold in Bullock's and Robinson's. (you may not see the current models, though.) These may be overruns from last season.

Δ **Nike Factory Outlet**, with Nike casual shoes, apparel and accessories (discontinued styles of all sport shoes including running, walking, basketball, aerobic and more.) None of the latest styles, only closeouts, at about 30% off. Tights, t–shirts, more. Clearance rack with discounts up to 70%. The busiest Nike Factory Outlet in the U.S. is in San Ysidro. Also located at Lake Elsinore and Desert Hills Factory Outlets.

Δ **Athletic and active wear shoes:**: Check out the swapmeet vendors as there is a pretty good selection with below store prices. Then there's the big sporting goods stores: Big 5, Cal Stores, Oshman's and Sportmart. They are always having huge sales. Road Runner's Sports is a big catalog company with an outlet store at 9020–B Activity Road (Miramar), 455–9825; discount prices, some clearance items. Price/Costco has great buys on leisure shoes. No need to pay full price for them, ever!

Δ **M & J Shoe Warehouse**, 3720 Sports Arena, 222–1177 and in the El Toreador Shopping Center, 637 San Ysidro. They buy bankruptcies, close–out inventories of shoes. Shoes are on racks and sell at good prices: ladies from $10 a pair; western boots, $59.90, famous brand shoes, $39 (value to $200).

Δ **Reebok Factory Direct** Store, 9401 Waples St., Ste 100B, Mira Mesa, 546–0343. Footwear + apparel, accessories, bags, hats, sox, shorts, sweat, exercise, T-shirts.

△ **Shoes Behind the Post Office**, 805 F St., downtown, 233-0645. Men's and women's.

△ **Jon's Wide Shoes**, 273 Third Avenue, Chula Vista, 422-1464. Ladies wide and extra wide; whole line for children, some men's.

△ Women's shoe catalog, hard to find sizes, 3 to 13, AAAAA to EEE. Send $1 to Gene's, 126 N. Main, St. Charles, MO 63301.

Sporting Goods

△ **Big 5,** one of the major chains of sporting goods stores which carries a huge selection of seasonal clothing and equipment. Their enormous buying volume allows them to discount prices 20 to 50% below retail. Running, golf, fishing, bowling, skiing, camping and hunting gear are sold. Look in the Sunday *Union-Trib* for their advertising supplement featuring current sale items.

△ **Gordon & Smith Clothing** has an end of the season clearance sale on surf wear, that people line up for all around their building at Lusk Blvd. Get on the mailing list to be notified of their August sale by calling 558-0225. Occasional end of year sale when there is overstock.

△ **Climax Distribution** holds a "clean out the warehouse" sale for skateboarding hardgoods (trucks, wheels, decks, hardware) and soft goods (T-shirts, shirts, shorts, pants, boxers, jackets, backpacks and accessories). Held twice a year at 3210-B Production Avenue, Oceanside, 722-1455.

⌂ For new sporting gear, try **Sportmart** on Balboa, Cal Stores (8 stores), Sports Chalet, Oshman's. There is a lot of competition in this area.

⌂ **Golf Mart,** discount golf supermart, San Diego, 298–9571; El Cajon, 462–0077; Del Mar, 794–9676; Encinitas, 944–1534; San Marcos, 741–0441. Balboa, 292–7292; Harborside, 239–0277.

⌂ **Reebok Factory Direct** Store, 9401 Waples St., Ste 100B, Mira Mesa, 546–0343. Footwear + apparel, accessories, bags, hats, sox, shorts, sweat, exercise, T–shirts.

⌂ **Cal Stores** has an annual Ski Swap and Sale. Call 223–2325 for exact date in October.

Used Sporting Goods Stores: (This is a great new concept!)
⌂ **Second Chance Sports**, 1968 Garnet, Pacific Beach, 581–9117, and at 4811 W. Point Loma, Ocean Beach, 224–9524. New and used surf boards, skiis, ski boots, skate boards, bicycles, motorcycle helmets, inline skates, balls, wet suits (long and short), diving equipment, fishing equipment, hockey and lacrosse gear, tennis rackets, snorkles, fins, tents, camping equipment and exercise equipment. Buy, sell, and consignment.

⌂ **Play It Again Sports**, 1401 Garnet, Pacific Beach, 490–0222; 9969 Mira Mesa Boulevard, Mira Mesa, 695–3030; two more locations with all sorts of sporting and outdoor equipment, new and used.

⌂ See the *Yellow Pages* for more second hand sports stores.

⌂ Look in the "Thrifties #780" classified ads of the *Union–Trib*. You'll find every kind of sporting gear that is manufactured. Inquire about the condition and age of the equipment. This is a good place to get that first pair of skis, first surf board and all kinds of sporting equipment, camping gear, etc.

∆ You can get your kids every kind of sporting stuff at yard sales: cheap, cheap, cheap. Even sail boats, rafts, etc.

Students (Employ One)

∆ Use a college or high school student to clean your house, do yard work, babysit, run errands, do your personal or professional bookkeeping, office work, set up your computer files, detail your car, serve at parties, wash windows. Call the student employment office at a school near you.

Sunglasses

In my next lifetime, I am going to sell sunglasses. That, my friends, is because I read somewhere that the average Californian has at least four pairs. What a market we have here! (Let's see, now. That's four times 24+ million..........Yea. I could probably live on that!!)

∆ **Sunglass City**, 1478 Garnet, Pacific Beach, 272-6041. Major brands at discount prices, Ray-Ban $49, Gargoyles $55, Porsche Carrera $139.

∆ **Price/Costco** has great prices on moderate to very expensive sunglasses. Ray-Bans, Liz Claiborne, Gargoyles. Big discounts.

∆ **Spectacular Eyewear** Factory Outlet, 4498 Camino de la Plaza, San Ysidro, 662-1154. Rayban and more at discount prices.

∆ Swap meets have Ray-Ban sunglasses and lots of inexpensive brands. Good buys.

Swap Meets

Δ Swap meets have been around for years and years and years, try 40–45 years for the El Cajon swap meet. They have become phenomenally popular in California where the weather lends itself to year–round outdoor shopping at the more than 200 swap meets in the state, with more than 2.5 million shoppers every weekend. They have become tourist attractions and people come from miles away. Shoppers are mostly educated middle class. Vendors are supplementing social security or retirement, maybe they have a large family, are supplementing their businesses or starting new ones, and some are there for the social aspect of it -- they don't care if they sell 50¢ or $50. It only takes a few thousand dollars to get started in a swap meet business. Vendors buy bankruptcy lots, factory close–outs, etc. saving 40–50¢ on the dollar. They are smart business people: it's easy money and a good place to work for yourself. They have to buy smart, sell cheap and treat people right, which makes it a great place to shop. About 70% is *new* merchandise, from A–Z, every weekend. Acres and acres of bargains, domestic and imports, including art, arts and crafts, artwear, automotive accessories, clothes and shoes for the entire family, baskets, beauty supplies, belts, bicycles, cellular phones, dance and exercise wear, eelskin and leather goods, flowers, furniture, gifts, hardware and tools, fine jewelry, natural stone and ethnic jewelry, photo supplies and equipment, plants, sheets and linens, sporting goods, sunglasses and more. Flowers are $1–$2.50 a bunch (value $5.98 up), 25 ft. telephone cords $2 (value $6.98), good buys on imported pots and decorator items, futons, wicker, and more. You'll find "garage sales" at the swap meets, too. Many people just go there for recreation or to get that $5 item that's worth $500; others go routinely every Saturday morning to scoop up the little "finds" at the garage sales in the back. I have several sets of bar wine glasses for parties in all sizes accumulated piece by piece at the garage sales at the swap meet for 25–50¢.

This is a good place to find second hand gourmet kitchenware. It's another place people go to browse for "therapy." San Diego's swap meets draw large crowds. They are becoming more and more fair-like, with entertainment and food. Here are the ones around the County and nearby:

△ **Kobey's Swap Meet**, 3500 Sports Arena Boulevard, in Point Loma, 226-0650, is open Thursday-Sunday, 7-3 p.m.. $1 entrance fee on weekends; 50¢ Thursday-Friday. Seniors, 75¢. There's usually a coupon for one free admittance with a paid admission are in the *Union-Trib* every week, good on Thursday or Friday only. If you pick up a copy of *This Week In San Diego* in any nearby motel lobby, there is always a two-for-one coupon good anytime. Kobey's (and the Oceanside Swap Meet) are the biggest swap meets in the area, with an entire array of goods, both new and used. The weekends draw crowds of over 25,000. A must on your list.

△ **Hemet Swap Meet** is on North Lion on Saturday and Sunday mornings.

△ **Santee Drive-In Swap Meet**, 10990 Woodside Avenue North, just off Hwy. 67, 449-SWAP. Open Every Saturday and Sunday, 6:30 a.m.-2 p.m.. Acres and acres of bargains and garage sellers. lst & 3rd Saturdays, ham radio & electronic swapmeet next door; 4th Saturday, fishing gear and sporting goods swapmeet.

△ **Spring Valley Swap Meet**, 6377 Quarry Road, east end of Hwy. 54, adults, 50¢, 463-1194. Saturday and Sunday 7-3 p.m.

△ **Oceanside Drive-In Swap Meet**, 3490 Mission Avenue, 6:30 a.m.-2:30 p.m. each Friday through Sunday, and on holiday Mondays, 757-5286. Everything here. All kinds of bargains in new and used merchandise. This is a must. One of the biggest in Southern California.

△ **Escondido Drive–In Swap Meet**, 635 W. Mission Avenue, 7–4 p.m. Wednesday, Thursday, Saturday– Sunday, 745–3100. Lots of goodies, lots of food concessions, fair atmosphere, farmers' market, indoor and outdoor, 50¢ Wed & Sat; 35¢ on Thursday, and 75¢ on Sunday.

△ **Tijuana Swap Meet**, east of the Race Track on Boulevard Agua Caliente (which becomes Boulevard Diaz Ordaz). On the right is Bazaar del Pueblo before you reach the cross road to La Pensa and Mesa de Otay. There is another one on the left, also. For information, call Sam Warren, Tijuana expert, in San Diego, 531–0765.

△ The **Orange County Swap Meet**, 291 State College Blvd., (714) 634–4259 Orange Coast College parking lot, (714) 432–5866.

△ **Rose Bowl Flea Market** in Pasadena, the second Sunday of each month, from 9–3 p.m., since 1968, (213) 588–4411. It is the world's largest flea market with over 1,500 dealers from all over the West and Midwest. Art Nouveau and Art Deco are strong sellers here. $5 admission. 1001 Rosebowl Dr., near the 210 Fwy., 134 Ventura Fwy., 110 Pasadena Fwy.

△ The **Paris Flea Market** is considered to be the leading shopping experience in the world, according to Weissmann Travel Reports, with over 3,000 sidewalk stands and permanent stalls. Kowloon, Hong Kong is second, and the Sunday Market in Kashgar, China is third.

Telephone Services

△ The Consumer Federation of America and the Telecommunications Research and Action Center provide **free pamphlets** on the following: "How to Choose a Long Distance Company;" "Equal Access: The New Long Distance System," and "Selecting a

Phone." Also, information for hearing and speech disabled. To order, call the hot line at (800) 332-1124 from 6 a.m. to 5 p.m. PDT weekdays.

△ Check several long distance services for current prices and ask if there are any specials. For switching, you may get a month's free service, or a gift, 1000 frequent flyer miles or other promotion. MCI offers five frequent flyer miles on Northwest Airlines for every one dollar I spend on long distance!! It adds up!!

△ The **800-number information** line is (800) 555-1212. You can see if an out of town company has a toll-free line. Great idea when an appliance or electronic device goes on the fritz

△ If you are dissatisfied with the service from a **900 number**, you can ask for a refund. You can block calls from your phone to all 900 and 976 numbers. Blocking is a free service for residential customers, $15 for businesses. Call the toll-free number on the first page of your phone bill.

△ Have your phone listed in a different name (such as your middle name) instead of paying extra for an unlisted number. Not only is it cheaper, but i helps to sort out phone calls, If a caller asks for the different name, it's probably a salesman.

△ If you are troubled by repeated anonymous hangups, the phone company will put a trap on your phone, and the harasser will be identified. A free service. (See "Resources."

Thrift Stores

There's nothing like a good junk store. They're like potato chips: sometimes you can't stop with just one....you have to keep going from one store to the next until they close the very last one! And, then there are times when you "just can't do it." Just go with the flow.............It's worth digging through the array of miscellaneous to find that treasure! I know bargain hunters who have gone on organized campaigns to hit every Thrift Store in town. One was in search of old silk ties to add to her one-of-a-kind silk and velvet patchwork quilt, an award winner in-the-making to be sure. Another said she wears only silk blouses and she goes from one thrift store to another to add to her collection.

Here's a thrift store story that'll get your attention: a man found an old map of Paris in nine pieces in a Salvation Army Store in Indianapolis that he thought, after rubbing the dust off of it, was *not* a reproduction but had actually been painted. He bought it for $3 thinking he could possibly sell it for $30–$40 to a dealer. He took it to the local university and had the head of the Geography Department take a look at it. The professor recognized it from a book he had read and sent him to an auction house in New York to have it appraised. Guess what! It was one of the few surviving copies of a map commissioned by King Louis XIV in 1671 valued at $12 MILLION!!!! It had probably come to America in the drawer of a shipment of French antiques.

All thrift stores price their clothing about the same. Here is the price list of clothing from the downtown Goodwill store: women's clothing (all items are *one* price, regardless of whether they are silk or linen or velvet or cotton): All blouses, $2.50; all jackets, $4.49; all sweaters, $3.89; all blouses/vests, $2.79 all dresses, $5.49; all skirts, $3.39; all jumpsuits, $5.49; all coats, $7.50; all slacks/joggers, $3.50. Men's clothing: all sportcoats, $5; all jeans, $5.50; all slacks, $4; all suits, $20 up. All girls' dresses, $3.29; all boys' shirts, $1.75; sweaters, $2.79. A lot of items in stock are new, complete with original store price tags, and many things look nearly new! (Please note: all sales are final! No returns!!)

Here are some of the larger chains of thrift shops with multiple locations:

Δ **Goodwill Industries**, Boutique, downtown, 696–6710; 4359 Home Avenue, (largest store) 262–6596; downtown, 696–6710; San Ysidro, 690–1795; El Cajon, 444–8370; Pacific Beach, 274–4960; Serra Mesa, 569–7925; Rosecrans, 225–5600;

Δ **Disabled American Veterans**, 881 Broadway at L, Chula Vista (largest store), unlisted phone; Downtown, 232–0141, and Oceanside, 433–5404.

Δ **St. Vincent de Paul**, 1550 Market Street, Downtown (largest store), 233–1800; .

Δ **Salvation Army**, 901 12th Avenue, downtown (largest store) 232–1378; with several other locations: Pacific Beach, Mission Bay, 272–6541.

Δ **Baras** Non–Profit Thrift Shops, 1445 University, Hillcrest; 4792 Clairemont Mesa, Diane Shopping Center.

There are dozens and dozens of thrift shops, too many to list, so check the *Yellow Pages* and head out for an afternoon of fun.

Tijuana

Here's what you can bring back across the border: booze (one liter every 30 days), food beef, most vegetables, some fruit, no citrus fruit, four lobsters per person, baked good, hand crafted furniture, clothing, cut flowers, medications, lots of pottery, leather purses, jackets and luggage, silver jewelry. U.S. residents can bring back $400 per person per month; non–residents, $200. It is a freeport, meaning you can buy imported articles there duty free, which translates to: less than you'd pay in the U.S. where import taxes have been levied.

If you're headed south, stop at the Customs Office. Take the *last U-turn*, head back north, park on the street and enter the U.S. Customs office and ask for their publication that covers what you can and can not bring back into the U.S. They told me they are really only looking for illegal items (illegal drugs and things forbidden by the U.S. Department of Agriculture because they do not meet our standards of safety), and purchases over the monetary limit on which you need to pay duty.

∆ **"Crossing The Border Made Easy"** by Paula McDonald, $6.95, contains Baja's best bargains and everything you need to make your cross across the border a breeze.

Wallpaper & Window Coverings

A lot of savings can be had here. Find what you want at any decorator or paint store, get the book pattern and number and then call a wholesale company to see if they carry it for less. Most companies have free UPS shipping and no sales tax. Compare prices. Try these:

∆ **Wholesale wallpaper & window companies**, 40–80% off, (800) 245–1768; Worldwide Wallcoverings & Blinds, (800) 631–9341; Style Wallcovering & Blinds, (800) 627–0400; Custom Windows & Walls (800) 772–1947; American, (800) 777–2737.

∆ **Home Depot** now carries a full line of wallpaper and window coverings.

∆ Wallpapers to go, 709 Center Drive, San Marcos, 480–1884; 4647 Kearny Mesa, 565–4550. Semi–annual sale, March/ Sept.

Weddings & Parties (Do–It–Yourself!)

You can put together your own fabulous **wedding** (or party) on a shoe string budget if you are willing to do a lot of the work yourself rather than pay someone to plan, buy, fix, serve and clean up everything for you. For a do-it-yourself party or wedding reception, get a good book on how to throw great parties or how to put on that fabulous wedding for any budget from the library or book store. Party goods stores have party and wedding planners, too, which outline what you need to do and how to plan for your size event. Have the reception at home or rent the little sternwheeler boat behind Tarantino's Restaurant and have your reception on the bay. The Heritage Park Bed & Breakfast Inn in Old Town is a wonderfully romantic site you can rent for a wedding and reception. You can have your wedding or party in any park or at the beach with a permit from the park. Each public park has its own rules to adhere to, including number of guests, glass containers, etc. Just call and ask for information on holding an event at Balboa Park, the Presidio, Torrey Pines, Mission Bay, Mount Soledad, etc. Check at Smart & Final for their wedding menu suggestions which tell how many containers of bulk salads, etc. you will need to feed "X" number of people. Their prices are great, too. Price/Costco now does party trays, too: 5 lbs. meat & cheese, about $19.95; or veggie tray (6 lbs veggies and dip, about $14.95; sandwich & antipasto trays, too). Honey Baked Hams puts on a great spread for about $6 a head for 60 people including two hams, roast beef, cheeses, olives, pickles, honey mustard, etc. Almost every restaurant will do catering (supply the food). Even an Oriental all-you-can-eat restaurant or an Italian or Mexican food restaurant or Rubio's Fish Tacos, 573-1779. A wedding lunch or brunch is usually less expensive than dinner. For a complete selection of wedding or party supplies including invitations, cake and candy supplies, wedding accessories, guestsbooks, invitations, rentals, and more, check Michael's and H & H Floral. Price/Costco and Smart & Final have the best prices on paper plates, napkins, plastic glasses in bulk. Pic'n'Save, Party Savers and the Paper Store in the Factory Outlet Shopping Mall in San Marcos are worth checking into also. Party rental stores rent champagne fountains, huge bowls, chairs, tables and cloths and everything you need. Check flower prices at the swap meets (go several weeks early and make arrangements with a flower vender), or go to Tijuana florists. The *Reader* has a wedding and party section in the classifieds where you can get goods and services. Sample the locally famous and very popular Black Forest wedding cake at the European Bakery, 3361 Voltaire, 222-3377, not cheap, but the best. Check Tijuana bakeries for wedding cakes at real savings or some of the major local supermarket bakeries or Price/Costco (sheet cake that serves 30-48!), or hire a student at an adult school cooking/cake decorating class. Some churches have a parishioner who specializes in making wedding cakes which is worth checking into (usually a senior citizen who is thrilled to have the opportunity to make it for you, at a great price.) Then gather up the friends and relatives and put them to work for you. It is recommended that you have a few paid employees at the event -- call San Diego State University's job listing board and get a student or two who do catering work for a few hours for you. For **music,** check under "Musicians" in the *Reader* classifieds for bands to rent, or call the award winning UCSD jazz ensemble, or hire Disc Jockey Steve Cosio Great American Music, 292-4158. He has the whole gamut of recorded music. (Tell him I said for him to give you a good discount!!) Get Buck to video the occasion (see Photography, this chapter), and have at least two friends run around with their cameras capturing you and the guests on film. (The candid shots are my favorite.) The bottom line is: with a little imagination and creativity, you can put on a wedding nothing short of a coronation, or have a fabulous party a la the lifestyles of the rich and famous for a very small percentage of what it would cost to have someone to do it all for you.

△ You can get big samples of **wedding cakes** at bakeries to take home for the mother of the bride, groom, etc. to taste.

∆ **Gown Pavilion**, 277 S. Rancho Santa Fe Road, San Marcos, 471–4500. Large selection of rental (and sales) of formal and informal wedding gowns.

∆ **Moonlighting Bridal Rental**, 4715 30th, Hillcrest, 282–0181. Bridal wear rentals, $115–$250, and bridesmaids, $49–$99. Will special order bridal wear for rent, time permitting. Will take bridal gowns on consignment.

∆ **Fashion Occasions Bridal**, 8341 La Mesa Boulevard, La Mesa, 697–9219, specializes in **used bridal wear** for the bride, bridesmaids, mother of the bride, etc.

∆ For a new wedding gown, you might try **My Bridal Gown**, 1050 Highland Avenue, National City, 474–4025, carrying designer gowns direct from the manufacturers at savings.

∆ **Bridal Fashion Center**, 1111 Torrey Pines Road, La Jolla, 551–2001; over 1000 designer gowns on display in a variety of fabrics and laces. Negotiate the price. Lay–a–way.

∆ *Down the Aisle In San Diego* by Marsha Starr; directory of wedding services, $500 in discount coupons, 125 pages, $9.95, available in bookstores or call (619) 697–1810.

∆ Pick up wedding invitations and (thank you's) and have them imprinted yourself. See "Paper Supply" in the *Yellow Pages*.

∆ In Mexico, they go in *"big time"* for weddings and good buys in wedding gowns and tuxedos can be found all over **Tijuana**. The signs on the store say: "Novias" (which means: sweethearts)

∆ Check the "Thrifties #780" classified column in the *Union–Trib* for used (or new!!)) wedding gowns, usually at very low prices. Some are unworn but had been altered and couldn't be returned.

Chapter 2
$MONEY SAVERS &
CONSUMER SAVVY

Whatever it takes to get more for my money, I am usually willing to do. Even if I won the lottery, I'd never abandon this philosophy. Here are a few tips I've picked up along the way that enable me to inevitably get more bang for the buck.

Δ KNOW THY PRICES!! How else will you know you've found a bargain? You gotta do your homework here. Jot down prices as you shop. Keep a record of them. I keep track of prices in the back of my check register (they're free) whether I'm shopping for a computer, sofa or comparing prices of laundry detergent.

Δ Comparison shop. Check at least six to ten sources before you make a major purchase. You'd be surprised at the difference in prices you'll be quoted and chances are someone is always willing to sell it to you for less if you keep looking. Let your fingers do the walking and use the phone. Always deal with the manager or person at the top who can give you the best price and tell them you are getting quotes, and don't tell them the quotes you already have.

Δ Keep all receipts. Have a receipt drawer, bowl or file and just toss all receipts in together. Many stores will refund the difference if you buy an item that goes on sale within two weeks.

∆ Keep a major mail order catalog like a Sears, J.C. Penney, Wards, etc. on hand for quick reference to compare prices of goods you see advertised in the newspaper.

∆ Don't hesitate to NEGOTIATE the price. This is the 90's, and stores are getting used to it. If you're new at it, start with garage sales. Make an offer, but always do it quietly and in private. Say: *"What'll you take for this?"* or *"Will you take X-amount for this?"* What have you got to lose? With the fine art of shutting your mouth and waiting a moment for their response, chances are they *will* lower their asking price. Most garage sales are for "getting rid of" rather than raising money, so it's worth your time to give this a shot. The author of a best-selling book on the art of negotiating says he never pays full price for anything, *even* at a department stores. Negotiating is a skill; you have to practice to be good. Never buy at the first price offered. Say you're on a tight budget, find something wrong with the product, make an offer and counter offer, don't take "no" for a final answer, and be gracious. Remember what Grandma used to say: *"You get more flies with honey than you do with vinegar!"* Charm your way into getting a better price!! Make it fun! Say: "Let's play 'Let's Make A Deal'" or "How about letting me make you an offer you can't refuse?" Make it a win-win situation. No one wants to deal with a person who is out to screw them.

∆ If a retailer advertises a special which is not stipulated to be in "limited quantities," and you make a trip to the store to buy it and it is not on the shelf, ask for a "rain check." This will allow you to buy the item later at the advertised price when they restock. When I went to Long's Drugs to buy L'Eggs hosiery (advertised at half price), they were out. The manager offered me a "rain check," a little form he filled in with the date, number of pairs I wanted, advertised price, and an expiration date. He told me when to check back to see if the rack has been restocked and gave me the phone number to call to see when they were in! I almost fainted!! This is a store that believes in customer satisfaction!! Here's another "rain check" tale: a friend said she went to Sears expressly to get some 100% cotton underwear for her allergic daughter. They were out. She asked the clerk for a "rain check." She was told they didn't give "rain checks." She went home and called the manager, who mailed her a "rain check" and ordered in the merchandise she wanted from another store. Another friend went to Target to get an advertised toaster oven. Target had sold out, but offered her a "rain check" and told her to come back in a week. She did, but they were still out, so they let her have a more expensive model at no additional charge! In 1971, the Federal Trade Commission issued the Retail Food Store Advertising and Marketing Practices Rule, which provides that you receive a "rain check," or a substitute or comparable item, or compensation, if an advertised special isn't in stock and the ad did not stipulate "limited quantities." The FTC suggests that if you have a problem involving this, to write to them: FTC Enforcement Division, Washington, DC 20580. Most stores want to make you a happy camper, so work with them on this. Speak with the manager because many employees do not know of this policy.

△ If a store overcharges you for an item, point this out to the manager. I was recently overcharged for some cantaloupes at Von's. They didn't charge the advertised price, and I paid over $3 more than I should have, but didn't catch it until I got home and thought about it. I called the manager who suggested I come down. He refunded the whole amount I paid for the cantaloupes and gave me two $1 Von's coupons! They appreciate customer loyalty and want to make amends for situations that really shouldn't occur.

△ Bargain hunting can involve a lot of trade-off's. Don't expect all the niceties of a department store when shopping discounters. Most off-price stores offer a "no-frills" environment, some with communal dressing rooms, or no dressing room! Remember, you're not paying for all those niceties that drive prices up, either. You're saving MONEY!!

∆ Many stores have specific days for sorting out items for clearance. Don't hesitate to ask the manager of your favorite store to clue you in on their routine.

∆ The better department stores offer FREE personal shoppers who will put together an outfit or a complete wardrobe for you on your budget. You can even finance your new wardrobe on a long term contract. And, they'll tell you if they know an item is going on sale in the not too distant future. The "pricier" stores also offer greater markdowns on sale merchandise than moderate-priced stores.

∆ Watch for clearance sales, end of the month sales, end of season sales, red tag sales and other advertised specials at major department stores in the newspapers. Weekend newspapers are loaded with sales. Wait for the major sales like Columbus Day, Memorial Day, Labor Day, anniversary sales, customer appreciation days, etc. to make a major purchase like carpeting or furniture. No point in buying just before a big sale and there's always a sale just around the corner.

∆ Get on the mailing list of your favorite stores. Even if you don't want to open an account, you can ask to be placed on the mailing list to receive advance notice of sales. Bullocks has private sales for their "special" customers, with drawings, entertainment, refreshments and giveaways you wouldn't believe . . .I won a Waterford crystal clock at their Fall-Preview Sale, and received several fragrance samples and a bag of potpourri!!

∆ Many stores offer a 10% discount on purchases made the day you open an account, and this can really add up when you make major purchases.

∆ Shop early on a sale day. Be there when the store opens for the best selection. If possible, shop the day before and ask the sales person to hold items for you until the sale begins.

Δ Beware. Don't assume you can return items. Carefully examine items before you buy, and always ask a reliable sales person or the manager for information on returns, refunds and credits.

Δ Nothing is a bargain if it doesn't fit and just sits in your closet. Just because an item is marked down to 10% of its original price doesn't mean that it is for you. Don't be seduced into buying something you won't wear or use just because it is an incredible bargain. We've all fallen into that trap, so live and learn. . . .*think about it!!*

Δ A good reason to charge auto repairs, appliance repairs, airline tickets, etc. is: if you car doesn't work properly or the bargain airline trip didn't materialize, your credit card company will credit your account if you provide proper documentation. Keep good records, receipts, agreements, etc. Check the back of your statement for their policy.

Δ Sometimes generic brands or products with the lowest price require more product to do the job, making them far more expensive than name brands.

Δ Consider time spent. If you're spending an extra two hours to save $5, you're putting a very low value on your time. If, however, you spend 60 hours painting the exterior or your house when the bid is $2000 and the paint and materials cost less than $200, you've "earned" $30 an hour and saved $1800 doing the work yourself.

Δ Putting off repairs can be costly. Failure to recaulk the tub for a few cents can do damage to the wall, which can cost 1000 times more to repair. A toilet that needs the ball replaced can add hundreds to your water bill. You can replace it yourself. Ask a sales person at Home Depot to tell you how.

△ Scrimping on little things like using less toothpaste or washing and reusing coffee filters can cause more stress and illness than it's worth. Being too thrifty can end up costing you.

△ There's not too much point in scrimping and saving unless you're able to enjoy spending when the right occasion comes along.

△ Treat yourself to the little luxuries that can make your life wonderful: a cup of gourmet coffee, a new plant or colorful new towels (on sale, of course). Show a healthy sense of self–love and reward yourself for all the money you've been able to save!

△ The best quality bed you can afford is worth it's weight in gold. It will last longer (15 year warranty on sagging) and gives better back support. A down comforter and pillows (on sale) will make for the perfect sleep (if you're not allergic to down).

△ Avoid consumer fraud. Con artists bilk $100 billion out of Americans in telemarketing and mail order, many of which are credit repair, health, insurance, or investments. For a free copy of "Too Good To Be True! A Guide To Consumer Fraud" write to the Consumer Information Center, No. 640Z, Pueblo, CO 91009.

△ To have your name removed from mailing and/or telemarketing lists, write to: Direct Marketing Association, P. O. Box 9008, Farmington, NY 11735; Telephone Preference Service, DMA, P. O. Box 9014, Farmington, NY 11735.

How To Complain & Consumer Protection Agencies

That feeling of being ripped–off or treated unfairly and not knowing where to turn is devastating, and we have all experienced it. Seek resolution and justice, and help prevent others from the same misfortune by bringing the matter before the appropriate authorities. Remember what Grandma used to tell you: "You gotta look out for Number 1......" (and don't step in Number 2).

First, sit yourself down and write a vicious, hateful, mean, nasty letter of complaint. Ventilate. Get into it. Say horrible things. Use disgusting language. Get it out of your system. Then, wad it up in a ball and throw it away because no one on the other end will read it if you send it! They'll think you're just another "crazy"! People *ignore* hate mail and simply throw it in the trash. After you've gotten that off your chest, sit down and write a coherent, specific letter detailing your dilemma. Include dates, copies of invoices, warranties, receipts and other appropriate documentation. Make copies of everything before putting it in the mail. Then, what do you do? Check the list below for an appropriate agency to contact.

△ The San Diego Mediation Center, 238-2400, will give advice and assistance, including **letter writing (a** free service).

△ Report the problem to the Better Business Bureau, 521-5888.

△ Call a radio talk show host (see "Resources") and ask for advice during "open phones." They'll give you good advice and tell you where to turn for assistance.

△ Write to Channel 10 KGTV Troubleshooter. They'll go to bat for you! Send a brief letter with any supporting documents to: Troubleshooter, P. O. Box 10, San Diego 92112. Include a telephone number where you can be reached during normal working hours.

△ Call the California Department of Consumer Affairs, (800) 952-5210. They offer live operators and recorded information.

△ Call the City Attorney General's Office **Consumer Protection Division**, 533-5600, 525 B Street, Suite 2100, San Diego, CA 92101. They can get your money back three ways: Small Claims, Contractors Licensing Board and the City Attorney's Office.

△ Write to: **Bureau of Consumer Protection**, Federal Trade Commission, Washington, D.C. 20580, and ask for a recommendation on how to pursue your complaint.

△ Send for the **Consumer Resource Handbook which lists**

contacts to help with consumer complaints, free, from the Consumer Information Center, Dept. 21, Pueblo, CO 81009.

△ Resolve disputes with **mail-order companies** by writing to Direct Marketing Association Mail Order Action Line, 6 E. 43rd Street, NY, NY 10017-4646.

△ For **automobile dealer complaints**, get the address of the district offices and/or the factory (available in your owner's manual), or call the corporate offices, using the toll free number, and find out to whom you should address your letter.

△ Check the Consumer Protection listings in the *Yellow Pages*.

△ See "**Consumer Complaint & Protection Coordinators**" in the white pages telephone directory (mainly toll free numbers!):

accountants
advertising
alarms (burglar)
athletics
automobile repair
banks
barbers
beauty salons
cemeteries
collection agencies/debt collection
contractors
cosmetologists
credit practices
(excessive charges)
credit unions
dance studios
dental examiners
dental auxiliary
doctors
employment agencies
engineers (professional)
escrow companies
finance companies
food-drug-cosmetic-hazardous
household-chemical-quality
franchise industries

funeral directors/embalmers
guarantees (deceptive or unhonored)
health professions
home furnishings
home improvement
insurance
investment fraud
loans
family counselors
nursing home complaints
optometrists
pest control operators
pharmacy
physicians-surgeons
podiatry
private investigators & private security
real estate
repair services
savings & loan
structural pests
tax preparers
TV repair
transportation (moving, busses)
veterinarians
warranties

Chapter 3
FREE & BARGAIN
THINGS TO DO

There are many, many, many things to do in San Diego that are free or low cost and the selection to choose from is absolutely wonderful. We live in a county filled with unique leisure opportunities: we have a bay and ocean full of water activities to the West, a desert and mountains to the East, a major metropolis to the North and a foreign country to the South! And nearly perfect weather year round! What more could you ask for? No wonder this place is known as paradise! And, even if you're on the tightest budget, there are enough free things to do to keep you busy for the next three lifetimes! So, if you are your basic "go*er* & do*er*," here are some great things to put on your calendar for the weekend. (For places that charge, don't hesitate to call first and ask if there are any discount coupons you should know about, or any organizational or corporate discounts, etc. OK? Okay!!)

Free & Bargain Things to Do

△ One of the best freebies in San Diego has got to be the **free admission to specified museums in Balboa Park on Tuesdays.** You could spend many memorable days in this spectacularly beautiful park without spending a single cent. There are over 1100 acres with gorgeous ornamental Spanish revival architecture with courtyards and fountains (the Museum of Art and the huge Spreckles Organ Pavilion are absolutely breathtaking), fountains and courtyards, an incredible array of massive trees, colorful seasonal flowers in bloom everywhere, and lush tropical and formal gardens. Rare and unusual fauna span the hills and canyons of the park. On weekends, there are street musicians to entertain you while you sit and "people watch." You can participate in sports, have a picnic on the endless green lawns, go on a guided walking tour, or participate in educational activities. Pick up a park map and schedule of activities at the Information Center in the Casa de Balboa (near the Space Center). Call 239–0512 for recording of hours of operation and directions to park.

There is **FREE ADMISSION** to specified museums to see the *permanent collections* (no traveling exhibits) *on Tuesdays* every month, as follows. *What a deal! One person alone can save over $31.50 in Balboa Park.* Think what you can save your friends and relatives when they visit!

FREE ON THE FIRST TUESDAY:
Δ **Museum of Natural History:** exhibits from the natural environment of our planet with emphasis on the plant and animal life in the Southwest; Desert Diorama; gems, minerals and crystals; Shore Ecology Diorama; dinosaurs, Antarctica; travelling exhibits; free on 1st Tues., 9:30 a.m.–4:30 p.m.; half–price Thursdays, 4:30 p.m.–6:30 p.m.; (Reg. price, adults $4, seniors & military w/I.D., $3, children 5–12 $1.50); 232–3821.

Δ **Model Railroad Museum:**   world's largest operating model railroad exhibit with four permanent model railroads and alternating toy train displays. Hands on exhibits and railroad artifacts; free on 1st Tues., 11 a.m.–4 p.m.; (Reg. adults $3, seniors 55+, military & students w/I.D. $2.50, under 15 free); 696–0199.

Δ **Science Center of Reuben H. Fleet Center:** a "hands–on" science center with over 50 exhibits; free on 1st Tues., 9:30 a.m.–6 p.m.; (Reg. adult $2.50, juniors $1.25, under 5 free); 238–1233.

FREE ON THE SECOND TUESDAY:

△ **San Diego Hall of Champions Sports Museum:** showcases over 40 sports, making the museum one of three multi-sports museums in the nation; free on 2nd Tues., 10 a.m.-4:30 p.m.; (Reg. Adults $3, seniors 65+ & military w/I.D. $2, children 6-17 $1, under 6 free); 234-2544.

△ **Museum of Photographic Arts:** contemporary and historic photographic exhibits of nationally and internationally known photographers; free on 2nd Tues., 10 a.m.-5 p.m.; (Reg. adults $3, 12 & under free w/adult); 239-5262.

△ **Museum of San Diego History:** local history and American cultural history from 1850 to present; free on 2nd Tues., 10 a.m.-4:30 p.m.; (Reg. adult $4, seniors & military w/I.D. $3, children 5-12 $1.50); 232-6203.

FREE ON THE THIRD TUESDAY :

△ **Museum of Man:** an anthropological museum with emphasis on American Indians, Pre-Columbian Mayas, and Early Man. Permanent exhibits include "Life Cycles and Ceremonies" and Egyptian artifacts; free on 3rd Tues., 10 a.m.-4:30 p.m.; (Reg. adult $4, juniors 13-18 $2, children 6-12 $1, under 6 and military in uniform free); 239-2001.

△ **San Diego Museum of Art:**   elegant collection of Italian Renaissance and Spanish Old Masters, American Art, 19th century European paintings and 20th century paintings and sculpture, and the Frederick R. Weisman Gallery for California Art; free on 3rd Tues., 10 a.m.-4:30 p.m.; (Reg. adult $6, seniors 65+ $5, military w/I.D. $4, children 6-17 $2, under 6 free); 232-7931.

△ **Japanese Friendship Garden:**   Small Japanese meditation garden in the Zen style with bamboo and rock surroundings. Includes an Exhibit House with Japanese cultural displays. Free the 3rd Tues., 10 a.m.-4 p.m.; (reg. adults, $2, students w/I.D., juniors 7–18, seniors 65+ & military $1; family unit $5, 6 and under, free;) 232-2780.

FREE ON THE FOURTH TUESDAY:

∆ **Aerospace Museum:** originals and replicas of historic planes and spacecraft. Highlights include a replica "Spirit of St. Louis," an A-12 Blackbird, WWII SPDA and an F4 Phantom. Includes the International Hall of Fame with portraits and plaques honoring aviation heroes; free on 4th Tues., 10 a.m.–4:30 p.m.; (Reg. adults $5, children 6–17 $1, active military w/I.D. and under 6, free; 234–8291.

∆ **Automotive Museum:** 50+ automobiles make up the museum's core collection, featuring historic, elegant, luxurious and power motor vehicles from a bygone era to present. Travelling exhibits; free on 4th Tues., 10 a.m.–4:30 p.m.; (Reg. adults $5, seniors 65+ & active duty military w/I.D. $4, children 6–17 $2, under 6 free); 231–2886.

Now, to really experience San Diego like royalty without emptying your pockets, after you've visited all the free museums on Tuesday, drop by Mr. A's (234-7951) on the top floor at 5th & Laurel (enter through the garage on 4th), for happy hour from 4 to 7 p.m. with complimentary hors d'oeuvres and happy hour–priced beverages (non–alcoholic drinks and coffee are very popular, too). There is a dress code (men need a jacket), so dress up a little for this one. The view from Mr. A's will knock your socks off. . . you can see the bay, ocean, Point Loma, Mexico and watch the planes land at Lindberg Field. Sit on the deck or at a window seat and wave to the pilots as they fly by. . . you can practically see the whites of their eyes. A sunset is really special here if you can catch one, and the city lights are spectacular after dark. I love to have my annual toddy at Mr. A's during the holidays when the buildings are decorated.

ALWAYS FREE IN BALBOA PARK:

△ **Timken Gallery:** features the Putnam Foundation collection of Old Masters from Spanish, French, Venetian, Flemish and American schools (one of the best west of the Mississippi) and a world famous collection of Russian icons; free daily, 10–4:30 p.m., Tues–Sat; 1:30–4:30 p.m. Sun.; 239–5548.

△ **House of Pacific Relations:** Open house with cultural displays, outdoor entertainment and refreshments on Sunday afternoons, March–October. Also open the fourth Tuesday, with free Hall of Nation's films. Free when open, Sun., 12:30 p.m.–4:30 p.m., and on the 4th Tues., 11:30 a.m.–3 p.m. with continuous films; international ethnic clubs; 292–8592.

△ **Spanish Village Art Center:** 41 studios feature works of local artists for display and sale; 11 a.m.–4 p.m. daily, free; 233–9050.

△ **Botanical Building:** redwood lath building containing rare tropical and subtropical plants. Exhibits are changed seasonally. Picturesquely framed by flower beds and a lily pond; free, Fri.–Wed., 10 a.m.–4 p.m.; 234–8901.

△ **Centro Cultural de la Raza:** a multi–disciplinary arts and cultural organization with exhibits and events that promote native American, Mexican and Chicano cultures; gallery hours: Wednesday through Sunday, 12 noon– 5 p.m.; free; 235–9050.

△ **Free concerts** at the gorgeous Spreckles Organ Pavilion in Balboa Park, Sundays at 2 p.m., 52 weeks a year. Free concerts on Mondays evenings at 8 p.m. from June through August; 226–0819. Twilight concerts from late June through August from 6:15–7:15 p.m. on Tuesdays, Wednesdays and Thursdays, 235–1105.

△ **Free walking tours** of Balboa Park. Explore the gardens, architecture and history of the park. Meet in front of the Botanical Building on Saturdays, 10 a.m., 235–1121. Spanish Colonial

Architecture tours, lst Wednesday. Meet at Visitor's Center, House of Hospitality, 9:30 a.m., 223-6566.

Δ May is National Museum Month, and in San Diego it is celebrated by offering either free or half price admissions to about 20 participating museums all month. Mark your calendar!

Δ The museums in Balboa Park are free the first Friday and Saturday of December, from 5-9 p.m. during the annual Christmas on the Prado.

Δ You can purchase a Balboa Park Passport which entitles you to visit the 10 major museums for one week for $18 ($44 value).

Δ All the museums above have great gift shops with unique and unusual items including beautiful shells, photographs, art cards, space gadgets, natural jewelry, etc.

Δ Learn folk dancing with the International Dance Association of San Diego County. Dance to the music of 35 different countries every Sunday from 1-5 p.m. in the Balboa Park Club Building, 422-5540. Costs a couple dollars. Ballroom dancing follows at 7 p.m. and on Friday evenings. See the *Reader* "Events" and the *Union-Trib* "Night &Day" section for more on dancing (country western dancing, swing dancing, jitterbug, etc.)

Δ Take free dance lessons at restaurants, usually an hour or two before the band comes on. Check the *Reader*, "Events, Dance."

Δ Cross the Spruce Street **suspension bridge** at First Street near Balboa Park. It crosses high above Highway 163 below. This is for thrill seekers. Don't look down!

Δ The *Entertainment* coupon book has "two-for-one" coupons for the Reuben Fleet Space Museum plus the San Diego Aerospace, Automotive Museum, Hall of Champions, Museum of Art, Museum of Man, Museum of Natural History, and the Model Railroad Museum if you can't make it down for free day (see chapter on "Resources.")

△ Tour the Old Globe Theater at 11 a.m. every Saturday, $3.

△ Admission to the zoo is free one day a year, on its anniversary, celebrated on the *first Monday* in October. Go early in order to get parking. Children are free the whole month of October. (Regular adult $13, children 3–11 $6, under 2 and military in uniform free; senior passes for 1 year, $19). Membership entitles you to unlimited entrance to the zoo *and* the Wild Animal Park, two guest passes, **4 two–for–one coupons and 6 discount coupons, Zoo Nooz Magazine**, free Skyfari, monorail, 231–0251. One membership, $55; dual membership, $68; Koala Kids Club, age 3–15, $15. Membership is a great gift for a family on a budget because it provides 365 days of wholesome family entertainment. And, the *Entertainment* coupon book has 25% off coupons for the Zoo. (See chapter on "Resources.") Discounts are available through AAA and credit unions, too.

△ **Wild Animal Park** is free on Founder's Day, *second Wednesday* in May. Visit Wild Animal Park during a full moon. Take the tram and see the animals feeding. Or, get in free with zoo membership, which entitles you to unlimited use of Wild Animal Park, 738–5021. And, the *Entertainment* coupon book has 25% off coupons for Wild Animal Park. (See chapter on "Resources.")

△ **Serra Museum** at Presidio Park, with exhibits and artifacts from the American Indian, Spanish mission and Mexican periods of California history, is free the second Tuesday of the month, 297–3258.

△ **Free walking tours** of downtown: 1–3 p.m. every Saturday at 255 G Street, 235–2222.

∆ **Free bus tour of downtown:** 10–12 noon Saturdays, twice a month, 235-2222.

∆ Listen to the radio shows, be the umpteenth caller and win tickets to plays, movies, sporting events, concerts, bay cruises, etc. I have friends who win tickets to premiers of movies, dinner for two, Padres and other sporting events, etc., all the time. One friend won a cruise to Mexico for four on the Love Boat. . . just listening to the radio! She has it down: has a couple radio of stations' numbers programmed into "redial" on the phone, and she wins something at least once a month or more.

∆ Drive the **"59–Mile Scenic Drive:"** Start at the foot of Broadway downtown and continue up Harbor Drive to Harbor Island, Shelter Island, Cabrillo Monument, Sunset Cliffs, Mission Bay, Pacific Beach, La Jolla, Old Town, Balboa Park and more. (Follow the blue and yellow "Scenic Drive" signs with a white seagull located every quarter mile.) Great places to stop and take photos. I am so glad I discovered this within a few months of moving to San Diego.

∆ Take in the great view from the top floor at the Hyatt Regency, Harbor Drive at Market Street. . . Pt. Loma, downtown, coastline.

∆ **Tour a navy ship:** Call for schedule, 532-1430x9 or 545-1133.

∆ Visit the Command Museum at the Marine Corps Recruit Depot with artifacts (including a tank) from 1846 to Kuwait. Enter Gate 4, Pacific Highway, 10–4 p.m., Tu–Su.

∆ Join any of the museums, galleries, zoos, etc. and get many freebies including unlimited entrance, classes, special admission to exhibits, passes for your friends and relatives, etc. See individual museums for benefits.

∆ **Sea World** adult admission is $28.95; children 3-11, $20.95;

and 2 and under are free. Discount coupons are available at Von's, $5; $10 off after 5 p.m., MacDonald's, $5; AAA $5 off. Student, military and senior discounts available. You can get a 12-month membership with unlimited passes, $54.95 for adults, $44.95 for children, 226-3939. I know families who ask grandma for membership for Christmas so they can go often. Shamu Club cards are available through a lot of credit unions including Mission Federal or employers, good for 20% discount on admission, 10% on merchandise. Group rates for 15 or more, 10% discount, call 226-3815. Sometimes, a second day pass is free. Summer Camp Sea World classes, 1 week, $60; with 12-month pass, $55; field trips for school groups, October–May. Call the education program at 222-6363x2452.

Δ Go to any hotel lobby or Visitor's Center (see list later in this chapter) and pick up a copy of *San Diego This Week,* which usually has a $3 off coupon for Sea World, and a two-for-one coupon for the Kobey's swapmeet, which may be where you end up going!

Δ For half-price tickets to *tonight's* performances at the theater, ballet, symphony and other performances, call 497-5000. See chapter on "Cultural Events."

Δ **Cabrillo National Park** offers one of the most incredible view points of San Diego plus trails, nature walks, tidepools, etc; Slide shows and lectures on the gray whale, sculpture and photo exhibits. Park entrance is $4 per car. You can get an annual pass for Cabrillo Park for $10, 557-5450. This is where I fell in love with San Diego. It was my first peek at west coast water, and I felt like Balboa discovering the Pacific! Whadda view! I was completely breathtaken. Go on a sunny day; you don't want the fog to cloud your view. Santa Anna days are absolutely glorious!

Δ You can get a Golden Eagle Pass at Cabrillo, good for *all* national parks for one year, for $25.

∆ Seniors age 62 and over get in free to all national parks with a Golden Age Passport issued free for the asking, with ID, at any national park.

∆ See the **whales** off the San Diego coast during their migration South from January to March, free, from Sunset Cliffs Natural Park or Point Loma Nazarene College, 3900 Lomaland, Point Loma. Ask the guard at the entrance where the public area is (drive through the beautiful campus to the ocean).

∆ One of the best short vacations I can think of is a 2 1/2 hour boat ride out to see the whales, especially on a warm Santa Anna day during whale watching season. The boats take you out near the Coronado Islands and guarantee sighting whales or you get to do it again! Trips cost about $12 per person and "two–for–one" coupons are in the newspapers and the *Entertainment* coupon book. (Call H&M Landing and ask if they have any coupons.) If you take a boat from Point Loma, first have the best fried fish or fresh tuna sandwich in San Diego at the Point Loma Seafood Market, 2805 Emerson Street at the wharf, 223–1109. Seafood lovers: you'll adore this place!

∆ The *Entertainment* coupon book has "two–for one" coupons for the Hornblower Yacht, Harbor Excursion, and the Catalina Flyer. (See chapter on "Resources.")

∆ **Walking tours** are a great way to get to know your city, and a good way to get some outdoor exercise. On a glorious day in San Diego what could be a better combination? All the following walks are free unless other wise indicated:

Walkabout International 231–SHOE
Walkabout sponsors over 150 walks a month, several per day, morning and evening, theme walks (historical, view walks, beach walks, see Christmas Lights, etc.) They also sponsor walking trips to Hawaii, Ireland, Washington, DC, San Francisco, etc.

Walkabout's great newsletter, $12 per year. Call for a sample.
Balboa Park tours . . . . See Above
Cabrillo Monument 557-5450
    Self-guided tour; tidepool explorations fall and winter, $4
    3rd Saturday, bird walk, 9:30 a.m.
    Sunday afternoon Military history walk, 2:30 p.m.
    Call for dates of mini-seminars on whales, the harbor, etc.
La Jolla Walking Tours, $7 453-8219
Coronado Historical Walking Tours, $5 . . . . 435-5892/435-5993
Gaslamp Quarter 233-4682
    Walking tours every Saturday at 11 a.m., $5
Downtown Information Center 235-2222
    Free two hour walking tours, 1 p.m. every Saturday, 255 G St
Encinitas walks (monthly) 753-5726
Old Town walks, 2 p.m. daily 291-1019/220-5422
Old Town Park Tours 491-0110
    For groups of 10, $6.50 for 2 hours
Quail Botanical Gardens, free tours Saturday, 10 a.m. 436-3036
Silverwood Wildlife Sanctuary Nature Walks 443-2998
Bird Walks, Saturdays, 8 a.m. 422-2481
Salk Institute tour . . . . 453-4100 x 1200
International Assn. of Walkers and Runners 276-7298
    8 a.m. every Sunday at De Anza Cove (over 25 years), free
(See the *Reader* and *Union-Trib*/Night and Day for more walks)

△ Check out the great views from the top floor of the Union Bank Building, 5th & B downtown; Mr. A's at 5th and Laurel; Del Mar Plaza sun deck at 1555 Camino Del Mar; Presidio Park above Old Town; Sea World Sky Tower (280 feet high); Mt. Soledad Park at the top of Soledad Mountain Road in La Jolla; Mt. Helix.

△ Take a picnic lunch and watch the free **kite flying** near the Hilton Hotel on Mission Bay, South of the Visitor's Center, or at Seaport Village. Some of these colorful and unique kites cost hundred of dollars.

△ Take the half-hour free guided tour around **Salk Institute** for

Biological Studies, Louis Kahn's most famous work in the West, while Nobel Prize winners labor inside, 453-4100 x 1200.

∆ **Tour the Union-Tribune Building**, complete with a film covering the history of the paper and a guided tour of the building from the editor's office to where they tie up the newspapers. Call 299-3131 for information on the next tour.

∆ Tour Channel 10 and find out what goes on behind the scenes. Call 237-1010x474 for further information. Form your own group of not more than 30, or ask to join a group that is booked.

∆ **Free bicycle maps**, routes and information are available at CalTrans, 231-BIKE.

∆ Get free assistance is checking out your genealogy through the Family History Library, 3705 10th, Hillcrest, 295-9808.

∆ The Coast Guard Auxiliary offers free **sailing and power boat lessons:** beginning, intermediate, advanced, navigation, seamanship, more. Classes are held throughout the County including Silvergate Yacht Club, 223-6054. Call the Auxiliary for other locations. Then, you can rent a boat using two-for-one coupons *Entertainment* coupon book (see chapter on "Resources.")

∆ Full Circle Tours offers many low cost one-day trips out of San Diego, and short excursions. Call for free schedule, 292-8859.

∆ Here's how you get to **Sally's favorite view** of San Diego Bay, the one that is on the promotional literature for San Diego that shows the San Diego Yacht Club, the bay, downtown, Mt. Helix and more. It is gorgeous. Take Rosecrans South past Shelter Island Drive, right on Talbot Street two blocks, left on Harbor View Drive, right on Harbor View Place, left on Bangor, left on Lucinda to Golden Park and stop! A breathtaking view. The homes are something to see, too. You must take all your guests to see this view, then drop down to Pt. Loma–Shelter Island Pharmacy and let them pick up postcards to send home with that view on it!

△ This one will cost you the price of a beverage of your choice. Check out the big picture above the bar at the Casa de Loma, 1304 Rosecrans in Point Loma. It is an approximately 6' by 8' slide of **"THE" view of downtown** and San Diego Bay that adorns promotional literature (above).

△ **Mexican dinners** anywhere are a bargain and a favorite place is Old Town. (In San Diego, generally speaking, inexpensive dinners are under $10; medium priced dinners are $10–$20; expensive dinners are $20–$30 and deluxe dinners are over $30. Compare that with NY or LA!)) Old Town is a great place to take the visiting friends and relatives, particularly in January when you can eat outdoors at the Casa de Pico in the Bazaar Del Mundo, 296–3267, or the Casa de Bandini, 297–8211; or El Fandango, 298–2860 ($6 or $7 items on the menu). Dine in shirtsleeves year round in this historic setting with lush foliage, flowers and birds everywhere. There is entertainment on weekends, with mariachis and flamenco dancers from 1–4 p.m. Definitely a favorite spot.

△ Visit the **Mormon Battalion Visitor Center**, 2510 Juan Street, Old Town, 298–3317, 9 a.m.–9 p.m., daily. Photos, videos, artifacts from the famous Mormon Battalion in Old Town dating from 1847.

△ If you move to a new location, call the Welcome Wagon at 488–9889. They will come for a visit and give you gifts and coupons from your new neighborhood merchants.

△ Take the **ferry boat** ride from foot of Broadway at Harbor Drive to Coronado Landing for $2 per person and roam the shopping center, have lunch, or board the Coronado Trolley and head for Hotel Del Coronado. Take your bicycle, 50¢ extra. Ferry boats leave every hour on the hour, 234–4111.

△ Spend the day at the **Hotel Del Coronado**, take the tour of the hotel at 1 p.m., or take the self–guided tour on tape available at the gift shop. Find out about the ghost of Kate Morgan, which 12 presidents have stayed there and what films have used it as a back drop. Lounge out back in the sun on their deck or walk on the beach. I go there for a stress break and play "bring me:" "Bring me a Blood Mary" and "Bring me a Club Sandwich." Just crossing the bridge makes me feel I have left town.

△ Visit the Coronado Beach Historical Museum, 1126–28 Loma Avenue, Coronao, 435–7242. Free admission. Mostly photographs showing early Coronado from its establishment, Tent City, the ferry boats, the beginning of North Island, plus exhibits and memorabilia are presented in an historic building, 10 a.m. – 4 p.m., Wedneday––Friday; noon–4 p.m. Saturday and Sunday.

△ Become a **volunteer**! You'll have a great time and meet a lot of people. I was a volunteer for **Sail America** when Dennis Connor came back with America's Cup from Australia. My volunteer "job" was to crank out beer from a tap at the B Street Pier. Dennis was a couple hours late, the crowd had grown big, and it was great fun. Volunteers could go into the VIP tent and see the celebrities, news anchors, the reigning Miss California and several local mayors and other officials. When you volunteer for an organization, you attend a few meetings and they'll assign you to whatever they need. Sometimes there are big parties held after events for all the volunteer workers. It's great fun. When Super Bowl was coming to San Diego, I called a year ahead of time and they already had enough volunteers! Ten thousand volunteers were needed and they already had enough!! Call the Superbowl Task Force or the Chargers headquarters a year ahead of the '98 Superbowl if you want to volunteer. You can be a volunteer at the **Mayor's** office and you may get to meet some very interesting officials and visiting dignitaries, or volunteer for the **Chargers,**

Padres, at rock concerts, golf tournaments, San Diego Historical Society's Designer Showcase, **etc. Channel 10** needs volunteers to work at the station, as do other TV and radio stations. If you volunteer at the Department of Parks and Recreation in Old Town to be a docent (tour guide), they of course train you and you get a card to go in to all the California State Parks free! You can volunteer at Humphrey's and see the concerts. You can volunteer to be an usher at a play and see the play for free. If you want to volunteer at an event, do call early and offer your services. Another type of volunteering is for service organizations, listed the first Sunday of the month in San Diego Section of the *Union–Trib*. If you volunteer at Palomar Hospital, you get discount tickets to movies and use of their gym! Channel 10 has a Volunteer Line for service organizations, 492–2121.

△ Browse **through antiques** in Ocean Beach's many stores; or on Adams Avenue and in Gaslamp Quarter. Don't miss the Unicorn!

△ Walk through **Heritage Park Village,** Juan Street at Haney, 565–3600, in Old Town and see the old Victorian homes that were moved there. Be sure to stop at Ye Old Doll House located in the Sherman–Gillman House, then have tea at the Heritage Park Bed & Breakfast, 295–7088. This is a very peaceful setting with NO cars. If you're interested in other old homes, contact the Save Our Heritage Organization and the San Diego Historical Society.

△ The **Coronado Bridge** is free if there are two people in the car. Get in far right lane.

△ Don't miss a sunset from the **Marine Room** on the ocean at 2000 Spindrift Dr., off Torrey Pines Rd., La Jolla, 459–7222; or during storm season when the waves are pounding on the windows! Beautifully lit at night. No happy hour, but one of the most spectacular views right on the ocean and rated one of the most romantic restaurants in San Diego.

△ Don't miss your chance to go grunion hunting at midnight on a full moon night at high tide. You must have these three ingredients to find the grunion. Best place: the beach at the foot of South Mission Blvd. There's always big grunion party going on!

△ Check out the **tide pools** at Cabrillo Monument or below the Ocean Beach Pier during a super low tide (December and January tides are very low). Get a *Farmer's Almanac* for the exact dates, and mark your calendar!

△ Take the **San Diego Trolley** to the border for $1.75, 233–3004; schedules, 685–4900.

△ **San Diego Transit** Bus monthly passes, $48 for adults age 18–60. One ride, $1.50 up. Seniors, disabled: $12.25 a month; youth pass, $24.50. Call 685–4900 for more information.

△ Take the **Coaster**, the new train, up the coast as far as Oceanside. Stops in downtown, Old Town, Sorrento Valley, Solana Beach, Encinitas, Carlsbad Poinsettia, Carlsbad Village, Oceanside; $6.25 maximum fare round trip, depending on where you get on. Monthly maximum, $95. Call 233–3004 or 685–4900 (recorded).

△ Sing along with karaoke. San Diego has a couple dozen bars that offer karaoke listed in *Reader* "Events" and *Union–Trib* "Night & Day"section.

△ Visit **Sunny Jim Cave**, below the La Jolla Cave & Shell Shop, $2. Take the 125 steps down to the ocean through the cave. This is a natural cave that was connected to the Shell Shop; 454–6080.

△ **State Parks & Recreation Camping** Information, (800) 444–7275.

△ **San Diego County Parks & Recreation** publishes a great $2 brochure describing all the County's parks and facilities, tennis courts, 694–3049.

△ San Diego Park and Recreation, 235–1100. Ask about tennis, golf, dance, etc. Swimming Pool info, 685–1322.

△ **Torrey Pines Hiking Trail** is free, parking $4, 755–2063.

△ **Open space hiking trails**: Mission Trails Regional Park, 668–2375; Las Penosquitas Canyon Reserve, 484–7504; Tecolote Canyon, 581–9952.

△ Hike up **Cowles Mountain**, a 1.7 mile trail that leads to the top of the peak. Great view to the ocean. Spectacular at sunset. Take flashlights for after dark. Park at Navajo Road and Golfcrest.

△ Watch the **Chargers** practice at UCSD during summer camp. Call 280–2111 for further information and dates.

△ **High Tea** at the Rancho Bernardo Inn, 277–2146, is a bargain at $5 per person, from 4–5 p.m. each day. High Tea is having its own little Renaissance these days and is very popular. Tea is normally served somewhere in the afternoon between 3 and 5 p.m. in individual china pots. A tea cart magically appears filled with finger sandwiches, scones and pastries and fancy cookies dipped in chocolate, accompanied by music from a pianist. The Hyatt Regency's tea is a bargain at $7.50 (up to $17.50). The U.S. Grant, Westgate, Le Meridien, Hotel Del Coronado, Horton Grand and the Heritage Park Bed & Breakfast have high tea for about $10 per person. No bargain, but don't miss tea at the Ritz Carlton, a Five-Star Hotel in Laguna, for about $17. What a view from the lounge! Get a window seat. This is a gorgeous hotel in a gorgeous setting! A "must-do" afternoon on the California Riviera.

△ Visit the **Ecke Poinsettia Ranch** in Encinitas. Call for dates of the holiday tour and mark your calendar, 633–4802.

Δ Check out the horse races at the **Del Mar Racetrack** during racing season *free* after the sixth race (about 5 p.m.). A lot of people go right after work! Take the Coaster train, $5.75 round trip from downtown. Satellite wagering, 755-1200.

Δ Ride the **Carmella Bella mini-sternwheeler** (summer only) behind Tarantino's Italian Restaurant during sunset, 5150 N. Harbor Drive, 224-3555. It's free for dinner guests. The restaurant is so popular they built the boat to handle the overflow of people during happy hour. Nice marina view.

Δ Tour a new addition to San Diego, the **Stephen Birch Aquarium**-Museum at Scripps Institute of Oceanography, 2300 Expedition Way, La Jolla near Scripps Pier; 534-3474. Admission: $6.50 for adults; children 3-12, $3.50. Discount coupons ($1 off) are in their literature in hotel lobbies everywhere and also in *San Diego This Week*. One-day scholarships for those who can't afford to pay. Membership: individuals, $35; family, $49; students K-college and seniors, $29.

Δ If you're into architecture and decorating, here are some **home tours** to mark on your calendar: Point Loma December Home Tour (over 40 years), 223-6394; North County Christmas Home Tour, 451-0122; Caridad International Tijuana Home Tour, 673-0210, 298-2186 or 283-9461. You get to peek into fantastic homes of the local rich and famous!!

Δ Browse around the **Oceanside Pier**, the longest pier on the west coast, stretching 1,940 feet out to sea. Beautiful panoramic view at the end of the pier from Fisherman's Restaurant and Oyster Bar.

Δ Many San Diego Adult School courses are free. You can attend classes in San Diego regardless of where you live. There are no boundaries. I have been taking *free* computer and wordprocessing courses at Midway, 3249 Fordham Sheet in the Sports Arena area, 221-6973, for a several years. I was a computer "dwid" but I hung in with it because I felt that if three–year olds can do it, there was hope for me. For a listing of free leisure, career and enrichment courses, see "Classes."

△ You can take as many **college credits** as you want for $15 per credit at community colleges throughout the State. It is one of the most wonderful bargains I have ever found. When I discovered this, I was the first one in line in September that year! I went from wife and mother (with two years of college) to part time student at Grossmont College to full time student at SDSU to high school teacher to writer, and if I can do it, you can do it, too! See chapter on "Classes."

△ **Palomar College** offers free planetarium shows programs for the public the first Wednesday of each month during the school year. Often overcrowded, reservations recommended, 744–1150.

△ Reuben Fleet Space Theater, 238–1233, offers programs the first Wednesday of the month called the Sky Tonight., which covers the start you'll be seeing over the next month. Adults, $3; juniors, $1.75. Afterwards, San Dieo Astronomy Association sets up telescopes outside for viewing, and you can ask questions of the experts.

△ To get to **Palomar Observatory**, 35899 Canfield Road, Palomar Road, take Interstate 15 North to 76 East to County Road S6, home of a 200–inch reflecting telescope, the world's second largest, used since 1949 to probe the mysteries of deep space. Free admission, 742–2119. A small museum next to the observatory has a replica of the scope and other displays. Open daily except Christmas.

△ Visit the observatory of San Diego State University **at Mt. Laguna from Memorial Day through Labor Day for their free summer program. See a slide show and view the sky through telescopes.** Call 594–6182 for more information.

△ Take a **helicopter tour of San Diego**, $95 each, a fabulous 30–minute tour, 291–HELO. Occasional specials for groups, $50. Mention this book for a 10% discount; seniors, 15% discount.

△ Don't miss the **Del Mar Fair** every summer during the last two weeks in June, ending the Fourth of July. About $7.50 admission, with discount tickets at supermarkets. It's the roast corn that gets me up there every year or so, not to mention the free concerts with big name entertainment.

△ Watch the **hang gliders** strapped to their apparatus take off from the edge of the 300–foot high cliffs at Torrey Pines on weekends near UCSD above Black's Beach, 452–3202.

△ Visit **Weidner's Begonia Gardens** and see dazzling flowers cascading out of hanging baskets and blooming from the ground during the season, April through September, November –December. Free. In Leucadia, 695 Normandy, 436–2194.

△ For the best view of a **sunrise**, take County Road S–1 to the top of the Laguna Mountains eastern edge and see the forest above and the desert below at one of the designated viewpoints. Also, try a sunrise from Shelter Island or from the intersection of Trumbull & Bangor on Point Loma. Wow! Good lookin' sunrise with the sun coming up over the bay, downtown and the hills.

△ Walk around the **Quail's Inn**, 1035 La Bonita Dr., 744–0120, at Lake San Marcos, rent boats on lake, feed ducks. Wonderful view. Beautiful gardens, trails, birds. The bar has a good happy hour, 4–6:30 a.m., with complimentary hors d'oeuvres.

△ Tour the **Self–Realization Fellowship** grounds and gardens on Highway 101 (215 K Street, Encinitas), 753–2888; or at 16455 Old Guejito Grande Road, Escondido, 749–3399. The Center on Sunset Boulevard in Los Angeles is 10 times larger than the one here and very interesting to browse, too.

△ Don't miss seeing the **ranuncula fields** in bloom in the spring around Easter behind Pea Soup Anderson's on Interstate 5 in Carlsbad. Wow. This is the flower capital of the world.

△ **Wander about the three–acre Grigsby's Cactus Gardens** with over 2,000 varieties of cacti and succulents, 2354 Belle Vista Drive, Vista, 727–1323.

△ Visit **Bates Nut Farm**, 15954 Woods Valley Road, Valley Center. Picnic area, farm zoo, gift boutique with gourmet honey, olives, etc; pumpkins in October. Open 8–5 p.m. daily, 749–3333.

△ Attend the **Starlight or Vista Moonlight Amphitheater** on a full moon night (or Wild Animal Park)!

△ Visit the **art district** between about 4th and 12th in the Gaslamp District downtown. Big annual art walk with champagne openings in April. Call 232–4395 for dates.

△ Don't miss the **Art Alive** exhibit in the spring (paintings and artwork recreated with flowers). Very special. Call 232–7931 for date.

△ Stay at the **Mission San Luis Rey** Retreat, 757–3659, in Oceanside for about $37.50 a day. Family week; holistic week (integrating mind, body and spirit); senior week; private room, two beds, the retreat activities, and lodging and meals, $115 each, less for kids!

△ Hear reknowned speakers like Wayne Dyer speak at the **Crystal Cathedral in Garden Grove**. Drive up or take a tour bus. See "Travel Agencies" in the classified ads of the *Union–Trib* for tour buses.

△ Free **wine tasting and tours** at the Bernardo Winery, 13330 Paseo Del Verano Norte, 487–1866; Deer–Park Winery is only a tasting room (the winery is the Napa Valley), with an auto museum with 49 restored antique cars, open from 1–5 p.m. every day at 29013 Champagne Blvd, Escondido, 488–1666; Ferrara Winery, 1120 W. 15th St., Escondido, 745–7632; Thornton Winery, 32575 Rancho California Road, Temecula, (909) 699–0099; free tours every Saturday and Sunday; tastings are $6; award–winning sparkling wines produced here. Their Cuvee de Frontignan was served at two state dinners at The White House. Wine tasting rooms, gold medal restaurant, gifts shop, case discounts. If you haven't had enough, the Temecula Valley has about a dozen more wineries.

∆ Watch the **hot air balloons** take off and land around sunset from several points in the San Dieguite Valley. Try El Camino Real and Manchester or next door to the polo fields on Camino Real and San Dieguito Road, or by the Doubletree Hotel at Camino Real and Carmel Valley. Watch while they are blowing them up, too. Sunset Balloons said to just call them at 481–9122 and they will tell you where they are going to launch that day, depending on the winds. You can get a discount coupon at hotels for a ride on Sunset Balloons.

∆ Take a **Grayline Tour** of San Diego or Tijuana. Call Grayline at 491–0011 and ask them to send you a "two–for–one" coupon!

∆ See the **birds sitting on the telephone wires** on Jimmy Durante Boulevard in Del Mar. Also, on the wires to the right of Interstate 8 West near Sports Arena exit. Tons of birds are always there. Wish I knew why. Maybe they enjoy that view??!!

∆ Attend the **Arts and Crafts exhibits** every weekend at several locations: at the end of Shelter Island; near the Hilton Hotel at Interstate 5 below Clairemont Drive; next to the Princess Hotel on Ingraham Street; and in Spreckle's Park on Orange Avenue in Coronado.

△ Ride the **Bahia Belle** around Mission Bay stopping at the Catamaran Hotel, San Diego Princess Hotel and the Bahia Hotel for $5. There is a "two- for-one" coupon in the *Entertainment* coupon book (see chapter on "Resources.") Music, dancing and cocktails on board. Stop off at any of the hotels and get picked up on the next trip around. Fun to do at sunset, 488-0551.

△ **Be an extra in movies or on TV!** Call Background San Diego's hotline if you want to be productions filmed here, 974-8970; or call Tina Real Casting, 685-3662. For a list of casting agencies, call the San Diego Film Commission, 234-3456. For more on this, see "How to Raise Quick Cash" later in this book.

△ **Produce your own TV show**, free, on Southwestern Cable, Daniels or Cox Cable. Call to get on the list for the next class to learn how. The deal here is that the FCC requires that the public be allowed access to television. The class is free and you'll meet others who will be your camera crew for your production.

△ Listen to a time share pitch and receive gifts or trips. I listened to Riviera Resorts pitch at the Carlsbad Inn and received a free weekend at a Marriott and dinner for two at Fidel's restaurant at the Inn. I have been invited to the Lawrence Welk Resort in Palm Springs for a weekend (value $250 a night), and toured the Coronado Beach Club, and received brunch for two at the Hotel Del. I think they got my name from a new car drawing at the Del Mar Fair Grounds!

△ Visit the Chula Vista **Nature Interpretive Center** which offers a unique opportunity to experience the vanishing salt marsh environment of San Diego Bay. Observation platforms overlook the Sweetwater Marsh. One of the last remaining habitats in the United States for some rare species of birds. Over 175 species in the marsh. Petting pools and interactive displays. Park at E Street and Bayside, just off Interstate 5. Buses run from the foot of E Street to the center for 50¢; admission is $3.50 for adults, $1 for children. Call 422–BIRD for further information.

△ Visit **Buena Vista Lagoon** off Interstate 5 between Carlsbad and Oceanside, another ecological reserve and haven for birds and bird watchers.

△ Bird watch at the **Silverwood Wildlife Sanctuary** with over 152 species of birds at the Audobon nature preserve. Follow the trails, 13003 Wildcat Canyon Road, Lakeside. Call 443–2998 for information and nature walk schedule.

△ **Antique aircraft viewing** is available from 1–2 p.m. the first Sunday of each month in front of the airport administration building at Gillespie Field, 1960 Joe Crosson Drive, El Cajon, 596–3900.

△ Check out the **Bancroft Ranch House Museum** of the Spring Valley Historical Society, 9050 Memory Lane, Spring Valley, 469–1480. This is a national landmark built in 1863, with artifacts and memorabilia. Free. Call for hours of operation.

△ **Bonita Historical Museum**, 4035 Bonita Road, Bonita, 267–5141, is an old fire station with a collection of old California artifacts. Free, open Th–Fri, 10–3 p.m., Sa–Su, 12–3 p.m.

△ **California Surf Museum**, 308 North Pacific Street, Oceanside, 721–6876. Vintage films and videos of surfing, historic photos, displays of boards, free. Noon–4 p.m., Th–Mo.

△ **Chula Vista Heritage Museum**, 360 Third Avenue, Chula Vista, 420–6916. Photos of big old homes, the old Otay watch factory, artifacts, free, 1–4 p.m., Tu–Th and Sat.

△ **Heritage Walk Museum**, 321 North Broadway, Escondido, 743–8207. Free, features Esondido's first library from 1894, a Victorian house beautifully furnished, a blacksmith shop (with classes!), paintings, etc. Open 1–4 p.m. Tu–Sa.

△ Check out the many farmer's markets for freshly picked veggies. See "Food," Chapter One.

△ Try your hand at **poker and bingo** at the Sycuan Indian Reservation Casino, 5409 Dehesa Road, El Cajon, 445–6066; or Barona Bingo, 1000 Wildcat Canyon Road, Lakeside, 443–2300.

Out of the area:
△ Visit the **Laguna Arts Festival**, about 75 miles up Interstate 5 to Laguna turnoff. The Pageant of the Masters features the re-creation of great works of art (paintings, sculptures and artifacts), with living models who look exactly like the original creations, thanks to highly technical lighting effects, makeup, costuming and backgrounds.   An orchestra and narration round out the presentation. Held during July and August for the past several decades, this one is always a sell–out. Call (714) 496–7050 for ticket information, or take a tour bus up. See *Union–Trib* classified ads, "Travel Agencies #169."

△ Drive to **Julian** in the fall and have a slice of apple pie during the Apple Festival. Call 765–1857 for dates.

△ Take the self–guided scenic auto tour through the **Borrego Springs** area, with its spectacular views of the badlands. Dirt roads, deep canyons, 6,000 foot mountain, campgrounds. Information is available from the Borrego Springs Chamber of Commerce or at the Desert Park headquarters in Borrego Springs.

△ Drive to the **Anza–Borrego Desert State Park** and stop at the underground Visitor Center to see an amazingly beautiful computer–run slide show of the 660,000–acre desert park's changing seasons. Park Headquarters, Palm Canyon Drive, two miles west of Borrego Springs. Call 767–5311 for information.

△ **Disneyland** discounts are hard to come by other than for military, students, seniors and corporate. Here's what I found: you can get a Magic Kingdom Club Card, (714) 490–3200 through employers, credit unions, and professional associations which entitles you to a $2–$8 discount on admissions, 10% discount on Delta Airlines, car rentals, and a 10% discount on merchandise Disney Stores nationwide (but not at Disneyland or Disneyworld!) I picked up a card from my credit union. In the fall through December 24, Disneyland offers a $23 Passport for Southern Californians with 90000–93599 zip codes and proof of residence, (714) 999–4565. In October, once the kids have gone back to school and attendance drops down, the Disneyland Hotel offers reduced–price package deals that include tickets. Call Disney Vacation Packages, (714) 520–5050. Sometimes it's better to stay at Disney for the convenience rather than trying to save a few bucks at a nearby hotel. You lose the savings by having to pay parking, you lose *time*, end up standing in longer lines because of it and see less.

△ Join the lottery to **win a liquor license**. I know someone who won! You put $5,000 in the lottery which is fully refunded if you don't win. The State has use of your money for the year. You won't earn any interest on the money, and it costs $25 to join, but if you win, you get a liquor license worth many thousands which you must keep and use for two years, then you can sell it!

△ Be on a **TV game show** in Los Angeles, free. I had a student who won a trip to Australia on *The Price Is Right*! Where to call for tryouts: *All New Dating Game* (213) 469–2662; *Card Sharks* (213) 520–1234; *Jeopardy* (213) 466–3931; at the *Price is Right*, contestants are taken from the audience, (213) 852–4002; *Wheel of Fortune* (213) 520–5555; *Win, Lose or Draw*, (213) 653–8551; *Concentration and Family Feud* have local numbers, (619) 223–2101 or 588–6600; *WhizKids* age 8–13, (213) 820–6391; *Scrabble*, (213) 284–8644;

△ For a **list of TV show tapings**, send a self-addressed stamped envelope to: L.A. Convention and Visitors Bureau, c/o TV Tapings, 515 S. Figueroa, Suite 1100, Los Angeles, CA 90071. The Home Show, (213) 520-5000; The Improv, (213) 394-8664. **Audiences Unlimited**: over 40 shows including "Murphy Brown," "Home Improvement," "Married with Children," "Roseanne," "Empty Nest," (818) 506-0043 (Hollywood), recording of the week's shows.

△ Get free tickets to the **Jay Leno Show** by writing at least four weeks ahead of time to 30000 West Alameda, Burbank, CA 91523. You can stand in line on the day of the show in the NBC ticket office in Burbank, where passes are given out on a first-come, first-served basis. For further information, call Guest Relations at (818) 840-4444.

△ **Tour NBC** in Los Angeles, (818) 840-4444.

△ Take a trip south of the border to **Tijuana**. Contact the Tijuana Convention and Tourist Bureau in San Diego, 298-4105. They will tell you in English about all the cultural events, attractions and sporting events, restaurants, etc. Don't miss the travel movie of all the sights in Mexico at the Cultural Center at 2 p.m. daily, in English. (At all other times, it is in Spanish, but it's beautiful even if you don't understand a word.)

△ Drive down to **Rosarito Beach** and have a Ramos Fizz at the famous Rosarito Beach Hotel. Winter rates and off-season are about one half the summer rates, include dinner and you'll have the place to yourselves. Senior discounts at age 45! Weekdays are cheaper than weekends. Ask about discount coupons when you call (800) 343-8582.

△ Call the Rosarito Beach Visitor Information at (619) 234-5652 and ask for an information packet.

△ About six miles past the Rosarito Beach Hotel is the Las Rocas

Hotel, newer, and on a wonderful site on the water. If you can get down there on a Santa Anna day in January or February and feel that warm sun and breathe that clean air and see the ocean and coastline forever, you'll thank me. A great place for lunch outside. The amazing thing is you'll have the place to yourselves (in winter, that is!) For more information and directions, call (800) 733-6394.

Δ Baja California Tours takes day trips, overnights, art tours, fishing tour busses to Baja for sightseeing along the Mexican coastline, 454-7166.

Δ Visit the *Oh! Disco* Laser Club in Tijuana, one of five world class discos (the others are in Rome, London, Paris and New York). It is located on Paseo de los Heroes a block past the statue of the Aztec Indian chief on the right. The usual rate of admission is $5, but with a big star performer, can be up to $50. Frequent lines to get in.

Δ Discover Baja Travel Club, everything you need to know about Baja, 275-4225

Leisure Resources

Δ The *Reader,* a free newspaper published every Thursday, contains a "Guide to Local Events" that lists what's doing in San Diego for the week. These happenings include major events and *free* things to do. Many people "in the know" rely on this source for their weekend leisure activities.   What I like about it is it lists outdoor things: what stars are in the sky, extreme high and low tides, the seasonal flowers in bloom along the freeways and in the desert, and other little things worth noticing that are unique to San Diego and make it such a fabulous place to live. Then, there is the section on upcoming "Lectures," "Drama," "Music," "Film," "In Person," "Sports," and "Special Events," and of course, "Night Life." You'll always find a number of "two-for-one" coupons for restaurants, too. The *Reader* is distributed free of charge throughout San Diego County at libraries, liquor stores, Seven-Eleven's and other locations and if you don't get one by 3 p.m., you don't get one this week. For a drop-off point near you, call 235-3000.

△ The Thursday edition of the *Union–Tribune* contains a whole section called "Night and Day" that tells what's going on in San Diego: special events, running, water sports, arts, theaters and night life. Still a bargain at $12.50 a month. Frequent special rates. Call 299-4141 for delivery.

△ *San Diego Magazine* does a great job of reporting forthcoming special events and happenings in town in its column, "What's Doing," and what I find especially helpful is that it comes out on the 21st of the preceding month so you have more advance notice. The August issue contains a special *Annual Guide to Dining and Night Life*. Back issues are available while supply lasts. Special introductory subscription offer, around $15 for 12 issues, 230-9292. Call and ask about specials, especially near year's end.

△ Pick up a great **free maps** at **visitor's information centers**, and a *Quarterly Calendar of Events,* if you can get one! They go fast.

```
Visitor's Information Center, I-5 & Clairemont Drive  . . . .   276-8200
Cabrillo National Monument at the end of Pt. Loma  293-5450
Downtown Information Center  . . . . . . . . . . . . . . . . . . . . . . . . 235-2222
Gaslamp Information Center . . . . . . . . . . . . . . . . . . . . . . . . . . 233-5227
International Visitor Info Center, lst & F Street  . . . . . . . . . . 236-1212
Balboa Park Information Center  . . . . . . . . . . . 239-0512 or 235-1100
Carlsbad Convention & Visitor Center . . . . . . . . . . . (800) 227-5722
Encinitas Visitor Center . . . . . . . . . . . . . . . . . . . . . . . . . . . . . 753-6046
Escondido Convention & Visitor . . . . . . . . 745-4751(800) 622-8300
Oceanside Convention & Visitor's Bureau  . . . . . . . . . . . . . 721-1101
```

△ **San Diego Convention Center monthly schedules** are available in the office end of the first floor toward the Marriott.

They are free of charge or to subscribe, send $10 to the San Diego Convention Center, ATTN: Subscription, 111 W. Harbor Drive, San Diego, CA 92101.

△ For a free *Calendar of Events* and a 196-page travel guide, write to: California Office of Tourism, POB 9278, Dept. T31-86A, Van Nuys, CA 91409

△ For a free copy of the *Los Angeles Visitors Guide*, contact the Visitors and Convention Bureau, POB 71608, Los Angeles 90071.

△ For a free *State of California Calendar of Events* which lists festivals and other major events throughout California, write to: California Chamber of Commerce, Sacramento, California.

△ For a free 200-page travel guide and a picture map of California, call the California Office of Tourism, 1-800-TO-CALIF.

△ My favorite source of what's available to do in San Diego County is a colorful 20" x 30" *pictorial* map, showing Cabrillo Monument, whales, sailboats, Old Town, the Tecate Border, the Desert View Tower on Sunrise Highway, all the lakes, the Cleveland National Forest, Mt. Laguna, Julian apple country, all the Missions, Mt. Laguna, the Palomar Observatory, the coast line highlights and much more. Produced by Carol Mendell, it is available at most Sav-On Drugs and some book stores for about $4. You can get it laminated at one of the many Teacher's Pet stores throughout the County, for about 45 cents a foot (less than $1.50). What's marvelous about it is you get an *"at a glance view"* of everything in the whole County. It's a great reminder to go see the things you've heard about and always wanted to see. On the back of the map is all the pertinent information about the places, including phone numbers to contact! I have a laminated one on my desk to inspire me to clean my desk off! I love to sit and look at it. It's a fabulous gift idea, too, especially for someone who wants to scratch around and familiarize themselves with every crack and crevice of the County.

△ There are over **100 San Diego–oriented** books written by San Diegans. If you can't locate them in the Local Book/Travel Section of your book store, ask the manager to see the Sunbelt Distributor's catalog (regional titles). There are over 100 titles but no store carries all of them; special orders take about a week (no charge). Here are some of San Diego's best titles:

Above San Diego
Adventures With Kids
Afoot & Afield in S.D.
Anza Borrego Desert
Backcountry Roads
Backcountry Wineries
Baja Book
Bicycle Rides of S.D.
Camper's Guide to San Diego
Camper's Guide to San Diego
Cuyamaca Hike Map
Cycling San Diego
Day Hikers Guide to Ca.
Day Outings From San Diego
Earthquake Faults of S. D.
Geology of Penasquitos
Guide to Julian Apple Stands
Haunted San Diego
Healthy Dining in S.D.
How To Beat a Traffic Ticket In San Diego
Indians of San Diego County
La Jolla
Mines of Julian
Railroad Stations of S.D.

San Diego Artists
San Diego on Foot
San Diego Originals
San Diego Pictorial
San Diego Trivia I & II
San Diego Travel Kit
San Diego Scenic Drive
SanDiegoSouthBay Interurban
San Diego County Writers & Publishers Resource Book
San Diego Visitor's Map
Sea Cliffs of San Diego
Sea Shells of San Diego
Short History of San Diego
Sin Diego
Smart Dining in San Diego
Successful San Diegans
Things to Do With Kids in San Diego
Torrey Pines Landscape Warner Springs
Weekenders Guide to the Anza–Borrego Dessert
Yesterday in San Diego

△ There are also regional books on fishing, boating, hiking, whales, birds, bears, snorkling, exploring Baja, the Cave Paintings of Baja, rocks, gems, wild–flowers, mountains, national parks, and, certainly not to be overlooked: the Great Hot Springs of the West!

Chapter 4
CULTURAL EVENTS
Theater, Music & Movie Bargains

If you love an evening of the performing arts, you know how much good tickets to a performance can set you back. But, if you're "in the know," you can see practically every cultural event in town at a discount, or for half price, for just a few dollars, or even free. It's all up to you. Check out the following mixed bag of performing arts bargains, and get set for some fabulous nights of theater, dance and music. Experience more, pay less!

△ **San Diego Theater League** 238–0700
The San Diego Theater League is a coalition of more than 90 San Diego theater, music and dance companies, which sponsors a number of programs that offer San Diego residents and visitors substantial savings on tickets. To insure affordability to anyone interested in the arts, the League sponsors ARTS TIX, POST TIXS, Bargain Arts Day, Family Theater Days and Sneak Previews. See individual listings below.

△ **Times Arts Tix** 497–5000
Times Arts Tix is a public service, not–for–profit organization, sponsored the San Diego Theater League and Wells Fargo. Times Arts Tix offers unsold *day–of–performance* tickets for half price, plus a 10% surcharge to more than 70 theater, music and dance events throughout San Diego County. Half–price tickets for Sunday's performances are available on Saturday. Call 497–5000, listen to the recorded daily listing of what is available for *tonight*, and hurry down to pay. Tickets are sold on

a first come/first served basis. (A word of caution: call early in the morning, and pick more than one performance because by the time you get down to pay for your tickets, the show you want may be sold out. The recording is not updated during the day.) Cash only. No checks or credit cards. They are located near Fourth Avenue and Broadway in Horton Plaza on the park between Planet Hollywood and Glendale Federal Bank. Hours are: Tuesday through Saturday, 10 a.m.–7 p.m. Parking is available in the green area (15 minutes), or in the Horton Plaza parking building on Fourth Avenue, and Arts Tix will validate parking for three hours. It is usually easier to get tickets for matinees and early-in-the-week performances than for weekends. If I have an errand to do downtown, I drop by and see what they have left on the show board. Full price advance tickets to events are also available.

△ **Post Tix** **497–5000**
Post Tix is the discount–tickets–in–advance–by–mail service of Arts Tix. For $10, you will receive a quarterly catalog with discount ticket offers up to 50% off for dozens of productions and performances. Call 497–5000 and request a free sample.

△ **Bargain Arts Day** 238–0700
Each spring, the San Diego Theater League presents Bargain Arts Day. Thousands of tickets for shows throughout the summer go on sale at ARTS TIX on a "pay what you can afford" basis. A tradition since 1992, hundreds of people lineup to purchase tickets for $5, $2, or as little as $1. For more information, call the League and ask to be placed on the mailing list.

△ **Family Theater Days** 238–0700
In the fall, the San Diego Theater League sponsors Family Theater Days (receive a free children's ticket with every adult ticket purchased). It's a great way to introduce children to the

theater, music and dance performances at an unbeatable price. Call the League for dates, and ask to be placed on the mailing list.

△ **Sneak Preview** 238-0700
Throughout the year, the San Diego Theater League offers Speak Preview performances for theater, music and dance companies, for only $5. These performances are not scheduled far in advance. Call the League and ask to be placed on the mailing list.

△ **Volunteer to usher** at plays and musical performances, and get in free! Call any theater, dance, or musical company and volunteer to become an usher (see *Yellow Pages*) or to do other volunteer work such as helping with mail-outs, answering phones, costumes, sets, printing, bookkeeping, fundraising, etc. You will usually get to see the performances on an availability basis. (Very few shows are totally sold out for all performances, so your chances of seeing even the biggest hits are good.) All theaters are crying for volunteers. I volunteered at the Old Globe, giving out programs for a few minutes before the performance, then shutting the door when the lights were dimmed, and watching the performance! I have a friend, a librarian, and a real nut for cultural performances, who said: "Let me tell you *my* schedule of volunteering. I'm at the San Diego Repertory Theater tomorrow, the symphony the next night. The following week I'm at the ballet, and then Old Globe." She says she sees almost everything that comes to San Diego, and rarely has to pay! (The Old Globe has a waiting list a mile long, and the opera uses professional ushers, but most performing arts need ushers and volunteers. It's best to try to sign up before the beginning of the season, although a few weeks ahead can work, too. Even last minute, sometimes.)

△ **TheaterGoers** 565-PLAY
A 15-year old organization of arts lovers offering the opportunity to go to the theater with other arts lovers. Their

activities include four to six performances a month (always the best seats in the house), dinner before or after a performance, monthly happy hour socials, occasional cast party get–togethers, theater trips to Los Angeles (sometimes two bus loads!), San Francisco, and a week in New York. Great for people who are new to San Diego or singles who don't want to go by themselves. Membership: $35 for singles; $50 couples; all renewals, $25. About 250–300 on the mailing list. For further information and a sample newsletter of monthly events, call 565–PLAY.

Δ The *Entertainment* Coupon Book usually offers **"two–for–one" coupons** for California Ballet, Christian Community Theater, La Jolla Playhouse, Gaslamp Theater, plus Mainly Mozart Festival, Starlight Civic Light Opera, San Diego Repertory Theater, San Diego Symphony, San Diego Symphony Summer Pops, La Jolla Chamber Music, Poway Performing Arts Co., and the Isaac's McCaleb & Dancers. For more information, see chapter on "Resources."

Δ **San Diego Symphony** 699–4205
Regular tickets to the symphony range from $15 to $60. Subscriptions for the season offer a 20% discount off regular prices. Winter bargain tickets include a program called "Tickets at 6," where select remaining seats during the winter are sold for $12; day of concerts, students, military and seniors 60+, half price. At noon during the summer symphony pops program, $19 cabaret table seats sell for $12. Call for the free summer concert dates, for information on the family program, education program or the volunteering program. Copley Symphony Hall which seats over 2000, is located 1245 7th Avenue.

Δ **Old Globe** 239–2255
Check out several good deals for Old Globe performances including day–of–show discount, half price, by phone, after 4 p.m., on the day of the performance (when available). Last

Minute Rush tickets when available for $8 at 8 p.m. Discounts on series tickets, and series previews offer the lowest price. Tours of the Old Globe are held every Saturday; adults, $3; students and seniors, $1. Call for group education program for students which includes in-school performances, attendance at regular performances, and question and answer sessions with actors.

▵ San Diego Opera 232-7636
The San Diego Opera, Southern California's oldest opera, (since 1965), has achieved top ten status in America. Five main stage productions are held each season (January–May) at the 3,000 seat Civic Theater, with tickets ranging from $23–$95. Rarely are tickets turned over to ARTS TIX. *However*, in an attempt to make opera affordable to everyone, one hour before the performance, 84 Standing Room Only tickets (numbered spaces in the back of the theater) are available for $15, *even when there is NOT a sell-out.* (If a seat is available, you can occupy it.) People have stood in line for two hours for these, so go early. Other bargains: seniors, students and groups of 12 receive a 20% discount. Pre-opera lecture series, under $5. Student dress rehearsals (available through their education program) are $3 for students, $7.50 for a chaperon with a minimum of 10 students. Freebies include five lunchtime concerts in front of the Civic Theater with world renown stars, performances at schools, and each opera is rebroadcast on KFSD 94.1 FM on the Tuesday following the last performance. Subscription benefits include a chance of better seating and advance notification of special events and recitals. For more information, tickets, and to be notified of free performances, call 232-7636.

▵ Humphrey's Concerts By The Bay 523-1010
Name entertainment at outdoor concerts featuring jazz, pop and country music stars and comedians, May to October. Call early in the season to volunteer to usher.

Δ **Spreckles Organ Pavilion** hosts free concerts in Balboa Park in the every Sunday, 52 weeks a year, from 2–3 p.m. Free concerts on Monday evenings at 8 p.m. from June through August. Movies, too. Call 226–0819 for schedule of performances and events.

Δ Free summer concerts, June –September
Symphony Pops 699–4205
La Jolla Concerts by Sea, Sundays, 2 p.m. 525–3160
Carlsbad Jazz in the Park, Fridays 6–8 p.m. 434–2904

Δ Listen to KFSD 94.1 FM, the classical music station; call in and win tickets to cultural events.

Δ **La Jolla Chamber Music Society** 459–3728

Δ To request good seats, check the theater seating charts in the front section of the white pages of the telephone directory.

Δ **Ticketmaster** Entertainment Guide 220–8497
A monthly guide to major concerts, performances and appearances throughout Southern California for $14 per year.

Δ If you live in an area near a college or university, call and ask to be placed on the mailing list for their cultural events: dance, theater, music. Great to take your kids to.

Δ Every semester, Mira Costa, Palomar and Grossmont Community Colleges offer bus tours to major cultural events in Los Angeles. Most offer **tours** to the Laguna Arts Festival, the Getty Museum, art galleries in L.A., etc. Because of early planning, they usually get very good seats (always ask about seating). You know you're in good hands when you travel with the colleges. Call the colleges listed in chapter on "Classes."

△ The "Travel Agencies #169" section in the *Union–Tribune* classified ads lists bus **tours** to theaters and events in Los Angeles.

△ If you hear of an event of interest coming to town, call and ask if there will be a final dress rehearsal or preview performance. Sometimes they are free!

△ **Westminster Presbyterian Church** (Pt. Loma) .. 224–6263 Spring and summer performances of plays that are reportedly excellent. Productions have included "Kismet," "Auntie Mame," "The Dining Room," "King and I" and "The Man From La Mancha." Tickets are $8 for adults; $3 for children under 13. (Any interested party can audition.)

△ **Better Worlde Galeria** .... 260–8007 Musical concerts, recitals and other events held on stage at 4010 Goldfinch in Hillcrest. Free, low–cost and "pass the hat."

△ Keep an eye on free events listed in calendars of events in the *Reader, Union–Tribune's* "Night & Day" section, *San Diego Magazine* and *San Diego Home/Garden.* Many public concerts and performances are held at the Athenaeum in La Jolla (454–5827), the San Diego Museum of Art in Balboa Park (232–7931), Del Mar Fair Concerts (755–1161). Ask to be placed on their mailing lists.

△ Get on the mailing list for events held at the California Center for the Arts in Escondido (738–4100); Poway Center for Performing Arts (451–0287; 440–2277.

Movies

No need to pay the high price of movies these days when there are so many alternatives. Most theaters offer bargain prices early in the day, usually up until the 5 or 6 p.m. showing. Some theaters offer bargain prices all the time. Here are a few to investigate: (Now you know where to go during the next heat wave)

△ Mann Theaters   . . . . First performance, $4
   Valley Circle, Cinema 21, Hazard Center 7, University Town Center 6, The Grove 9, Rancho Bernardo 6, Sports Arena 6, Plaza Bonita 6, Oceanside 8

△ United Artists . . . . Bargain matinees daily, $4
   Horton Plaza, Glasshouse Square, Chula Vista, Escondido

△ Pacific Theaters . . . . $2.50 all day Tuesday at some theaters
   Grossmont Trolley, Cinerama 6, Sweetwater

△ AMC Theaters . . . . $3.50 until twilight (about 6 p.m.)
   Fashion Valley 4, Santee Village 8, Wiegand, Plaza 8

△ Edwards Theaters . . . . $3.75 before 6 p.m.
   Mira Mesa 7, Mira Mesa 4, La Costa 6, San Marcos 6, Flowerhill 4, Del Mar Highlands 8

△ Century Twin, 4370 54th, 582–7690 . . . . $2.^{99} anytime

△ Clairemont Theater . . . . $2, all performances
   4140 Clairemont Mesa Blvd, 274–0901

△ The *Entertainment* book contains **two–for–one coupons** for the following theaters: United Artists, Pacific and AMC. Mail in for up to 12 tickets at $4–4.^{50} each, or pick up tickets at participating Mail Boxes Etc. (See chapter on "Resources")

△ Get discount movie passes at many credit unions, adult schools.

∆ The **Cinema Society** is a cultural arts organization that premiers sophisticated commercial and art films once or more a month during its season, from fall to spring. Other activities include cocktail parties, celebrity salutes, discounts to film festival trips, special receptions, discussions, and a trip to the Palm Springs Film Festival. About 700 members, with chapters in Encinitas and La Jolla. Membership fee is $175 per person for the season, and tickets are transferrable. Newsletter before each program. For more information, call 454-7373, a 24-hour recording.

∆ **Silent Film Series**, "At the Movies," is a series of four evenings of silent film classics which are shown while the San Diego Symphony performs the score. Pre-show activities include shorts, celebrity guests and discussions. September through April. For more information, call 699-4205.

∆ **Visual Arts Foundation** offers the Sunset Cinema Film Festival in conjunction with Cox communications and "Night & Day" section of the *Union-Tribune*. Every August, they show free family-oriented films under the stars. In San Diego, they put a projector and sound system on a barge and anchor it 70 feet off shore, and show movies to hundreds of people at Embarcadero Marina Park North behind Seaport Village, at Tidelands Park in Coronado and at Bonita Cove in Mission Bay Park, and on land, in Solana Beach Poway and Escondido. For dates, call 454-7373.

∆ For classic, foreign and off-beat films, check the *Reader's* "Guide to Local Events," ("Films"). UCSD, SDSU and other colleges and community colleges, libraries, museums, and art galleries offer unique movies, usually free or very low cost. If you want to be placed on their mailing lists, give them a call.

∆ Rent **videos for 99¢** at Long's Drugs; frequent "two-for-one" coupons in their ads, posted in the stores. Many public libraries offer video rentals of great movies for $1 or less. (Chula Vista Library has great videos.)

Chapter 5
FREE & BARGAIN TRAVEL

Here are some wonderful travel opportunities you may not be aware of. You can add a lot more travel to your life, for *free* (or without paying full fare, at least), if you know of the opportunities available to you, are a little bit flexible, and are willing to do some extra planning. First, you declare to the universe that you want more travel. You'd be surprised how powerful that is. I did it, and, *voila!* More travel was mine!! I went to the AAA Travel Show at the Convention Center and won a $3,800 cruise for two on the American Hawaii Cruiseline within three weeks after declaring it!! Not convinced yet? I volunteered to be bumped in Minneapolis (see below), and Northwest Airlines gave me a round trip ticket to anywhere they fly in the continental limits *or* Mexico *or* the Virgin Islands!! Then I won a trip to Vegas at a time share, and a night at the Hilton, and a weekend at the Marriott!! And, now I have enough frequent flyer miles again on Northwest for another free ticket, and I only took two trips to earn it (to Washington, DC and Hawaii) and I already received a free bump ticket.

Here are some interesting travel bargains for you to consider. Remember, flexibility is the key. I can consider getting *real* flexible to get free airline tickets to somewhere I want to go!!

Air Travel/Cruises

Δ Be a **courier**, and fly free, or up to 70% discount. Every year, thousands of people travel the world as a courier. I *know* people who are doing it: college professors, retired people, students, and even those who only have a two-week annual vacation. A professor friend took a flight to London with a 30 day return, then took a London courier flight to Africa, then India. A courier is a person who escorts the delivery of a document, parcel, freight or *something* on board a passenger flight. The Federal Aviation Agency dictates that "cargo" that is sent on a passenger plane must be accompanied by a passenger. Many international corporations and businesses need important cargo or documents delivered *immediately,* in person, and checked through customs. Regular freight sits for days before being cleared. It may not be economically feasible for the corporation to send an employee, who has other responsibilities. Why should they pay an employee *and his round-trip ticket* when they know you and I are willing to travel for them as a courier for just the price of the ticket? Courier companies have sprung up to meet this modern need, and act as brokers between the corporation that needs the personal escort and the individual who wishes to act as the courier. The courier broker charges a percentage of the ticket price, unless the company agrees to pay for your ticket *and* the commission to the courier, too, which does happen. Trips to the orient originate from Los Angeles and San Francisco, to Europe from New York, and to South America from Miami. The down side is: you can't take luggage. You sacrifice that for the cargo you are escorting. But, you know....I can jam a lot of things into my carry-on luggage for a free ticket! You travel on short notice, and the flight might be cancelled, but that is fairly rare. Δ Courier Flights are on regular scheduled airline, not charters. Δ Your documents state the content of each bag you accompany. Are you transporting drugs? The freight has been inspected by the courier company prior to being manifested. Δ Courier representatives meet you at departure and arrival of each end of the trip and take care of the paperwork. You receive a one way ticket, an envelope of documents (cargo manifests) and a letter of instruction for the return flight. No alcohol on flight before or during. ∆ Cost: You pay a percentage of the regular fare plus departure taxes. Some companies charge a registration fee of $20 to $50 a year. Some require a deposit of $100 to $500, refundable on return; if you miss the return flight, your deposit is forfeited. ∆ You must be 21 years of age, have a valid passport, have conservative looks, be self assured, and wear business clothing. ∆ Each company and each flight will have it's own advantages and restrictions, so get in touch with the following: International Bonded Courier (flies out of Los Angeles, (310) 607-0125.) Now Voyager, 74 Varick St. New York, NY 10013, (212) 431-1616; World Courier, (718) 978-9552. ∆ The Learning Annex offers a three hour workshop on how to be a courier, 544-9700. ∆ Pick up a copy of "The Insider's Guide To Air Courier Bargains," by Kelly Monaghan, 223 pages, soft cover, $14.95, at book stores and local libraries. Several courier services are listed (library "call" number: 387.742/Monahan.)

∆ **Volunteer to be bumped** and get a voucher for $$ of your next flight or free airline tickets to anywhere the airline flies within the continental limits of the United States (whichever they currently have budget for). Airlines book more than 100% of their seats, knowing that a percentage of passengers will be "no shows." However, if all show up, someone won't be able to board. They will be "bumped" off the flight, so to speak. To compensate them for this inconvenience, and to insure good will, the airline gives the bumped passenger (more & more frequently, vouchers, or a ticket to anywhere the airline flies, or cash, and sometimes both, and books them on the next flight out. If the flight isn't until the next day, the airline will frequently give vouchers or cash for hotel rooms and meals, until their budget for doing so has expired. You're dealing with a frenzied airline employee who is no doubt dealing with a freaked out ticket holder who is being told there isn't a seat for him, so remember what Grandma used to tell you: *"You get more flies with honey than you do with vinegar."* (You're more likely to receive more goodies with a more friendly attitude, OK?? OK!!) A Saratoga man volunteered to give up his seat on an overbooked San Jose/Seattle flight, and in exchange, American Airlines gave him a ticket with a $900 value, and he continued on to Seattle on the next available flight. A Los Angeles frequent-flyer scooped up between $4,000 and $5,000 in tickets over the past few years by being bumped. A woman and her daughter, returning to San Diego from Boston, volunteered to be bumped, received round trip tickets to anywhere the airline flies, booked the next flight out, volunteered to be bumped again, and they now have four round trip tickets to anywhere Continental flies! Approximately 130,000 people are bumped a year, and 80% of those are *volunteers*, so if you want free tickets, keep reading.

Here's how to get bumped: Plan it!! Reserve on the busiest flights...Sunday nights, Monday mornings, Friday evenings when the business people travel, and before a major holiday and just after a major holiday. Business people have to get where they are going, but if you are on a leisure trip and it really doesn't make any difference to you when you get there, you can volunteer to be bumped. Check in early. Be one of the first in line to present your ticket. Ask if the plane if full, because if it isn't, no point in getting your hopes up. If it's full, tell them you want to volunteer to be bumped. Some airlines keep a list of those volunteering, some don't. If they need your seat, you'll be located, and you can negotiate your benefits. Remember, your luggage has already been placed on board and will arrive ahead of you. If you're getting on the next flight, who cares? For further information on being bumped, write to the U.S. Department of Transportation, Washington, DC, and request their free guidebook, *Fly Rights*, also available by phone, (202) 366-5959. How they made a such a fascinating topic so boring is absolutely beyond me!

△ If you're taking a flight, always join their **"frequent flyer"** program even if you don't think you'll ever use the airline again. Many people think the Frequent Flyer Program is for business travelers only. Not at all true...it's for you and me! The reservationist will assign you a number right then and there, at no cost to you. You will be placed on the mailing list to receive their newsletters outlining their inaugural specials, double miles, etc. I am a Northwest frequent flyer. With one trip to Washington, DC (receiving double miles for flying into National Airport), a trip to Hawaii plus my MCI miles, I have enough miles for another free ticket! I volunteered to be bumped on my Washington trip, so *I've already gotten one free ticket!* Whadda deal!!

Here are the airlines and their numbers to call. You'll be assigned a number and will receive their newsletter of forthcoming special fares. Get them all!! The, you'll know the best fares, who is giving double miles, etc.

Alaska	(800) 654-5669
America West	(800) 247-5691
American Airlines	(800) 433-7300
Continental	(800) 525-0280
Delta Airlines	(800) 323-2323
Northwest Airlines	(800) 447-3757
Southwest	(800) 445-9267
TWA	(800) 325-4815
USAir	(800) 872-4738

△ **Discount Fares/Travel Brokers/Consolidators** I first found out about discount travel when I was aboard a ship in the Mediterranean en route to see the Pyramids in Egypt. A lady standing behind me in line waiting for dinner one night mentioned in passing that she was on the same trip, *half* fare! *Needless to say, this ruined my whole trip!* She told me she belonged to three discount travel clubs. A few months later, I saw a list of several in travel magazine. Here's the way they work. Airlines and hotels, tour operators and cruise lines all suffer from an abundance of unsold tickets on almost every trip. Since they can't have a "clearance sale" and risk offending traditional travel agents who sell their offerings at full price, these travel suppliers turn to clearinghouses or brokers or consolidators who buy their unsold seats in huge lots at huge savings, and resell them at discounts ranging from $100 to $2,000 per person off the published retail price. The only catch is that these special savings are secret. Clubs are strictly prohibited from advertising the original supplier of their offerings....only their members receive this highly confidential information. After paying a membership, you receive a telephone *hotline* which is updated with the latest offerings. Verify the seat confirmation with the airline you will be using, and check their rates to see what you're saving. Longer trips are usually available about four weeks in advance, short trips may be available only 10 days or a week in advance. Many cruises are put on the hotline up to six months in advance.

Δ It's worth checking out available fares through these travel discounters:

Traveler's Advantage . . . . (800) 255-0200
Membership, $49 a yr., 3 mo. trial, 24 hr. bookings, lowest fares, no booking fee, 5% cash bonus, coupons; + hotels worldwide at 1/2 price. Good deals.
Moments Notice . . . . (212) 486-0500
Tours, packages, flights.   Hotline: (212) 873-0908
Travel Avenue . . . . (800) 333-3335
Fares, tours, cruises, rebates on fares over $300. Plan your trips. Special rates.
UNI-Travel . . . . (800) 325-2222
Consolidator. Specializing in Europe.
Council Travel . . . . (619) 270-6401
Specializing in travel for students, everyone. Hawaii/$199
Last Minute Travel (good prices) . (617)-267-9800
South Florida Cruises . . . . (800) 327-7447
Best Fares (Magazine) . . . . (800) 635-3033
$58 for 12 issues; coupons, 64 pages. Travel deals galore.

Δ If a deal seems too good to be true, the deal may not fly. Those ads that read "Hong Kong $499, "Paris $299" may not be available.

Δ The consolidators (and others) may only have one seat available at the advertised price.

Δ Strangely enough, some presumed "cheap fares" are actually higher than you'd pay elsewhere. It pays to shop around!!

Δ Pay for your ticket on your credit card, and if the trip does not go, you can get the charge backed off your credit card. You won't have to hassle with getting your money refunded.

Δ Order **special meals** on board flights with a day's notice. The dairy vegetarian is absolutely exquisite gourmet food! Everyone around me was lusting after my fresh looking meal. Also available, low fat, low calorie, non−dairy, low salt. Kosher meals require longer notice.

Δ The **week's best airfares** are published weekly in the travel section of the *Union−Tribune*.

Δ You can re−book your non−refundable ticket (for the same date) if the fare is lowered after your purchase, and lower fare seats are available. You can get a refund on your non−refundable ticket with a doctor's excuse.

Δ Apply for a **Master Card or Visa** through an airline and earn frequent flyer miles for every $1 you spend. For example, I have a Northwest Visa. I earn frequent flyer miles for the number of miles flown, plus an additional frequent flyer mile for each $1 the ticket cost (charged on the Visa card.) I know a retired couple who charge *everything* they can on their Citibank card through American Airlines to get AA frequent flyer miles: the dentist, groceries at Lucky, all department stores, newspaper subscriptions, gas, dentist, vet, doctors, airline tickets, hotels, restaurants, rental cars (anything where they will take plastic), and they have gone to Europe, free, on their frequent flyer miles!! They pay their Visa bill monthly, so there is no accumulated interest. They're livin'!

ᴧ Some long distance phone companies offer frequent flyer miles. **MCI and AT&T** give five miles for every $1 spent on long distance, which can add up! It costs you nothing to switch, and they give you a free hour of long distance for doing it. Other companies are now doing this, too. It all adds up!! If you are currently subscribing, all you have to do is call and ask to start accumulating mileage!! I already had MCI, so I called and got 1000 miles for re-signing up through Northwest Airlines!

ᴧ Check the **Travel Transportation #170 classified ads** for travel opportunities in the *Union.* Also, check the *Reader and Los Angeles Times.* People sell tickets they have won, non-refundable tickets they bought at a discount and now can't use, frequent traveler coupons, and more. Always negotiate on the price. You can ask: "Will you take $__ for the tickets?" or "How much will you take for them?," as it is sometimes difficult to sell tickets through the classifieds. Not everyone is aware of this marketplace, and it might be your chance to score. Make sure the tickets are transferable. Call the airline and check. Airlines tend to "look the other way," but this would be a good negotiating point for a lower price.

ᴧ Always **ask for least expensive airline fare**; otherwise, you will only be asked: "Do you want first class or coach?" Frequently there are other fares far less expensive than coach, so you have to ask for the least expensive way to get where you are going and then see if what they have will fits your needs.

ᴧ Call local Better Business Bureau, 521-5898 re: complaints against travel agencies. See "Consumer Complaints," Ch. 2.

ᴧ **Free Guide to Paris:** *The Insider's Good Value Guide To Paris.* Write to French Government Tourist Office, P. O. Box 2658, Lake Ronkonkoma, NY 11779.

ᴧ **Half-Price Coupon Books:** *Entertainment Publications* has coupon books for several European cities (London, Amsterdam, etc.) 1/2 off hotels, entertainment, food. Or, one for just hotels all over Europe, about $53 each. Hawaii, $46. Call (800) 374-4464.

△ If you're looking for **bargains under the warm Mexican sun**, consider traveling the first two weeks of January when it is less crowded and many hotels offer special rates. High season in Mexico is mid-January to mid-April, low season is mid-April to December 15th, with a sur-charge for Thanksgiving. The Christmas rate is higher than high season because of a sur-charge.

△ Call the **Mexican Government Tourist Office** for free information, (800) 262-8900

Cruises

△ See cruise discounters above.

△ **Always ask for the least expensive cabin**, then ask for the guaranteed room rate **(upgraded up to better quarters)** in the event they sell out all the least expensive cabins. This policy is basic to the industry, although the language may differ somewhat. My travel agent suggested this on my first cruise and we ended up being upgraded two price levels in accommodations (yet paid the lowest fare!) You have to book early to get the least expensive cabins because they always sell out fast.

△ Many cruise lines have a **standby fare.** You pay for your ticket in advance, and three weeks before the cruise, you are notified whether you are on. Call and ask....it's worth a shot!!

△ Cruise Lines (Lowest Rates) (800) 327-3021.

△ **Ocean Liner Queen Elizabeth II** offers a standby fare. A real bargain is a minimum cabin in one direction during low season (early December and early April and the lowest) Call (800) 221–4770 for schedule of rates and departures. They offer incredible specials from time to time, including one way on the Concorde for 600 bucks (about a $3000 value!!).

▵ Get a **free cruise** for two if you can teach a seminar aboard a cruise ship. Or teach aerobics, bridge, give dance lessons, a tax seminar, do handwriting analysis, read auras, etc. Write to the individual cruise lines and offer your services.

▵ **Free Cruises for Single Men Over Age 50** (Here's one that the ladies throw tomatoes at me for when I speak before groups.) Single men over the age of 50 can go free on certain cruise lines as a Cruise Host. Because there are so many more single women on cruises than single men, the owner of Royal Cruises, who has received a great deal of publicity for his creative idea, decided to supply the ladies on board with dancing partners, called Cruise Hosts. The bottom line is: women would rather have someone to dance with on their vacations than not have someone to dance with; in fact, the program has been phenomenally successful. The deal is: men of average or better height who are fairly good dancers with reasonable social skills are provided free passage *and* a bar tab....in exchange for dancing and socializing with the ladies. It's a tough job, but somebody's got to do it, *right?* There are conditions, of course...the men cannot fall in love and sit in the corner sipping wine with *Ms. Right* all through the cruise, or he may find himself swimming home. For further information, contact the **Cruise Host Program** at: ▵ Royal Cruise Line, 1 Maritime Place 1400, San Francisco, CA 94111, (415) 956–7200; (800)–227–4534; ▵Royal Viking Line, 95 Merrick Way, Coral Gables, Florida 33134; Regency Cruises, 8880 N.. 20th Street, Miami, Florida 33171; ▵ Delta Queen Steamboat Co., Box 288, 2139 University Drive, Coral Springs, Florida 39071. ▵ Crystal Cruises (wants men no younger than 65), 2121 Avenue of the Stars, Los Angeles, CA 90067; (310) 785–9300. ▵ Cunard Line (Queen Elizabeth II, Vistafjord and Sagafjord) uses an agent, who charges

$150 per week of cruising. Contact Lauretta Blake's Working Vacation, 4277 Lake Santa Clara Drive, Santa Clara, CA 95054-1330. (408) 727-9665. ▵ Regency's Regent Sun, Regent Star and Regent Sea also use Lauretta Blake, above.

▵ If you've never taken a cruise and want to get away for a few days, you can board the Norwegian Cruise Lines or Azure Seas from L.A. to Catalina and Ensenada for a **3 or 4 day cruise, from $279.** Call your travel agent.

▵ **Windjammer Barefoot Cruises** (tall ships in the Eastern Caribbean), have occasional specials with l/1 off second person, (800) 327-2601.

▵ **Crew on a yacht**. Go down to the marina areas (Shelter Island, Harbor Island, Mission Bay) and pick up a copy of the many free marine publications that are available in the yacht sales offices and marine supply stores. Look in the "Crew Wanted" classified section. Many captains are looking for compatible people for a long trip and require no experience. Also, there is a "Crew Announcement Board" in many marine supply stores. Place your ad, or respond to one.

▵ Check the library or bookstore for a copy of *Work and Sail Your Way Around the World* (Writer's Digest).

Local & Regional Travel

▵ **Low Cost Trips and Tours** are available through most of the local community colleges. One of the good things about traveling with the community college system is that you have the security of knowing you are under their insurance coverage. Their schedules contain day trips to L.A. museums, theater and or to special events like the Laguna Arts Festival (at least two buses!).

∆ **Free Map of California** with national parks, and other tourist information including discount coupons, is available from the California Department of Commerce, Office of Tourism, POBox 9278, Van Nuys, CA 91409.   Ask for "The Californias" information packet.

∆ Gadabout Travel Club has a newsletter of **tours for senior citizens** for $4 per year, with trips galore. You don't have to be a senior to travel with them, 291-3402.

∆ Cunningham Tours, 292-5522, many local tours to regional attractions including Laughlin, Crystal Cathedral, Rosarito, Ensenada, Hollywood, Julian, Tahoe, San Francisco, more. Call for calendar of events.

∆ Check bus tours listed in travel classified ads of the *Union-Trib.*

∆ Baja Expeditions, 2625 Garnet Avenue, 581-3311.

∆ If you're calling to make air reservations to **Las Vegas**, be sure to ask if there are any specials. They frequently throw in the hotel room.   Southwest Airlines frequently offers fares to Vegas, sometimes as low as $19 per person, with 21 day advance purchase. ∆ **Las Vegas "Turnaround"** for $10 available through Carlsbad and La Mesa park & recreation departments.   A "turnaround" is a 24 hour trip.

Other Travel Opportunities, Information & Tips

∆ **Always ask if there are any promotionals or special fare rates.** You never know what this might bring. I told a friend who needed to go to a wedding in Sacramento to be sure and ask if there were any specials when making reservations. He did, and let me know right away that he was told: " *Yes, there are. Go to Burger King and get a Whopper and fries, and you'll get a two-*

for-one coupon for airline tickets." If he hadn't asked, they would not have told him. (Their marketing department is in charge of promotions. The ticket sales counter is in charge of ticket sales; however, if someone *asks* if there are any specials, they are required to announce them. It's not like the world is against us, its just that certain departments have certain functions, and if you came to the ticket office without being lured in by their promotion, they have no reason to want to inform you of it. They already have your business.)

Δ *Entertainment* publishes "two-for-one" coupon books for 115 cities, including Los Angeles, San Francisco, Orlando, Manhattan, Hawaii, plus "Bed & Breakfasts"; "Travel America" Available for a discount with the coupon in the back of San Diego *Entertainment* book. Call (800) 374-4464.

Δ American Wilderness Experience, free catalog of trips, (800) 444-0099.

Δ The sister cities of San Diego are Yokohama and Edinbougho. Contact the visitor's centers before going to get lots of special treatment.

Δ Students (full time) who apply for an American Express card can get travel certificates for reduced round-trip flights, (800) 545-5036.

Δ Friendship Force, an adult exchange program (stay in homes), 130 U.S. chapters and 180 clubs in 45 countries. Over 1,600,000 have met each other, (404) 522-9490 or write to ICNN, 575 S. Tower, Atlanta, GA 30303.

Δ **Go Camping, America**, camping information, (800) 47-SUNNY.

Δ *Guide To Free Attractions*, by Don Wright, ISBN No. 0-937877-03-4, $14.95, 640 pages.

∆ **Hotel Rooms for less** if you ask! Questions to ask: Are there special promotions? Does it make a difference if you're there on a week day or weekend? A room with vs. without a view? Do they use a "frequent flyer" program (earn mileage)? Do they give senior, student or military discount? Are there are any two–for–one coupons available? Do they honor AAA membership? Do they give a discount for professional, employment, organizational, credit union, or other membership? Are there any cheaper rooms? Call for rates on their 800 toll free number, then call directly and see if there is a difference in room rate. According to a national publication, many hotels quote a higher rate over the toll free line! For deep discounts at hotels, negotiate–negotiate–negotiate. You'll do best with advance reservations, purchase and a minimum stay. Keep asking questions about discounts, and add one final question: "Is that your lowest rate?" They will tell you. Ultimately, ask "Who gets the lowest rate?" (if you think they won't throw you out!!) You can *ask* for the corporate rate even if you don't work for a corporation.

∆ Stay in regional **hotels at 50% off** with your Entertainment coupon book. I loved the famous glass Bonaventure Hotel in Los Angeles. Use coupons for hotel rooms all over California: San Francisco, Carmel, Hollywood, Anaheim, Universal City, Beverly Hills, Long Beach, Costa Mesa, Orange County, Laguna, Apple Tree Pine Valley, Dana Point, Catalina Island, San Clemente, Glen Ivy. Or, put your visiting friends and relatives up in San Diego, half price, at some of the best hotels. Or, take a romantic holiday there yourself!!

∆ **Consumer Reports Travel Newsletter**, $39 per year includes annual *Travel Buying Guide*, (800) 234–1970. Available at most libraries, and is a goldmine of info. Ask for free sample.

∆ If you are travelling because of an **emergency or bereavement**, say so. Many airlines have discontinued the policy of giving you the lowest rate available as a gesture of good will, but check around. Policies change from time to time, so check with several airlines. Northwest as of this writing offers 70% off the no-notice fare, which is very high. Some airlines evaluate on a case by case basis, so hone up on your "sweet talk" skills. (You may do better with a consolidator or Last Minute or Moment's Notice, mentioned above; or look in the Travel classified ads of the *U–T*.)

△ Through Intelli Travel International in La Jolla, for $495, you can take training and become a travel agent, get a license and card that entitles you to all **travel agency discounts** including 7 day cruises for about $398, extreme discounts on "familiarization" trips, 40% of commission back on travel, 25% commission on trips you book for clients. About 40,000 members. Call (800) 873–5353.

△ **Return a rental car** to its city of origin. You pay gas. Need major credit card. Check *Yellow Pages* under "Automobile Transporters and Drive Away Companies" for return opportunities. Check *Reader* classifieds, too, for individuals who need their cars driven across country, or to ???

△ **Summer prices drop by degrees at the warm resorts**. Palm Springs has room rates in the summer you won't believe. You can have a hotel room fit for a King for a song, with use of the spas. Your chance to get away for a day, escape in the air conditioning where the rich and famous frolic and play.

△ Go to work for an airline, railroad, travel agency or cruise line. Airline/travel employees **receive free travel benefits** for themselves and certain relatives, and some award a limited number of passes for friends!

△ You can always *ask* for a **free upgrade** on planes, trains, in hotels, etc. The way you ask has a lot of influence on whether you get it.

△ This is a little sophisticated, but you can say: "I wanna fly non-rev." Think about it.

Δ There are walking tours available in major cities worldwide. **Walkabout International** takes groups to various cities in the U.S., sometimes Hawaii, and Europe. I wanna do this!! For more information on walks locally or trips, call 231-SHOE.

Δ For a **directory of state travel offices**, send a self addressed stamped business size envelope to: Discover America, Travel Industry Association of America, 2 Lafayette Center, 1133 21st Street NW, Washington, DC 20036. Send for free literature from states you are interested in visiting. Washington, DC has the most freebies: almost every museum is free!

Δ Wards, Sears, Auto Club of Southern California and American Association of Retired Persons (AARP) have **travel clubs** that offer group rates on trips.

Δ **Home Exchanges** Trade homes with people from all over the world. See *Frommer's Swap & Go: Home Exchanging Made Easy;* Intervac International home exchange network, over 40 years, (800) 756-4663; Better Homes & Travel, (212) 689-6608; Vacation Exchange Club, POBox 820, Haleiwa, **Hawaii** 96712, (800) 638-3841.

Δ Travel with a **special interest club**: Shakespeare tours of England through the Old Globe, go to New York every Easter for a week a plays with TheaterGoers (565-PLAY), art oriented tours of other countries through the museums or get out of town with the Sierra Club and backpack and hike through California and the surrounding region. See telephone directory for numbers.

Δ **University Campus accommodations**, (all ages), over 300 listings in the U.S. or abroad, available for an average price of $18 a night, lower if you are a student, with access to cultural and recreational offerings, and inexpensive meals to boot. The U.S.

and World Wide Travel Accommodations Guide provides detailed information on lodging at campuses in this country, Canada and Europe. It's available for $11.95 plus $1.05 postage from Campus Travel Service, P. O. Box 5007, Laguna Beach, Calif 92652

∆ **YMCA** has more than 28,000 beds around the world, including Hawaii, Australia, Israel, Hong Kong, Finland and Yugoslavia, many with spas an swimming pools. Most rooms cost less than $20 per night. Travel packages are available to many U.S. cities and to Europe. Mainly for students and young people, but older people frequently use their services. The Y's Way International, a 24 page catalog describing accommodations and travel packages, can be obtained by sending a legal–size envelope with 52¢ stamp to: Y's Way International, 356 W. 34th Street, NY, NY 10001.

∆ If you are planning a trip, pick up a copy of the Sunday **Los Angeles Times.** The Travel Section is huge; lots of deals & steals.

∆ **Travel Store**, 739 4th, 544–0005, downtown, is the "ultimate store for travellers" for San Diego. Travel tips, books, maps, luggage. Coffee bar. Council Travel's office is in the back.

∆ If you **put together your own travel group of 15 people,** sometimes only 10, contact your travel agent, and *you go free.* And, everyone in the party gets a 20% discount.

∆ **American Youth Hostels** are not by any stretch for youth only. Anyone can and everyone does use them. San Diego AYH Council, 338–9981; Point Loma Youth Hostel, 3790 Udall, 223–4778; For a 24 page booklet "AYH Discovery Tours," write to AYH, POBox 37613, Washington, DC 20013; (202) 783–6161.

∆ **Inter Hostel,** travel programs for those over age 50, (800) 733–9573.

∆ **Elder Hostel**, for seniors. Stay in college dorms, 2 weeks food and lodging for as little as $400. Write to: 80 Boylston St., Boston, MA 02116, 96170, (Boston) 425-8351. There is an elder hostel group through Grossmont College Community Education, 465-1700, x650. Another chapter at SDSU.

∆ **America at 50% discount:** For an annual fee of $19.95, you'll get a 50% discount any time of year at more than 900 hotels, over 2000 with restrictions, across the country, 25% discounts in selected hotel restaurants, auto rental discounts to 20%. Call (800) 248-2783 for more information. Discounts on condominiums, cruises, plus 5% instant rebate on airfare. Call (899) 828-5004.

∆ For a **free travel planner** and information for an **Amtrak vacation**, write to: Discover the of Magic Amtrak, POB 7717, Itasca, IL 60143.

∆ Slide shows and **travel movies** are available at REI, 3029 University Avenue, 295-7700, and through AAA Travel Agency.

∆ If you're going to do any international travel, regardless of your age, get an **International Student Identity Card**. An International Student Identification Card is about $15, and will entitle you to discounts for transportation, museums, tourist attractions and restaurants abroad. Receive *Student Travels*, a travel magazine from the Council on International Educational Exchange, covering inexpensive student air fare, Eurailpasses and applying for the International Student Identity Card, (212) 661-1414, x 1108.

∆ Recreation Vehicle Industry/AARP catalog of low-cost resources for RVers. Write to: AARP Travel Industry Relations, ATTN: Hal Norvell, 601 E Street, NW.Washington, DC 20049.

∆ For information on **freighter travel**, write to: Associated Container Transportation, Paceline Suite 8101, 1 World Trade Center, NY, NY.

△ **Travel/Study Programs** If you are 18 to 70+, you, and some trips allow your children, are eligible to take advantage of travel opportunities provided by the extensions of the colleges. You don't have to be a an enrolled student, or you can enroll and earn credit if you desire. Travel/study tours are different from other tours available, as academic tour leaders avoid the tourist routes and show you the real culture of the area. Trips are planned to Mexico, Ancient Egypt, Greece, the Holy Land and Italy. For a brochure of travel study programs, call UCSD at 534-0406x60 or SDSU at 594-5152. Travel/Study programs are available through the Museum of Man, the Smithsonian Institute and other museums throughout the country. See ancient cave paintings, archeological finds, etc. that are not available to the general public by touring with a museum. Write or call your museum of choice to ask about their travel programs

△ **Travel for Those With Disabilities** Send for publication of travel opportunities for those with disabilities: Consumer Information Center, Pueblo, CO 81009. Tours featuring wheelchair accessible transportation, lodgings and sightseeing are available for those able to care for their personal needs or who are accompanied by someone who can help.

Chapter 6
HEALTH & MEDICAL BARGAINS

Health & Medical Services
Prescription Drugs
Medical Insurance
Dental Services & Insurance
Medical Research Centers (Earn $$)
Bargain Spas

This chapter contains information on health and medical services for less (some free), discount prescription drugs, medical insurance that won't cost you an arm and a leg, dental services and insurance for less, medical research centers where qualified persons can get free medical care (and get paid for it!), plastic surgery for less, and deluxe spas at a discount. Here are some great resources you should know about:

Health & Medical Services

△ **The San Diego Info Line** 230–0997
The San Diego Info Line is a free service sponsored by United Way which successfully puts thousands of callers in touch with San Diego County Health and Human Care services, and other health related services. Most of these services are free or low‑cost, based on a sliding scale according to income. More than 1000 medical, psychological, emergency, birth control, abortion, shelter, abuse, elderly, personal, child care, family and other

229

organizations are in their database. The Info Line exists to help you quickly locate an appropriate organization for assistance, some of which are difficult to find on your own. The Info Line also has a Rolodex file chocked full of self–help groups for everything from loneliness, depression, and grief, to various illnesses. For information and assistance, call between 8 a.m. and 8 p.m. weekdays, 11 a.m. to 6 p.m. Saturdays, Sundays and holidays.

△ **Ask–A–Nurse** 696–8100
Ask–A–Nurse is a 24–hour, free community service, offering free medical advice over the phone. The nurses receive over 200 calls a day. A great service for new mothers, mothers with young children, or for sudden illness or emergencies. Staffed by registered nurses who answer questions and make referrals to many types of services. Keep this number with your other important numbers.

△ **Free medical care/hospitalization** 492–4444
If your income falls below $600 per month (for one person), you are eligible for free medical care through County Medical Services. Call for income requirements for additional family members. Legal residents, age 21–64, without medical insurance can apply for medical care through the County Medical Services. You must be able to verify that you earned less than $600 (for single) a month income in the previous month.

△ **San Diego Council of Community Medical Clinic** 265–2100
San Diego has 21 community medical clinics which offer free and low cost comprehensive primary care services. Call for clinic nearest you.

△ The **County of San Diego Department of Health Services** offers a variety of services and clinics, free or low cost, as follows:
General Information 692–8448

Immunizations for children 692–8661
Sexually transmitted diseases clinic 692–8550
Tuberculosis control and testing 692–8600
Women, infants, children 236–2300
Prenatal care network 565–3351
Child health & disability prevention 692–8428

△ Middle income families who are not insured can apply for free pregnancy health care under Proposition 99, 492–4444; or 565–3351, or (800) 675–2229.

△ **Planned Parenthood** 683–7526
Provides examinations, **birth control, pregnancy counseling and options,** and education.   Planned Parenthood is **free** or fees are based on a **sliding scale** according to income.   Several clinics throughout the County.

△ **Facts of Life Line** 683–7543
A 24–hour recording, sponsored by Planned Parenthood, with selections including information on where to get help, pregnancy counseling, sexually transmitted diseases, and legislative updates.

△ Pregnancy, parenting & adoption services 231–2828
△ Door of Hope (under age 18 pregnancy housing) .. 279–1100
△ Abortion Aid 287–5783
△ Abortion Hotline 298–9352
△ Abortion Alternatives 583–5433

△ **County Public Health HIV Testing (free)** 236–3848
A 24–hour recording, with information on the 7 locations for free testing, including 1700 Pacific Highway, downtown. No names or addresses taken, no appointment needed.

△ **Asthma Hotline,** (800) 727–5400.

△ **American Breast Centers** . . . . (800)262-6648
For a complete **mammogram, $60**. Breast cancer is the number one killer of women, yet more than 90% of women survive who have their breast cancers detected through mammography.

△ Villa View Community Hospital 583-0605
Mammograms, $60.

△ New blood test can **predict heart attacks** (costs less than $100), measures body levels of renin, a natural hormone produced by the kidneys that helps regulates blood pressure, according to Dr. Michael Alderman, New York Hospital–Cornell Medical Center.

△ **Alzheimer Disease** Education/Referral Center. . (800) 438–4380 Report on gene mutation may be responsible for nerve cell death.

Additional Medical Information:
△ Even if you're not a senior, read the Senior column in the Union–Trib on Sunday, for listings of **free medical services** including **blood pressure, health screenings, cholesterol, hearing,** etc. These services are usually not just for seniors.

△ Ever wonder what's in **your public record medical record file**, and who put it in? Write to: Medical Information Bureau, POBox 105, Essex Station, Boston, MA 02112, or call (617) 426-3660. Free.

△ National **Digestive Diseases** Information Clearing House, Box NDDIC, Bethesda, MD 20892. Write for free, helpful information on how to deal with various digestive ailments.

△ **Become an organ donor.** Talk to you family and let them know your wishes. Your next of kin must give consent upon your death. Contact the Living Bank, (800) 528–2971, the only national organ registry in the United States. Ask for information and a registration packet. For body donation, call UCSD Medical School donor program, 534–4536.

△ ***Prescription for Nutritional Healing***, James F. Balch, M.D.– Phyllis A. Balch, C.N.C., Avery Publishing Group. A practical A–Z reference to drug–free remedies using vitamins, minerals, herbs and food supplements, $16.95. (This book is great!)

△ **Surgical Fees Can Be Negotiated**. Here's how! Contrary to popular opinion, surgical fees are not fixed in stone. You can save money by bargaining with your doctor. First, determine the lowest prices available for your surgery by checking with surgeons in your area. Then find out what your insurance company says is a reasonable charge. Armed with this information, ask if your surgeon will accept the insurance payment as full payment. Or, explain to your physician that you can only afford to pay so much, that your insurance will cover only so much and tell him if other doctors are charging less for the surgery. Your physician may direct you to speak to his office manager about the fees, or state that the fees are fixed and non–negotiable. Most will accept a lump sum payment of less. As a last resort, you may tell the surgeon you will be forced to go elsewhere if he will not lower his fee.

△ **UCSD Free Smokers Helpline, (800) 7 NO BUTTS**

△ **Do–It–Yourself Medical Kits** are available at local pharmacies. There are **at least 35 or more** on the market that **test for various deficiencies, pregnancy, gum disease, stool check, diabetes, and others**. Inquire at Long's, SavOn, Thrifty, Von's and other pharmacies.

⌂ **Optimum Health Institute** of San Diego 464–3346
6970 Central, Lemon Grove. The OHI offers one to three week
sessions for detoxification from diet, illness, stress, or substance
abuse. Classes, meals (all raw foods and wheatgrass juice) and
room, $295 a week, shared; $425 private. Commute for less.
People attend from all over the world, and rave about what this
program does for them (cleanses the system).

⌂ **Self–Heal School of Herbal Studies and Healing** 224–1268.
Classes in herbal medicine, nutrition for the 90's, energy healing.
Also, one–hour consultation (with 3rd year student), $20.

⌂ **Whole Being Weekend** .... 594–6805.
Three– day retreat, $75 includes cabin and all vegetarian meals
and dozens of holistic workshops. People of all ages, young to
old.

⌂ Get a **free chiropractic adjustment** at health fairs and street
fairs. There is usually a chiropractor booth at all fairs.

⌂ Here is a comparison of a **generic pain reliever** and a name
brand pain reliever: Tylenol, 100 count, acetaminophen 500mg,
$8.^{99}; Von's Pain Reliever, 100 count, acetaminophen, 500mg,
$5.^{25} (with occasional two–for–one sales!) Same ingredients!

⌂ Student **massage**, $10, Body–Mind College 453–3295
    Free massage/and lecture, School of Healing Arts . 581–9429
    Student massage $20, School of Healing Arts 581–9429
    IPSB Massage School, $25 (by student) 490–1154

⌂ **Free health videos** are available at Blockbuster Video (Back
Care, Heal Yourself, Infant Care, and more).

⌂ Consumer Reports Books publishes *The New Medicine Show*,
$7.95, a practical guide to everyday health problems and health

products, including remedies for common complaints, diet and nutrition, skin and hair, teeth and gums, women and health, blood diseases, and information on drug frauds, generic drugs, and more. Available from Consumers Reports, free of charge with a subscription. Available at libraries.

Medical Care in Tijuana

Many people who **don't have medical insurance in the U.S. go to Tijuana** for medical care. *I am neither advocating nor not advocating this*, but I will say that Mexicans go to Mexican doctors all the time, even rich Mexicans, and I know many Americans who have told me they go to Tijuana for Xrays, tests, prescriptions, examinations, alternative therapies for terminal diseases, orthodontia, and even deliver their babies there (in order to have dual citizenship which entitles the parents to purchase Mexican land). There are doctors on every corner. You can locate specialists (Medicos) in the *Tijuana Yellow Pages. (See Chapter on Resources.)* If you've had a little Spanish, you can probably fake your way through the Spanish *Yellow Pages.* I can. There are doctors who have nice offices near the Zona del Rio (River Zone) Shopping Area, and those that have medical offices you probably wouldn't want to walk into. Ask the doctor where he got his medical degree and how much training he has had before making your decision. Many have done graduate work in the United States.

People who live in border towns across the U.S. are going to Mexico for medical treatments and prescriptions. Doctors in Mexico report that Americans comprise one in four patients. They go for prescription drugs, physicals, allergies, ear aches and other medical treatment. People who go there say they are happy with the service. Although most would prefer getting care in the U.S., health care here is unaffordable or their insurance excludes coverage, or has such a high co-payment that it is cheaper to go to a border town. Doctor visits average about $25. In the U.S., a first visit to a pediatrician is about $65; a surgeon, $125; family practice visit, $55, twice the price you pay in Mexico.

Prescription Drugs

△ To get the **best prices on prescription drugs,** let your fingers do the walking and comparison-price shop, since the wholesale cost of drugs varies like the Dow Jones Industrial. Here are some stores to call for prices: Price Club (you don't have to be a member to buy prescriptions at Price Club or Costco), Fedco, SavOn, Thrifty, Long's, Drug Emporium, Von's and Save Mart Drugs, AARP, and Tijuana drug stores (See Tijuana, this chapter.)

△ Many **prescription drugs** can be purchased for less in Tijuana at pharmacies (the signs say: *Farmacias*), which are on every corner. There are many on both sides of Second Avenue, above and below Revolucion. Many of the drugs are made in Mexico City, so bring your prescription and any literature you might have to compare ingredients. Be sure to check to see if the dosage and milligrams are the same. Compare prices at Le Drug Store (Revolucion at Fourth), then check prices at pharmacies on a side street away from the business area for the best prices. Farmacia Fenia on 2nd Avenue between Madero and Nigrete is a discount drug store (20% off). Many prescription drugs are available in Tijuana without a prescription, like blood pressure medications, some tranquilizers, birth control pills, antibiotics, Tagamet, and more. Retin-A, both the Mexican and the American version, is available without a prescription. The Mexican version is selling for anywhere from $3 up for the small tube. The American version, which sells in the U.S. for about $16 for the small size, sells down there for varying prices, both lower and higher.

∆ If you are taking an expensive drug that you feel you can't afford, write to the drug company (your pharmacist will give you the address), and tell them it is a hardship. Many companies will send the prescription to you, free.

Medical Insurance

∆ **Kaiser Permanente** . . . . (800) 245–3181
Kaiser offers about the most reasonably priced medical insurance around, although it keeps going up every year.   Their preventative medicine program is excellent, because they want you to stay healthy.   I've had their coverage for years.   No complaints.   A single subscriber membership is $85 (under 30) to $146 (age 64) a month; subscriber and spouse and one or more children, $216 (under age 30) to $387 (age 64).   This includes all preventative care and full hospitalization with no deductible.   Call for rates for subscriber, spouse and children, and for a no–obligation information packet.   Their pharmacy prices are usually very good, but it's best to comparison shop for savings.

∆ **National Association of Self–Employed** . . .   (800) 827–9990
Health insurance for the self–employed.

∆ The **Medical Consumer Discount Club** . . . .   299–6232, #22
A program for people with no insurance.   Over 500 doctors participate, offering savings on medical bills for members.

∆ **AARP (Association of Retired Persons)**   . .   (800) 523–5800
Supplemental hospital plans for persons age 50–64, and over 65, starting at $11.25 per person.

Additional Information:
∆ If you have a **pre–existing condition** and can't get health insurance, here's a tip that was shared with me: go to work for

any major company that has group insurance. Usually after about one to six months, you will qualify for their group health plan. Most group insurance companies take pre-existing conditions, excepting certain major health problems. When you leave, you can opt to pay to continue coverage, depending on insurer. Some allow you to continue for one year only. Kaiser is very good about letting you continue coverage (tough to get in on your own). The federal government is the only employer (I unearthed) who will allow any pre-existing medical condition (if you can get hired).

△ If you have difficulty getting insurance, you might consider enrolling in a college to get college student medical coverage. Be sure to check age limit, although there may be none. Contact student services for information at any college. You must carry a minimum number of credits.

Dental Services & Insurance

△ **SmileSaver** . . . . (800) 638-3384 x249. SmileSaver is one of California's largest dental insurance plans. With membership as low as about $6 a month, you'll get exams and x-rays at no charge, one cleaning for $10, fillings $30, and a savings up to 30-50% on other services including cosmetic procedures. No deductibles, acceptance guaranteed. Choose from list of dentists. Individual coverage: $6 per month; family, $10.25. Coverage must be in effect 30 days before it can be used. Optional **orthodontic coverage** available.

△ **San Diego Children's Dental Health Center** . . . . 234-8131 Dental care for low income children between the ages of 4 and 17 years.

△ **University of So. California Dental School** (714) 824-5011 In Irvine (Orange County), with a dental clinic, and an orthodontia clinic. Patients are seen either **free**, or on a sliding scale. Call for information and an appointment.

∆ Many San Diegans who are fed up with the high costs of **dental care** are heading to **Tijuana**. A clinic frequented by San Diegans is the American Dental Clinic, (619) 338-9600 (new building). There is a female dentist (smaller hands make sense to me!) and I know several people who have gone here and are very satisfied. English is spoken. Prices are reasonable ($129 porcelain crown, usually $350-$500 or more in San Diego). They can give you a ball park quote over the phone if you call and say what you think you need done. Also, a neighbor took her daughter to Tijuana for braces and saved a lot.

Medical Research Centers

In recent years, San Diego has become an acclaimed center for **medical research**. The advantages of participating in medical studies are: free medical evaluation and treatment by experts in their fields, the opportunity to take advantage of the latest developments in diagnosis and treatment for a variety of medical problems, and financial compensation for participation. A study lasts anywhere from one day to several months. You may or may not be taking a placebo or a drug; you won't know. Either way, they won't let you suffer if you need medication. You can drop out, or you'll be dropped out. Check with your doctor before participating. Of course, your doctor may not want you to participate because he might lose you as a paying client.

Much money for medical research comes from the National Institutes of Health in Washington DC, or from pharmaceutical companies who are introducing new medications. If you participate in medical research, you are not a total guinea pig. Inquire about the history of the medication you'll be taking, and the known or potential risks. You will have a lot of information to read about the study before they accept you, and you must sign a consent form.

I learned a lot when I participated in a 12 week asthma study at the Clinical Research Institute (see below). I became a happy, asthma–free camper, and gained a better understanding of what asthma is, and how is affected me. My breathing went from 62% of capacity for my sex, height, etc., to 114%!! I was the only one in my group who did so well, *and* I was the only one taking oriental herbs in addition to the medication!!! *Hmmmm!!!* We had EKGs, blood work, breathed into a tube connected to a computer, received medication, some allergy testing, received a meter to blow into at home and a form to record the information on, and we were paid $350 at the end of the study!! I haven't had an asthma attack since! I also learned a lot from reading a book I bought at the Loma Theater Bookstar entitled *Asthma and Hay Fever* by Leon Chaitow, N.D.,D.O., Thorsons Publishing Group, which offered proven drug–free methods to combat the causes of asthma. I learned to avoid milk like the plague; mold and dust, too, and to stay tuned to my breathing. Haven't had a wheeze since I participated in the study. According to a doctor I talked with since, I may have had a worm that was killed by the medication! Who knows?!

The following companies are engaged in medical research. Call and inquire about current studies and compensation, as new research studies come up every year. Most pay you to participate, although certain studies may only give you medical care. Compensation varies from under $50 for travel expenses, but many pay $300–$700. A 30–day sleep study paid $3000!

∆ The **Clinical Research Institute** 271–1690
Studies have included: asthma, menopause, jewelry allergy, pneumonia, heartburn, high cholesterol, asthma, infant nutrition, osteoarthritis, menopause and osteoporosis. (This is where I did

my asthma study, and they were wonderful to me.) Call for current studies and compensation.

Δ **University of California San Diego (UCSD) Medical Center** ranks in the nation's top 10 for research funding received from the National Institutes of Health. Many UCSD studies are done in conjunction with the VA Hospital. Studies have included:
<pre>
    diabetes   543-3716
    high blood pressure   543-3716
    Alzheimer's disease   622-5800
    obsessive-compulsive disorders   534-4306
    psoriasis, wrinkles, shingles, atopic dermatitis . . . 543-5820
    female baldness 552-8585 x2169
    panic attacks   534-4306
    genital herpes 552-8585 x2169
    anti-anxiety   497-6648
    arthritis   543-5820
    asthma   294-3787
    insomnia, forgetfulness, panic, loss of interest . . . 622-6111
</pre>
Call the above numbers for current studies and compensation.

Δ **California Research Foundation** 291-2321
    North County 675-3251
Studies have included stomach pain, ulcers, arthritis of knee or hip, angina, yeast infections, asthma. Call for current studies and compensation.

Δ **Clinical Neuroscience Research Center** 452-9232
Studies include depression, anxiety, panic attacks. Call for current studies and compensation.

Δ **ClinTrials** . . . . (800) 38-ASTHMA
Call for current studies and compensation.

Δ **Allergy Medical Group** 291-2321

Studies have included eczema, atopic dermatitis, ulcer, prostate, ear infection, sinusitis, Alzheimer's, depression. Call for current studies and compensation.

△ **Allergy & Asthma Research Center** 292–1144
Studies have included hay fever, asthma, allergy, hypertension. Call for current studies and compensation.

△ **Asthma & Allergy Treatment/Research Associates.** 436–3988
Studies have included asthma, heartburn, acid indigestion. Call for current studies and compensation.

△ **Bruce Prenner, MD, Allergist** 286–2801
Studies have included asthma and allergies for children and adults. Call for current studies and compensation.

△ **Scripps Clinic & Research** Foundation 455–9100, 554–9598. Studies have included skin cancer, Crohn's disease, ulcerative colitis, cancer, insomnia, male hair regrowth, depression. Call for current studies an compensation.

△ **Dermatology Associates** 753–1027
Studies have included skin problems, eczema, cold sores. Call for current studies and compensation.

△ **Sharp Rees–Stealy** . . . . 234–6261 or 699–1552
Studies have included asthma, heartburn, blood pressure, arthritis, heart flutter. Call for current studies and compensation.

△ **San Diego Endocrine & Medical Clinic** 265–3011
Studies have included osteoporosis, cholesterol. Call for current studies and compensation.

△ **San Diego Arthritis & Osteoporosis Medical Clinic** 287–1966
Studies have included osteoporis. Call for current studies and

compensation.

△ **Feighner Research Institutes** 544–0100; 464–4300
Studies have included depression, anxiety, Alzheimer's. Call for current studies and compensation.

△ **Center for Stress Studies** 574–0252
Studies have included anxiety, depression. Call for current studies and compensation.

△ **James Goldberg, Ph. D**. 425–6109
Studies have included Panic disorder. Call for current studies and compensation.

△ **Pacific Institutes of Health** 574–6932
Studies have included PMS. Call for current studies and compensation.

△ **Pacific Research Network** 294–4302
Studies have included **Alzheimer's disease**, male impotence, stress, depression, anxiety, migraine, sleep. Call for current studies and compensation. Additional offices in Indio, (800) 748–5646.

△ **Behavioral Medicine Research** 571–1188
Studies have included **Alzheimer's disease**. Call for current studies and compensation.

△ **VRG International** .... (800) 666–7777
Studies have included asthma, prostate, yeast, bronchitis, urinary. Call for current listing of local studies and compensation.

Additional medical research information:
△ For **cancer research studies** in San Diego, call the National Cancer Institute, (800) 422–6237 or (800) 4–CANCER. I have

friends who have been involved at Scripps and at UCSD.

△ For information on clinical trials on a wide variety of diseases and rare disorders, write to NORD, Box 8923, New Fairfield, CT 06812-1783.

△ Compuserve offers an on-line computer search of clinical trials.

△ To inquire about **research studies** going on in the San Diego area, contact:

National Institute on Aging . . . . (301) 496-1752
National Institute of Arthritis . . . . (800) 283-7800
National Institute on Dental Research . . . . (301) 496-4261
National Institute/Diabetes, Digestive &Kidney . . . . . (301) 496-3583
National Eye Institute . . . . (301) 496-5248
National Heart, Lung and Blood Institute . . . . (301) 496-4236
National Instit. of Allergy & Infectious Disease . . . . (800) 874-2572
Neurological Disorders . . . . (301) 496-5924
Pharmaceutical Manufacturers Assn. studies . . . . (202) 835-3450
Office of Alternative Medicine . . . . (301) 496-1712

Plastic Surgery

△ **UCSD Medical Center Plastic Surgery** 294-3746
Plastic surgery performed by an intern or resident (a medical school graduate from who is specializing in plastic surgery) at UCSD Medical Center can cost less than elsewhere, depending on the procedure. You might be surprised at their prices. All services are completely supervised by Board Certified Plastic Surgeons.

△ In one of my bargain hunting workshops at Mesa College, a young woman jumped up and announced that she had her thighs "vacuumed" in Tijuana by a plastic surgeon, and she said that I should let everyone know that this procedure can be done down there for much less than up here. I know some people will read this and scream, but I am not advising you *to* or *not to* do this: I am telling you that Californians are having plastic surgery in Tijuana for less than they can in San Diego (facelift, eyes and neck, $2300; nose, $1000; tummy tuck, $1600). Inquire about credentials. Get all the information you can from plastic surgeons here and be knowledgeable about the procedure, the dangers, etc. before you consult a plastic surgeon in Tijuana.

∆ Call the American Society of Plastic and Reconstructive Surgeons at (800)–635–0635 and (800) 332–FACE and request free brochures on procedures, and check the library or book store for information on plastic surgery.

Bargain at Spas!

Most spas have reduced rates during the summer months, and some offer the summer rate during most weeks that have a major holiday. Remember to ask if there are any specials, or if any discount coupons are available!

∆ **Rancho La Puerta Health Spa**, in Tecate, is the sister spa to the ultra deluxe health Golden Door spa in San Marcos. It's located a few minutes South of the border in Tecate, about an hour's drive from downtown San Diego, with over 30 exercise classes a day, swimming, running, hikes, pampering. Single rate, Saturday to Saturday, $1685 a week. (The Golden Door is $4250 a week, and $3750 in the summer.) Call for brochure, (800)–443–7565. Family week is held one week in the summer. Children up to age 3 are $300; up to age 17, $600, including all meals and lots of activities.

△ **Desert Hot Springs Hotel & Spa** offers day use passes for $5 on weekdays, $6 on weekends. Admission entitles guests to use the spring–fed pools and dressing rooms with lockers and showers, from 8 a.m. til 10 p.m.. Call (800) 843–6053 for further information and directions (about 2–2 1/2 hours from San Diego airport).

△ **Oak Meadow Fitness Ranch**: 3 days, 2 nights, $250, hiking trails, pools, in Escondido, 749–9426.

△ **Cal A Vie Spa** in Vista offers a $500 discount during the summer ($3818, normally $4318) and a $500 discount on holiday weeks; 945–2055.

△ **Glen Ivy Hot Springs**, Corona, CA, less than 2 hours from downtown San Diego, (909) 277–3529. Daily admission including use of outdoor mineral baths, indoor/outdoor therapy pools, red clay mud bath, outdoor hot spas, olympic–size swimming pool, sunning deck and sauna, Monday through Friday, $12.50; Saturdays, Sundays and holidays, $14.75. No reservations required. The Entertainment Coupon Book usually has a two–for–one coupon for Glen Ivy. See chapter on "Resources."

△ **The Palms Spa** in Palm Springs, (619) 325–1111, offers 13 optional fitness classes, three low–calorie meals, pools, saunas and spas, from $129–$209 per day, including accommodations. Ask about specials.

△ The **Oaks at Ojai**, Ojai, CA, (800) 753–OAKS, $963 a week, treatments extra. (Located between Los Angeles and Santa Barbara).

*For additional information on **major spas**, including current rates and brochures, call the Spa toll–free number, (800)–ALL–SPAS.*

Chapter 7

JOB INFORMATION

HOW TO RAISE QUICK $CASH

About 95% of job openings are *not* listed in the classified ads. And, if you are applying for an advertised position, you may be competing with hundreds of applicants for the same job!! Here are a some of the "hard to find" employers in San Diego, job hotlines that list recorded job openings, and other helpful job info. Later in this chapter, you'll find some interesting ways to raise quick cash.

Finding a Job

Most of the following employers have 24-hour job hotlines, listing jobs currently available; others handle employment through their Personnel Department, Office of Human Resources, or Employment Office. These organizations hire employees in positions from custodial and non-professional, to clerical and professional. Call to see what's available:

Federal Government . . . . (818) 575-6510
This is a central job hotline (located in Los Angeles) for *all* of California, broken down into areas, including San Diego. Listen carefully to directions. Jobs for San Diego area by occupation. You can also select to hear listings for all over the country, by occupation. The Federal Government Walk-in Job Center, is located at 880 Front Street, Room 4280, downtown. No phone.

State of California 237–6163
Post Office 221–3351
San Diego Unified Port District 291–0110
San Diego County 531–5764
City of San Diego 682–1011
City of Escondido 432–4585
City of Chula Vista 691–5095
City of Coronado 552–7807
City of El Cajon 441–1671
City of Imperial Beach 423–8300x134
City of La Mesa 667–1183
City of National City 336–4306
City of Poway 679–4300
City of Lemon Grove 464–6934
City of Santee 258–4100x5
UCSD Medical Center 682–1001

San Diego Community College District 584–6580x6580
San Diego County Office of Education 292–3500
Grossmont/Cuyamaca College 465–1700
  Ask for tape 8081 or 8081
San Diego State University .... 594–5801 or 594–5861
University of California (UCSD) 682–1000
City Schools 293–8002

△ Call all school districts. A list of districts is available at the San Diego County Office of Education, 292–3500.

△ While you have the *Yellow Pages* in hand, call all hospitals. They hire hundreds of employees.

△ Thumb through the *Yellow Pages* for other ideas. Who knows, you might create the ideal job match for you. (Remember, there are several *Yellow Page* books for the different areas: San Diego, North County, Inland, East County, South Bay, etc.) The downtown library has a telephone book room, with all San

Diego directories, plus directories from major cities across the country.

△ The Employment Development Department (State of California) has job listings posted in the lobby of their offices. Call for further information.

Downtown 525–4520
El Cajon 441–2300
Oceanside 754–5080
East San Diego 265–4800
South Bay 482–6096

△ The Chamber of Commerce publishes an annual directory of major employers in San Diego, available at libraries. It lists the largest employers (those who hire the most employees), and provides the name and phone number of the personnel directors.

△ The *San Diego Business Journal* publishes a list of top employers by occupation (accountants, engineers, etc.,) with the name and phone number of the personnel directors. They publish another list of top general employers. Both are available at libraries.

△ The San Diego Career Center, 8401 Aero Drive (near Montgomery Field), 627–2553. Free individualized career planning and counseling, vocational assessment, career information library, nontraditional jobs information, job search skills, career exploration classes, computer labs. Call for hours.

△ Job Search Assistance Workshop, a free one–day workshop held almost every Friday at the San Diego Career Center, 8401 Aero Drive, 627–2553.

△ **Job Placement Preparation/Civil Service Review** is a *free* three–hour workshop on preparation and practice for the civil service test, held once a week at Point Loma Campus, 3249 Fordham Street, near the Sports Arena, 221-6973.

∆ If interested in leaving the area for a job, ask the librarian for the directories of jobs in other cities, with titles such as: *Job Banks: Los Angeles; Job Banks: Orange County; Job Banks: Chicago*, etc.. I was surprised at all the titles I found in the downtown library, including *101 Ways to Find An Overseas Job*.

∆ Paras Newsstand, 30th and University in North Park, 296-2895, carries newspapers from major cities throughout the United States, and the world. Check the classified ads for jobs.

∆ San Diego Career Planning & Assessment Center, 8401 Aero Drive, 627-2553, offers help with career goals and career assessment, and more.

∆ **Peace Corps Recruiting Office** . . . . (800) 292-2461 or (800) 242-6709

∆ Each community college has a job placement board with jobs countywide posted. Walk on campus, ask where the job placement board is, and take a look. You don't have to be enrolled to do this, but if you enroll in a class, you can get job counseling, etc.

∆ Economic Development Department (EDD) of the State of California, 1354 Front Street, 525-4522, has a job board with positions throughout the county posted. Anyone can go in and take a look. They sponsor a free networking group for professionals who are seeking employment, with 50-200 attending. They can also direct you to other services for job seekers, including career counseling and filing for unemployment. Offices throughout the county. Call 525-4522 for office nearest you.

△ Look for these books, or similar titles in libraries or book stores: *Jobs In Paradise, Work and Sail Your Way Around the World, Directory of Overseas Summer Jobs, How To Get A Job On A Cruise Ship, Summer Jobs in Britain, How to Make Money in Music, Art, Photography, How to Get an Overseas Job, Job Seeker's Guide to 1000 Top Employers, Job Seeker's Guide to Socially Responsible Companies, etc.*

△ San Diego Center for Worktime Options . . . . 456–4424 Career consulting and management consulting to explore and implement non–traditional schedules. Learn how you can get flexitime, job sharing, telecommuting, and flex–place. Part-time, temporary, or full–time options to suit your schedule.

Free Job Training/Career Change

△ The ROP Program (Regional Occupational Program) offers quality free job training for anyone in the County, no tuition, for all income levels in all areas from accounting to welding, with computer, construction, medical, insurance, interior decorating, food service, travel and other occupations. Call East County 579–8323; San Diego, 292–3611, for further information.

△ San Diego Community College Continuing Education (adult education program) offers dozens of free business skills classes including all office skills (computers, desktop, accounting, data entry, DOS, business math, medical office skills, shorthand and typing, plus 10–key, typing and shorthand tests), plus vocational courses including appliance repair, auto body paint and repair, auto mechanics, electronic assembly, basic electronics, construction, landscape construction, pipefitting, sheet metal, shipfitting, blueprint reading, plumbing, heating, air conditioning, printing, graphic arts, upholstery, VCR/TV repair and welding. Call 584–6500 and ask where you can pick up a schedule of their courses.

They can direct you to one of 10 locations throughout the city where you can get a copy. They no longer mail it.

△ Grossmont/Cuyamaca Community College District, 8800 Grossmont College Drive, El Cajon, 465-1700, offers training for entry-level opportunities in insurance, clerical and accounting, plus career assessment, career planning, resume writing and interviewing techniques.

△ Don't know what kind of work you want to be in? Send for a *free* copy of the 32 page *Whole Work Catalog*, which contains *hundreds* of books written on how to enter careers in art, fashion, advertising, public relations, health, catering, human services, animals, outdoor careers, law enforcement, high tech, real estate, making money in music, freelancing, mail order, retailing, franchising. Also, alternative careers, working from home, self-employment opportunities, starting a word processing service, getting money to start a business, temporary employment, freelancing, career guides, career assessment, resume writing, interviewing techniques, job hunting guides, plus financial aid for college, etc. Write to: New Career Center, P. O. Box 297, Boulder, CO 80306, or call (303) 447-1087. (How I wish *I* had known about all these options and alternatives when I was in a career change!!)

△ Low income individuals can seek job training, on-the-job training, skills, counseling, referrals to other services, etc., from a variety of sources including Occupational Training Services, 560-0411; Metropolitan Area Advisory Committee (MAAC), 474-2232; Foundation for Educational Achievement, 299-0999; Greater Avenues For Independence (GAIN), 338-2749; or call the County Info Line, 230-0997.

Start Your Own Business

If you're interested in starting up your own business, here are some resources you may want to look into. Drop by a newsstand or major book store and look over the magazines on money-making opportunities, including *Venture, Entrepreneur, and Spare-Time Money Making Opportunities*. These magazines are actually catalogs of mail-order books that cost about $75 or more on how to start various business. They are great for ideas, but you can do better by looking over books with similar titles in libraries or book stores. There are hundreds of titles available. (See *Whole Work Catalog*, above.)

Δ For a free Business Start-Up Kit is available from the U.S. Small Business Administration. Anyone can use their free Business Resource Center with resources for anyone who runs a business or is starting one. Info on your competition, potential new customers, your market, plus business planning software. Counselors will help. All services are free. Located at 500 West C Street, Suite 550, downtown, 557-7272.

Δ Government loans are available from the U.S. Small Business Administration to start up or expand a small business for those who have been turned down by two banks. Call 557-7250x4 for further information.

Δ **Free counseling** on how to start up a business is available from S.C.O.R.E. (Service Corps of Retired Executives), 557-7250.

Δ **Association of Home-Based Businesses**, monthly meetings, 591-1151.

How to Raise Extra $Cash

Could you use some extra cash in today's tight economy? Wanna fatten your wallet a little? You'll never get rich with the following ideas, but you can raise come quick cash to ease the crunch, pay off some bills, or just for fun. Try these:

△ Earn approximately $20–50 cash for one hour participation in various **market research**. *Qualified* volunteers (each study has its own requirements) can participate in several categories including: taste tests for new food product and fast foods, evaluating products, evaluating the effectiveness of product advertisements, and more. You can meet people, have a lot of fun, receive gourmet snacks, and make a few bucks! A friend participated in a mock jury for three hours and was paid $75. Another discussed ordering fitness wear from a catalog for two hours for $50. Another taste–tested cereals for $50. Anther evaluated new car advertising for $50. Another evaluated five kinds of vanilla ice cream for $35. Watch for advertisements of market research companies in the display ads and classified ads of the *Reader* ("Notices" or "Personals") on Thursdays, or in the *Union–Tribune* ("Personals"), usually on Sundays. Here are a few companies to call to participate in market research:

Taylor Research 299–6368
Luth Research 283–7333
San Diego Survey 265–2361
Directions in Research 299–5883
Fogherty Group 550–3878

△ **Audition for acting in TV commercials** and bit parts. Check the *Reader* classified ads (Stage Notes) for places and dates to audition.

△ Be an extra in movies and TV shows that are filmed in San Diego.   Call casting the hotlines for casting companies:

Background San Diego 974-8970
Tina Real Casting 685-3662

△ Screen Actor's Guild (SAG) Hotline 278-7695
SAG Membership $1050

△ Send $5 for a copy of "How To   Make Money As A Hollywood Extra," (51 pages of resources) to: Glenn David, P. O. Box 5314, Hemet, CA 92544.   Ask for his schedule of workshops in San Diego.

△ **Be a host parent (singles, OK) for international students** who come here to study English for short periods, from about a month to a few months.   Earn $350 or more a month.   A private room is required by most, with a private or shared bath. Meals to be provided would typically include a light breakfast. Most students require a full dinner with the family, although some students only want breakfast.   The home must be in a convenient location for the student to take the bus to school. Check "Language Schools" in the *Yellow Pages.* and look for schools with host programs that are in your area or convenient by bus to the school.

△ **Take in a runaway, pregnant teen, or senior,** and receive income.   Contact Social Services through the County by calling the Info Line of San Diego County, 230-0997.   They will be able to direct you to the proper agencies.

△ **Have a yard sale.** Advertise it in the classifieds of the *Union/Tribune*, the *Reader* or your neighborhood newspaper. Put up good signs at major nearby intersections with date, time, address and arrows pointing to direction of sale.   Print your signs with an inch-wide felt pen which is really easy to read from a distance, available at office supply stores and drug stores.

△ Do as a lot of people are doing: attend yard sales, rummage sales, estate sales and auctions and buy up the great buys whether or not you need them. Take them home, mark them up, and have a yard sale of your own every few months, or sell your stuff at the swap meet.

△ Clean out your closet and sell your unwanted clothes at Buffalo Exchange in Pacific Beach and Act III on Lake Murray and La Mesa. They pay cash for used clothing, about 40% of the agreed upon selling price. (If you leave things on consignment, you usually get about 60% of the selling price, but if you want cash today, it's usually about 40%. So, if you take in a sweater that you both determine will sell for about $10, you'll get $4, today.) They are "picky" about what they will take, so call first and tell them what you have. A smart move is to ask: "What are you looking for?" They sometimes drive a hard bargain, so be prepared. (*For a list of resale and consignment shops, see chapter on Goods & Services*).

△ Get cash (up to $28!) for your used Levi's 501's in good condition at Pia's Vintage Shop, 1570 Garnet, Pacific Beach, 483-6175, or at Fair Mairs, 4879 Newport, Ocean Beach, 222-0220, and at Buttonfly Stores, downtown, 237-0504; Hillcrest, 297-9135; Pacific Beach, 581-6735; College area, 287-5779; El Cajon, 444-0689 and San Ysidro, 428-2327.

△ Take your unwanted furniture, decorator items and dinnerware to a furniture consignment store. You usually get 60% of the agreed-upon selling price, the store gets 40%. You will sign a three-month contract, and the price gets lowered 10% at the end of each month until it sells. Most items sell, but some things do get returned at the end of 90 days, if unsold. *For listings of furniture consignment stores, see chapter on "Goods & Services."*

△ **Find something to sell at the swap meet.** Home made food is a good one, and an easy one. The Escondido swap meet has hand-made tamales. You can do it, too. All swap meets could use a little more of the Del Mar Fair type foods: roast corn, barbecued chicken, deluxe french fries, home made zucchini bread, cheese breads, brownies, cookies, chili, etc. A spot costs around $20, and you're your own boss. People sell at swap meets to supplement incomes, to make a living, or for the social aspect of it. Call the swap meet office and ask for their publication on how and what to sell at swap meets, how to buy wholesale, and other tips. Book stores and libraries have additional information on how to sell at flea markets and where to get wholesale merchandise. I was impressed with the wholesale resources they have in the downtown library's Business Book Section.

∆ Sell your newsworthy home videos to KNSD, KFMB, KGTV, or KUSI news. Local stations pay around $50 or so, unless it's something really big. L.A. stations pay about $125. See if you can locate a video on how to shoot and sell video news. There used to be one. I no longer have a source, but feel sure that a similar title is available.

∆ Grow house plants, or tomatoes or lemons or avocadoes, etc., in your yard for profit. Sell on weekends at your own yard sale, or become a local supplier for a nearby restaurant, or small grocer.

∆ Breed pedigreed dogs or cats, or tropical fish or birds. Pick up a "how to" book at the library or book store.

∆ Make homemade soups or desserts to sell to local restaurants. and pick up some extra bucks. I have a friend who makes and sells hot sauce for chicken wings. He sells it by the gallon to restaurants.

∆ Participate in medical research and get paid. *(See chapter on "Health and Medical.")*

∆ Get a part-time job in a retail store, restaurant or business.

△ Get a seasonal job (summer, Christmas, etc.)

△ Consider signing up with a temporary agency.

△ Consider a second job at night or on weekends.

△ Do free-lance work in your field. Advertise your services in the neighborhood newspaper: typing, carpentry, accounting, resume writing, etc.

△ Look into overtime work at your job.

△ Consider getting a better job, with more pay, more benefits.

△ Rent a spare room.

△ Do housecleaning, child care, painting, pet care, hauling, yard work, sewing, running errands.

△ Sign up for part-time work with a caterer.

△ Get people to sign petitions at stores. See *Reader* classified ads for job listings.

△ Sign up to work part-time at conventions. Calling the San Diego Convention & Visitor's Bureau, 231-3101, and ask about opportunities.

△ Learn to prepare tax returns and make extra money during tax season. Instruction is usually only a few weeks, free, and provided by the employer.

△ Work at the polls on election day and earn about $30-40 a day. Call the Registrar of Voters, 560-1061.

△ Deliver flowers on special occasions such as Valentine's Day, Mother's Day, etc. Call a major florist near you.

△ Start a day care center. Get a "how to" book at the library or book store.

△ Counts heads for the Census Bureau every ten years. It's a federal job, with good hourly pay.

△ Apply for a grant or student loan and head back to college (*See chapter on Classes, Money for College.*)

△ Borrow money from friends or relatives, who may be more willing to give you a low or no interest loan, and a flexible repayment schedule.

Δ **Borrow on your whole life insurance policy** which has a cash value if it has been in force for any length of time.

Δ **Pick up a new skill** by taking free job training classes that could lead to a part-time job, perhaps a whole new career.

Δ Head for the business book section of the library or book store, and find a book on ideas for home-based businesses you can start on a shoe string. There are dozens of titles available in this field.

Δ Enter the Pillsbury Bake-Off. The grand prize is $1 million, the largest ever awarded. Call (800) 598-8753 for complete rules and an entry form. Head for the library or book store and ask for the book on how to enter cooking contests, and other contests.

Δ Earn $15-20 selling your plasma to blood centers. They draw whole blood, separate out the plasma, and return the red blood cells to you. Call Alpha Therapeutics, 233-6553; Pyramid Biologics, 298-4022; Hemabiologics, 682-5252; Bayer Corp., 233-7763. Some restrictions apply. Qualified Rh negative mothers can earn up to $300 a month.

Δ *Teen-Age Money Making Guide* by Allan Smith, (Success Advertising & Publishing), is a book containing useful **advice to help ambitious teens start profitable business enterprises**. Many other titles deal with this subject, and it's never too early to have your kids learn about making money!

Δ Call the San Diego County Info Line, 230-0997, which can put you in touch with the proper Social Service Agency that will lend certain individuals a few hundred dollars for emergencies.

Chapter 8

CREDIT INFO
AND
LEGAL GOOD DEALS

This is an important chapter. I hope everyone reads it because there are some real *eye-openers* in it...things that could change your future for the best!

Credit & Credit Cards

Following is information on credit card rates, getting credit for those with credit problems, credit clean-up and bank loans.

Δ For a list of the ten lowest-rate credit cards available and those with no annual fee, check the Personal Finance Section of the *Union-Tribune* on Mondays.

Δ Making only a minimum payment on your credit card can be very costly. It would take 33 years to pay off a $2000 debt paying only a minimum payment. You would repay $9,125.98!

Δ You can request a lower interest rate on your major credit card and ask them to waive the fee. If you pay 17% or more, send more than the monthly minimum, mail your check on time and have a good credit history, call and ask them to drop the fee and lower the rate. Suggest that you're considering switching to a no-fee/lower rate card company.

Δ If you've been turned down for a Master Card or Visa due to divorce, bad credit or bankruptcy, you may be eligible for a "secured" credit card. Here's how secured credit works. "Secured" in this case means that your credit limit will be established by the amount of money you have on deposit in savings with them, as "security." Most bank cards require $1 on deposit for every $1 of credit you want. If you want a $500 credit line, you'll need $500 on deposit. Some banks require less on deposit, some more. Their interest rates may be higher, but some offer lower rates because you have cash on deposit with them.

Δ Secured credit cards are offered from First Consumer's National Bank of Portland, Oregon, an annual percentage rate of 19.5%, and 3% interest on your secured deposit. Your credit line is 150% greater than your security deposit: with $400 on deposit, you get a $600 credit limit; $1000 deposit, $1500 credit.; $100 deposit, $150 credit. Criteria: must be 18+, have gross income of $1,000 per month or more, phone in your home, and a street address, not a P. O. box, and no liens. If you've filed bankruptcy, it must be discharged; accounts must not be more than three payments behind in the last six months. No application fee. Annual fee of $39 is billed on first statement. The majority of applications are approved. Call (800) 876-3262; ask for secured Master Card info.

Δ The City Attorney's Consumer Fraud Unit has prosecuted a few San Diego credit clean-up clinics who have taken fees, but failed to deliver the services they promised. Typically, what they do is charge $75-$300 or even $6000 up front and promise to clean up your bad credit and obtain credit cards for you regardless of your past credit. If they do obtain credit cards, it is usually done through a bank that issues "secured" credit cards, where your credit line is the same amount or than you have on deposit as "security." Erasing bad credit is a questionable promise and rarely successful since only information that is outdated or erroneous can be eliminated from your credit report. Using the Fair Credit Reporting Act (FCRA), the credit repair company will dispute everything in your credit report in the hope that something inaccurate will show up, or the credit reporting agency will not be able to confirm the information. If it cannot be confirmed, it must be removed. California law states that a credit reporting agency does not have to reinvestigate disputed information if "it has reasonable grounds to believe that the dispute by the consumer is frivolous or irrelevant." Since credit repair companies investigate *everything,* they are frequently dismissed as "frivolous." Inaccurate and outdated information is best remedied directly by the consumer. For a copy of *Credit Repair Clinics: Consumer Beware*, send $1 to Bank Holders of America, 560 Herndon Parkway, Suite 120, Herndon, Virginia 22070.

△ Here's essentially how to clean up your credit yourself: First, get your credit report (see Credit Reporting Agencies below) and dispute everything on it that is negative. Send by certified mail. They will either remove items as requested, tell you they won't change your credit file and give reasons, or if the party involved fails to respond within 30 days, the information you wanted removed will be. Many companies can't be bothered to go through back records, so this can work for you. If not, you are allowed to send in a 100 word consumer explanation, which will be included in your credit report. If you have unpaid debts on your credit report, determine an affordable plan to pay off your debts, and contact your creditors with your proposal. Send an explanation of your repayment plan to the credit bureau. This will let potential creditors know you are satisfying the debt. Bad credit stays on your record for seven years, after which it can no longer be reported. Pay your bills on time for six months, and get a secured credit card. If your bills are paid on time, you improve your credit rating. Check the library and book stores for books on solving credit problems and how to clean up your credit.

Δ Get a copy of your credit report from the three major credit reporting agencies below. Send your request with your full name including "Jr.," maiden name, current address and addresses for the past five years, social security number, and date of birth to: TRW, POB 2350, Chatsworth, CA 91313; (800) 392–1122. TRW gives one free report a year.   Equifax, (800) 685–1111, charges $8. Trans Union, (800) 851–2674, also charges $8. All companies give free copies if you have been denied credit within the past 30 days.

Δ TRW Credentials Service is credit service that sends you a quarterly report of inquiries into your credit report. You may receive unlimited copies of your credit report, are informed about who is seeing your credit, and are notified if anything negative has been put into your file. Membership is $29–44. You'll receive a toll free number to call anytime about your credit, a newsletter, and a financial profile (you can input information into your credit file). Call (800) 262–7432 for further information.

Δ Mission Federal Credit Union, with numerous San Diego locations, is open to membership by any parent of a student in school, alumni of local colleges and universities, senior citizens and retired persons, in addition to educators and school employees. They offer a Visa Card at 12.9% interest, no annual fee. Secured cards available, processed normally, 12.59% interest, 150% on deposit.   Call 552–6860.

Δ If you have *no* credit, get a secured Master Card or Visa (see above). Many department stores will then give you instant credit if you have a major credit card. Instant credit may offer a low credit line, under $1000, but this will be increased automatically as you establish a good credit history with them by paying your bills on time, and always pay more than the minimum required.

Δ If you're plagued by piles of unpaid bills, get free help from Consumer Credit Counseling Services, 1550 Hotel Circle North,

Suite 110, San Diego, 497–0200. All services are free at their five local offices and can run as high as $100 a month elsewhere. Call for an office near you.

△ If you have been turned down for credit or financing by banks, you still can *get* credit; but you have to pay more interest and points. Banks give "A" loans to those with perfect credit histories, etc. Other financial institutions and private investors offer "B" and "C" and "D" loans for those who have late or missed payments or have bankruptcies a few years old, but have recent good credit. There are a lot of variables in interest rates, some very high, so be sure to shop around for the best deal. Check several sources. Look under "Mortgage Loans" and "Loans" in the *Yellow Pages* or the "Money to Lend" classified column of the *Union–Trib.*

Legal

Having legal problems is like having a serious illness, so do what you can to resolve the problem as quickly as possible so you can get on with living. Here are a few sources where you might get a free first, second or third opinion, and learn a few things about the law.

△ Attorney Referral Service 231–8585
Free half–hour initial legal consultation through the Attorney Referral Service of the San Diego County Bar Association.

△ Lawyer referral service of the Legal Aid Society of San Diego, 262–0896; North County, 722–1935.

△ San Diego Mediation Center 238–2400
A *free* service to help you handle disputes concerning neighborhood, domestic, juvenile, landlord–tenant, consumer–merchant, employee–employer, small claims, etc.

△ Lawyers Day at the Mall 231–0781
San Diego County Bar Association members offer free informal consultations on a one–on–one basis at six area shopping malls. An annual event held every May. Call for exact dates.

△ A lawyer, Bill Handel, is on KFI *Radio* (640 on your AM dial), every Saturday morning from 7–9 a.m. offering **free legal advice**. to those who call in. Get your question and thoughts organized, and call (800) 767–4KFI about 10 minutes before the show starts. Let the phone ring until someone picks up. Who knows how long this will last, but he's doing it for now, and what a character he is.

△ Free legal info 233–9797
Recorded information tapes on consumer law, bankruptcy, tenant/landlord, family law; personal injury, criminal law, workman's comp, business law, professional negligence, tax more.
△ San Diego Volunteer Lawyer Program 235–5656
Free legal services on specific matters for low income individuals. Contested custody, HIV and AIDS–related cases, etc. No criminal, DUI, personal injury or landlord/tenant.

△ University of San Diego Legal Clinic 260–4532
Services for low income: civil, juvenile, environmental, immigration and mental health cases. Available September to November and January to May.

△ Save thousands on funerals. The average cremation is about $425; a traditional funeral $825; a pine box that looks like casket, $180; membership fees, $10–$25. For more information, call the Continental Association of Funeral and Memorial Societies, (800) 458–5563.

△ Caring Cremation Services, $545 .... (619) 282–0505
  Accu–care Cremation Center .... (800) 323–1342

∆ For a free catalog of legal books on: employees rights, family law, homeowners, landlords, tenants, harassment, bankruptcy, patents, how to buy a house/sell one, neighbor law, homestead your house, legal guides to living together, small claims court, fighting tickets, do your own divorce, call Nolo Press, (800) 992-6656.

∆ A legal services plan, about $8.^{95} a month from Montgomery Ward Enterprises, (800) 323-4620. No attorney legal fees for consultation and advice by phone or face-to-face consultation, etc. More than 7 local attorneys participate in this plan.

∆ Prepaid Legal, unlimited phone consultations with an attorney, will preparation and annual update, representation for traffic tickets, law suits, IRS audits, 10 page contract and document review, phone calls made and written on your behalf. Discounts on bankruptcy, and other legal services. $25 a month, 297-7265.

∆ Women's Legal Center . . . . 699-5700 Emphasis on family law, landlord/tenant, bankruptcy. Reduced fee based on income and complexity of case.

∆ Lawphone, legal plan sponsored by TRW Credentials (see above), $120 per year, network of private attorneys for legal counsel, (800) 443-6338.

∆ Neighborhood House: free tenant/landlord counseling 263-7761

∆ Tenant/Landlord Rights Hotline 262-0663

∆ Reader's Digest's *Family Legal Guide* is an excellent reference covering everyday legal problems: how to select an attorney; buying, selling, financing real estate; zoning; public use; pensions; condemnation; landlord/tenant; insurance; marriage contracts; divorce; income tax; social security; wills; laws of intestacy; estate taxes; estate administration; employer/employee; consumer; defamation; auto accident; personal injury, etc.

Chapter 9
$FREE & LOW COST
CLASSES AND SEMINARS
For Personal Enrichment, or Leading to a Degree/Certificate
Plus MONEY FOR COLLEGE

California offers the best continuing education for adults in the country, with more tax dollars in the system than in any other state. You can return to school and earn a high school diploma *(free of charge)*, work toward a community college or university degree *(still a deal)*, pursue vocational courses leading to a certificate *(many are free)*, enroll in job search and counseling *(free)*, or check out the leisure classes *(free; some fee–based)*. Like they used to say in the old country, as long as you keep learning, you'll never grow old. *Think about it.*

Adult School/Continuing Education
For Credit, Career or Fun!

Free or low–cost leisure and credit courses are offered through adult education in every school district in San Diego County, funded by local, state and federal tax dollars. County residents can attend any adult school in any district; there are no "boundaries." If you don't know where the nearest adult school is, your local high school should be able to tell you.

For a schedule of hundreds of free classes offered by San Diego Community Colleges Continuing Education Centers, drop by the Point Loma Campus, 3249 Fordham (Sports Arena area), between 8 a.m. and 9 p.m., M–Th, and 8–4 p.m. on Fridays, during the fall, spring or summer sessions, or telephone 221–6973 and ask about one of their locations nearer to you. Sorry, but they no longer mail the schedules. You may enroll any day of the school year, as most courses are individualized. Among the free classes offered are:

All computer training classes, including word–processing and desk–top All job search, Civil Service Review, resume & interviewing classes
All job training classes
All academic classes leading to a diploma
Appliance Repair
Assertive Parenting
Building Maintenance
Cake Decorating, Breadmaking, Pastries, Desserts
Child Development
Childbirth Preparation
Desk–top Publishing
Effective Writing
Electronics
English as a Second Language
Family & Consumer Studies
Floral Design
Health education
Home Planning
Household Repair and Maintenance

Introductory ceramics
Jewelry Making
Landscape
Literature Survey
Machine Shop, Welding
Management classes
Menu Planning
Microwave Cooking
Most Senior Classes
Music: Chorus, Orchestra
Musical Experiences, Music Appreciation
Office Skills
Plumbing, Heating, Air Conditioning
publishing (which I've taken for years!!) The computer lab is open on Saturdays, too.
Sewing, Wardrobe Planning, Tailoring
Super–Saturday Workshops (one-day workshops
Typing Certification
Upholstery
Writer's Workshop

ROP – Regional Occupational Program

The San Diego County Regional Occupational Program offers a variety of free job preparation classes for adults, leading to careers in areas from agriculture to welding, including telecommunications, travel/tourism, commercial art, banking, etc. Call the 24-hour information line at 292-3611, or outside San Diego city, call the toll free line at (800) 479-4900. Classes are held in El Cajon, Linda Vista, Coronado, Chula Vista and North County.

Community College Workshops (& Trips!)

In addition to the traditional, semester-long credit programs, most community colleges offer short-term, non-credit workshops, which are mainly held on Saturday mornings. You may enroll at any of the colleges, regardless of where you live. Most offer one-day short trips to regional sights and events, also. To get on the mailing list to receive their free schedule of workshops, call the following numbers. I receive them all! See you in class.

△ Grossmont Extended Studies 670-1980 x365
△ Southwestern Extended Studies 421-6700, x384
△ Mira Costa College Community Services 757-2121x485
△ Palomar College Continuing Education 744-1150
△ UCSD Extended Studies 534-3400
△ SDSU Extended Studies 594-5152
△ National University Community Education
     Mission Valley. . . . . . 563-7292; Vista 945-6292

Other Classes & Seminars

△ **The Learning Annex**, Mission Valley, holds a variety of three-hour personal growth and business classes, 544-9700.

⚠ **Free classes for women** on health issues and topics of general interest are offered by several hospitals. Call to receive a current schedule, and to be placed on the mailing list of these not–to–be–missed, usually free, workshops:

Sharp Women's Education Program . . . . (800) 729–0229
Scripps Hospital Women's Health Source . . . . (800) 248–6848
Alvarado Parkway Institute Women's Program 697–0396
Mercy Hospital Women's Program . . . . (800) 628–2880
UCSD Medical Center 294–5338

⚠ Check the "Reader's Guide to Local Events: Lectures" each Thursday in the *Reader*. Most of the lectures featured are free. "Lecture junkies" follow this column with a passion, and head out to hear the free speakers at book stores, churches, etc.

⚠ Older Adult Workshops can usually be attended by anyone of any age, provided the majority attending are seniors.   Get on the mailing list of the senior center nearest you; watch for workshops in the Senior Scene column of the *Union–Tribune,* and check out *Senior World's* calendar of events. Lots of free classes! I discovered and started attending senior classes in my neighborhood when I was in my 30's!

⚠ The Foundation For Educational Achievement, low cost language classes and short regional trips (Mexico, California), 571–1003.

⚠ The **U.S. Small Business Administration** offers a number of low–cost business start–up classes, plus seminars for managers, supervisors, and self–employed. For a schedule, 557–7250.

⚠ Home Depot has classes every weekend on "how to" install ceiling fans, tile, faucets, replace roofing, etc. The schedule is posted above the entry doors, or check at the Information Desk.

Local College Fees

Δ **Community college** tuition fees are $13 per credit, or about $300 per semester for residents, more for non-residents. Financial assistance available. (If you have a degree, the fees are $50 per unit.)

```
Mesa College (Kearny Mesa) ......................627-2600
City College (Downtown) ..........................230-2400
Educational Cultural Complex (E. San Diego) ......527-5258
Miramar College (Miramar) ........................536-7800
Grossmont College (El Cajon) .....................465-1700
Cuyamaca College (El Cajon) ......................670-1980
Palomar College (San Marcos & Escondido) .........744-1150
Mira Costa College (Oceanside & Encinitas) .......757-2121
```

Δ **San Diego State University (SDSU), 594–5200:** annual tuition is about $2,000 per year for residents. Financial assistance available.

Δ Food and housing in university housing at SDSU will average about $6000 a year

Δ Estimated standard total costs of one year at SDSU including tuition and fees, books and supplies, food and housing, transportation, miscellaneous and personal expenses:

```
Living with parents ........................ $6,996
Living in university housing ................ 10,334
Living Off-Campus ........................... 11,418
```

Δ Over 5000 classes are offered through the "Open University" at SDSU. Gain college credit without the admission process. Anyone can attend any class without prerequisites, 594–5152.

Δ **University of California, San Diego (UCSD), 534-2230**: the average annual tuition fees are about $6,000 a year. Financial assistance available.

Δ **University of San Diego (USD), 260-4600**: the average annual tuition is about $14,000. Financial assistance available.

Δ **Point Loma Nazarene College (PLNC), 221-2200**: the average annual tuition is about $11,000. Financial assistance available.

Δ There are a number of other private colleges and universities where you can get a degree on weekends while holding down a full time job. See "Colleges, Universities and Schools" in the *Yellow Pages*.

Δ According to the Census Bureau, the average bachelor's degree holder earns $1,000 more per month than those with a high school diploma. Those holding law and medical degrees earn $5,000 more, on average.

Δ The cost of college text books averages around $600+ per year.

Δ The cost of tuition and living on campus at Stanford, Yale, Harvard, Vassar and Bryn Mawr is about $25,000 a year, plus books, personal expenses and transportation.

$Money for College

Millions and millions of dollars of money that doesn't have to be repaid is available every year for college students of all ages. Much of it is never awarded because no one applies for it, or it is applied for after the deadline, which is usually early in the spring prior to the fall semester.

Grant money and college loans are available to all American families, whether you earn $20,000 or $100,000. Home equity will no longer be a factor in determining eligibility for free and low cost federal grants and loans. The federal government wants to grant or lend you money to get your education. The more education you have, the more society will benefit.

Grant money is a gift assistance, based on need, with no obligation for work or repayment. Loans require a future obligation for repayment. Scholarships can be awarded for merit, heritage, occupational major, etc., and do not have to be reimbursed.

Some grants and loans are harder to qualify for than others, but most have nothing to do with high scholastic grades. Many, many are available to women and minorities to encourage them to compete in the academic world. You can save thousands if you're willing to do some legwork. Find out what's available for you. Here are some worth looking into:

∆ Most community college extended study programs (see above) offer a three-hour workshop on scholarships, grants and loans for higher education, for about $25, at least once a year. Call the colleges listed above for the next offering.

∆ *Student Guide: Financial Aid Programs* is a free 74-page booklet from the U.S. Department of Education which describes federal grants, loans and work-study programs for college, vocational and technical school students. For information or to request a free application, call (800) 433-3243, or write to: Federal Student Aid Information Center, P. O. Box 84, Washington, DC 20044-0084.

∆ *Financial Aid Handbook,* is a free publication available from the financial aid office at SDSU. Call 594-6323 to have a copy mailed to you.

△ Federal Pell Grant ($400 to $2,300), depending on your family's contribution (must be $2,100 or less to be eligible), does not have to be repaid, available to all undergraduate students, including those attending college less than half time. By 1997, maximum will be $4,500.) For information, call (800) 433-3243.

△ Cal Grants, up to $5,200 per year, from the State of California, are available to qualifying individuals. If you are a California resident, your grade point average is better than 2.0, and your family income qualifies, you are eligible. Forms are available at all high school counseling offices and at college financial aid offices.

△ Federal Supplemental Educational Opportunity Grant (FSEOG). Based on financial need. Priority given to Pell Grant recipients. For further information, call (800) 433-3243.

△ *Free Money For Undergraduate Studies* (Facts on File) by Laurie Blum, lists financial-aid grants and scholarships by subject and geographic location.

△The American Council on Education, 1 Dupont Circle, NW, Washington, DC, (202)-939-9300, publishes the *Complete Grants Sourcebook for Higher Education,* which should be available at libraries and financial aid offices of high schools, community colleges, or directly from the American Council.

△ *Bear's Guide to Finding Money For College* (Ten Speed Press) by John Bear, Ph.D.: offbeat, creative ways to finance your education.

△ Nellie Mae (New England Loans), the largest nonprofit provider of college loans in the country, offers free up-to-date information on low cost government and other loans for students and parents, (800) 634-9308.

Δ Stafford (Federal) student loans, formerly called Guaranteed Student Loans, are for dependent undergraduate students and are based on need. Students can borrow up to $2,625 for freshmen, $3,500 for sophomores, $5,500 for juniors and seniors, $8,500 for graduate students. Interest well below current rates. No interest while in school, no family income limits. For further information, call (800) 433-3243.

Δ PLUS (Federal) student loans, 9% capped interest rate. No adverse credit history. For further information, call (800) 433-3243.

Δ Perkins (Federal) Loans, formerly known as national direct student loans. Borrow up to $3,000 a year, for a total of $15,000 for undergraduate study; $5,000 a year for graduate study. Interest is only 5 percent and doesn't start until the student leaves school. Inquire at the Financial Aids Office at any college.

Δ Check libraries and book stores for the *Directory of Financial Aids for Women* by Gail Ann Schlachter (Los Angeles Reference Service Press, Inc.).

Δ The Business and Professional Women's Foundation (BPWF) offers hundreds of thousands of dollars in one-half year scholarships of up to $100 to women seeking education for entry into or advancement in the work force. Last year, they awarded over 430 such scholarships. To be eligible, you must be a woman 25 years or older, a U.S. citizen, in need of financial assistance, be in an accredited program and be graduating within 24 months. For an application, send SASE, business size with two first class stamps to: BPW Foundation, 2012 Massachusetts Ave. NW, Washington, DC 20036.

Δ For a free 32-page booklet and information on the **Clairol Scholarship Program**, open to women over 30 who are returning to school, write to: Role Models, Clairol Take Charge Awards, 345 Park Avenue, New York NY 10154

△ Scholarship Research Group, 5868 East 71st Street, Ex. Suite 129, Indianapolis, Indiana 46220, guarantees 5 to 25 sources of scholarships and other financial aid for which you are personally eligible, for $42.50. These sources may already be available, free, above. If you are interested in this service, inform them that you know about the above listed sources of grants and scholarships, and ask if they have 5 to 25 *different* sources before you fork over $42.50. They may only have information on federal grants and loans mentioned above.

Other helpful information:
△ Send your kid to college for *free* at one of the military academies: Naval Academy, West Point, Air Force Academy. Contact the academies directly for requirements (this works best if you have your heart set on it by junior high). They pay all tuition, room and board and give the students over $700 a month to go.

△ Check with the information desk at any library or bookstore for books on money for college, including money you do not have to repay (scholarships and grants). Consider loans *after* you have received all monies you do not have to pay back.

△ Local residents are welcome to use the **libraries** of any local high school, community college and state university, without enrolling, since they are funded by your tax dollars. However, book checkouts are not allowed unless you are an enrolled student. Neighborhood residents near private universities are also welcome to use the libraries.

△ Start saving for your children's education when they are young. Check with your financial advisor about avoiding taxes on your child's investment income. Check into prepaid, guaranteed tuition at the university of your choice.

Chapter 10
ALL–YOU–CAN–EAT RESTAURANTS, SUNDAY BRUNCHES GREAT SEAFOOD FINDS HAPPY HOURS

Since dining out is the Number One pastime these days, this is an area that you can really spend a lot on. If you want to save money, it's very simple. Just try this for 2 months: DON'T EAT OUT WITHOUT A TWO FOR ONE COUPON. PERIOD. There are tons of them out there every week: in your neighborhood newspaper, in the *Union–Trib* "Night & Day" section every Thursday, and in the *Reader* every Thursday and mailed to you in your junk mail. These restaurants pay for the ads because it works for them. They like the business, so don't hesitate to use them. Always tip on the total bill. They've done you the favor of saving you money –– do them a favor and treat them right. Remember: what goes around, comes around. Then there are the awesome "two–for–one" coupon books: *Entertainment* ($40) and *Dine–a–mate* ($30) (see chapter on "Resources"). They can save you many hundreds of dollars. And, for those who are sensitive about using a coupon, *Entertainment* has come out with a new Gold Card that you can use in lieu of coupons for 25% off the total bill. People save tons with these books: why pay full price when you can get two for one? There are coupons in three classifications of restaurants: fine dining, with some of San Diego's best known .. on the water .. in hotels .. great restaurants like Humphreys, Elarios, Brendory's, Athen's Market, Brasserie La Costa ($28), Cafe Taxxi in La Jolla, Cecil's Coronado, La Escale, Crab Catcher, Little Russia ($20), Then there's Family Dining: mid priced restaurants, ethnic restaurants, great restaurants. And there's the smaller restaurants, and fast food. Coupon books pay for themselves by using them just a few times.

△ Many restaurants have "early bird specials," usually between 4 and 6 p.m., before the dinner crowd crunch. Good prices, and a good option to save some $$. Senior specials, too. Just ask!

All-You-Can-Eat Restaurants

△ **Asian Gardens**, 4768 Convoy Street, 268-1911, and 7102 El Cajon Blvd., La Mesa, 697-7422, offers over 20 Chinese items in their buffet seven days a week. Lunch, $4.25; dinner, $4.86. Drive-through, too.

△ **Baja Beach Club**, 7305 Clairemont Mesa Blvd, Clairemont, 576-7009; Mexican buffet, carnitas, tostadas, fajitas, enchiladas, BBQ ribs, lunch 5.95; dinner, $6.95.

△ **Bali Hai**, 2230 Shelter Island Drive, 222-1181, serves a luau buffet luncheon with Polynesian dishes, chicken or beef, salads, desserts, Monday through Friday, for $6.50, includes beverage! Seniors, $5.75. The view of the bay and downtown is to die for.

∆ **Bit of Sweden**, 2850 El Cajon Blvd at Utah, 284–8939. Since 1963, they have served a lunch buffet Monday–Saturday with 20 salads, 10 hot items, desserts, homemade pies, $5.49; buffet dinner is $6.99 weekdays; $7.85 all day on Sunday. Seniors 10% discount. Listed since 1984 in Birnbaum's *Travel USA Today Book* as one of five best bargain restaurants in San Diego and AAA.

∆ **Bob's Big Boy**, 3036 El Cajon, breakfast, $3.99 with eggs, bacon, sausage, hotcakes, french toast, potatoes, fruit, rolls, cookies, biscuits, some salad items, $3.99; breakfast buffet Saturday & Sunday til 2 p.m., $5.49. Lunch salad bar with baked potatoes, zucchini marinara, pasta alfredo, shells, $5.49.

∆ Cafe India, 3760–5 Sports Arena Blvd., Pt. Loma, 224–7500. Vegetarian buffet, weekdays, $4.95; 11–3 p.m., weekends, $6.95, dinner, $6.95.

∆ **China King I Mandarin & Szechwan Cuisine**, has a 14 course Chinese buffet for $3.99 always at 1041 4th Ave, downtown next to Horton Plaza, 233–3389; at 131 Fletcher Parkway in Parkway Plaza, El Cajon, 579–3904, lunch, $4.25; dinner, $5.25.

∆ **Hsu's Schezhwan & Mandarin**, 9350 Clairemont Mesa Blvd., 279–9799. All–you–can–eat Mongolian barbecue, 5–9 p.m., $8.95.

∆ **Khyber Pass**, 4647 Convoy Street, Clairemont, 571–3749; excellent Afghan cuisine lunch buffet with a dozen items, $6.95. Not available for dinner.

∆ **Mandarin Plaza**, 3760 Sports Arena Blvd at Hancock, 224–4222; has a 20–foot lunch buffet bar with over 25 items plus soup & salad bar; $4.95, seven days, 11–4 p.m. After 4, $6.50. No MSG.

∆ **Mandarin Szechuan**, 3373 Rosecrans (Midway & Rosecrans, Loma Square), 224–3838, oriental buffet luncheon with beef, chicken and seafood dishes **seven days**, 20 items plus salad bar, $4.95; dinner, $6.55. NO MSG.

△ **Polynesian Garden**, 4768 Convoy Street, 268-1911, featuring Chinese selections including broccoli beef, roasted pork or fried seafood, $4.25 for lunch; $4.86 for dinner, plus tax.

△ **Godfather Pizza**, all the pizza you can eat, Monday-Friday, $4.69, 11:30-2 PM. Weekly discount coupons in your junk mail.

△ **Fairouz Cafe**, 3166 Midway Drive, 225-0308, all you can eat vegetarian lunch, everyday, $5.25, with 26 salads, humus, beans, spinach, lentil and chicken lemon soup. Dinner includes chicken, lamb, beef, eggplant, and other regional specialties, $10.99. Coupon in *Entertainment* book.

△ Home Town Buffet, 7 locations including 5881 University Ave. at College, 583-7373, plus Santee, Chula Vista, Oceanside, National City, El Cajon. Full buffet with standards like meatloaf, chicken & dumplings, fried chicken, baked fish, ham, whipped potatoes, etc. Lunch, $5.49; dinner, $7.19.

△ **Petro's Place**, 6618 Mission Gorge at Zion, 280-4888. Greek and American buffet, 7 days. Menu varies daily, with gyros, chicken, fish, spanokopita, falafel, mousaka, pastichio, dolmades, keffedes, BBQ chicken. Lunch, $5.39; dinner, $6.99.

△ **Sizzler**, with its several locations in San Diego, has an all-you-can-eat salad bar for lunch or dinner that is enormous, with over 50 items to choose from including hot dishes, meat balls, fried chicken, soups, hot pasta, taco bar, pasta salads, fruit and vegetable salads, and desserts. Menu items such as steak or chicken are available for an additional charge to accompany all this. Monday through Saturday, $5.99 for lunch; $6.99 dinner and all day Sunday. The new one at Midway and Rosecrans, 224-3347, is attractive, large, and fun.

Δ **Soup Exchange**, located at 7777 Fay, 459-0212; 7305 Clairemont Mesa Blvd, 576-0622; 7985 La Mesa Boulevard, 697-8561; over 60 items on salad bar, six soups, baked goods, frozen yogurt, baked potato bar, fresh chocolate chip cookies baked every hour, and a nacho bar. One item (soup or salad) lunch, $5.35; soup and salad, $6.35; dinner includes ribs, lemon chicken, $6.95; Sunday includes brunch for $6.95 until 2 p.m., with eggs, bacon, toast, waffles, bagels, plus all the other regular items! Discount coupons are in the *Pennysaver*. Several other locations throughout the county.

Δ **Soup Plantation,** located at 3960 W. Pt. Loma Boulevard, 222-7404, 6161 Mission Gorge Road, 280-7087; 9158 Fletcher Parkway, 462-4232; several other locations. You get quality with quantity, including over 60 salad items including Caesar and wonton chicken, a bread bar with assorted freshly baked muffins, six assorted soups and chili, baked potato works, pasta, and a fruit and yogurt bar. Lunch until 4 p.m. for $5.99 includes soup and salad, $5.59 for soup or salad alone. Dinner is $7.19 for both items. Coupons in the *Union* and your junk mail. Senior discounts 10%; 20% between 4-5 p.m.

Δ **Tarantino's**, 5150 North Harbor, 222-0010, serves an Italian luncheon buffet Monday through Saturday, with several seafood items that vary daily: salmon florentine, deep fried fish, smoked mussels, seafood salad, beef and chicken dishes, excellent variety of salads. Desserts, nice view of the marina, $7.95.

Δ **Wendy's** restaurants have all-you-can-eat salad bars worth mentioning, with 24 items, $2.59 for one trip, $3.39 for all you can eat.

Δ **Carl's Junior Restaurants** have an all-you-can-eat salad bar with 24 items, for lunch or dinner, $2.99. Take-out available. Several locations throughout the county.

Sunday Brunches

So many of the all–you–can–eat brunches in San Diego fall into the extravagant category, and run well over $15 (**Humphrey's**, $17.95, 224–3577; **Hotel Del**, $21.95, 435–6611). But, here are several wonderful ones that are beautiful, bountiful and under $10:

∆ **El Torito**, 8910 Villa La Jolla Dr, 453–4115, 445 Camino Del Rio S., 296–6154. Buffet: 12 Mexican specialties, ceviche, corn cake, tamales, enchiladas, fish of the day, barbecue ribs, chicken ranchero, hot vegetables, omelet bar, sausage, waffles, sundae bar, Mexican pastries, fruit salads, tossed salads, carnitas, fresh taco bar, beans, rice, champagne, desserts, $8.95, senior discount.

∆ **Bali Hai**, located at 2230 Shelter Island Drive, 222–1181, a favorite restaurant because of the incredible view of the city and bay, serves a Sunday buffet brunch until 2 p.m. for $8.95, includes ham, eggs, sausage, pastries as well as a variety of oriental and traditional lunch buffet specialties in a tropical setting.

∆ **Bay Club**, 2131 Shelter Island Drive (**The Bay Club**), 224–8888, serves a buffet breakfast in an elegant marina setting, daily til 10:30 a.m. and Sundays til ll:30 p.m., with omelettes or eggs to order, fruit, potatoes, breakfast meats, danish, muffins, juice, $8.95. Ask about coupons.

∆ **Shanghai**, 1930 Quivera Way, Marina Village, 226–6200, serves a Sunday bottomless champagne buffet (no breakfast items) in a lovely, peaceful marina setting, mainly luncheon items, barbecue salad, egg rolls, wontons, paper–wrapped chicken, shrimp with lobster sauce, almond chicken, hot and spicy beef, sweet & sour gotlet chicken, subgum vegetables, egg foo young, mandarin lo mein, fried rice, dessert items, fresh fruit, 11–3PM, $9.95.

△ **Hornblower Cruise** Sunday Champagne Brunch Cruise, 234–TOUR, 11–1 p.m., buffet brunch, $29.95. What a deal if you use your two–for–one coupon in *Entertainment* book. *See chapter on "Resources."* The bay is gorgeous. Go on a Santa Anna.

Great Seafood Finds

For you seafood lovers, here are deals you won't want to miss:

△ **Barrett Cafe** (since 1946), 34 miles southeast of San Diego on California 94 at the corner of Barrett Lake Road, 468–3416, serves an all–you–can–eat fish dinner which includes cod fish, hush puppies, wheat pilaf, refried beans and salad. Natives and tourists from all over the world come to sample this fish fry at $8.95; $6.95 seniors.

△ **Rubio's** Restaurants, 32 locations including 3555 Rosecrans, 223–2631. The originator of the fish burrito was Rubio himself. A real San Diego success story. Fish burrito and fish taco plate with rice and beans, $4.26 includes tax. Absolutely egg–cellent. A must. Fast food environment, but the food is great.

△ **Brigantine**, 2725 Shelter Island Drive, 224–2871, and other locations including Old Town, Del Mar, La Mesa, Coronado and Escondido. Half price on selected seafood bar items like clam chowder, shrimp cocktail, fish taco; Sunday & Monday, 4 to closing; Tuesday through Saturday, 4–7 p.m.

△ Peel–your–own–shrimp every Tuesday, 75¢ a bowl, for over 10 years, at **Humphrey's**, 2241 Shelter Island, 224–3577, during happy hour, 4:30–6:30 p.m.; Wednesdays, 50¢ oysters on the half, jumbo shrimp, ceviche.

△ Life is not complete until you've had a fried fish sandwich or a *fresh* tuna sandwich (the best in the West) from **Point Loma**

Seafoods, 2805 Emerson St., Pt. Loma, 223-1109. Great soups, seafood platters and salads, and a complete fresh fish market with live lobsters. Eat outside or in the covered area by boats.

△ Half-price on many oyster bar items during happy hour at **Quiigs** in Ocean Beach, 5083 Santa Monica, Ocean Beach, on the ocean, 222-1101, 2-7 p.m. Great view, great sunsets, great place to watch the ocean during storms, $1.50 champagne during happy hour.

△ World Famous **Puerto Nuevo** Mexican style lobster is served with rice and beans (and limones) in several restaurants in a group off the right hand side of the road a few miles south of Rosarito Beach. Inquire at the Rosarito Beach Hotel lobby for directions to exact location just down the road from the hotel.

△ Some of the best seafood restaurants in town offer two-for-one discount coupons in the *Entertainment* coupon book. See chapter on *"Resources."*

Other fresh seafood ideas:
△ **Catch your own lobster** and abalone off Point Loma, or west of La Jolla Cove from the first Wednesday in October to the first Wednesday after March 15th. Find out more about this at any marine supply store or diving center. △ **Catch your own fish** at one of San Diego's many freshwater lakes: Lake Poway, a 60-acre trout-filled lake; for bass, try Lake Hodges. Call the Lakes Fish Line, 465-3474, for recorded information on this week's big catches at the lakes, plus information on when the lakes will be restocked with fish. △ Go **deep-sea fishing** on a half-day or all day trip with a two-for-one coupon. △ Go **clamming** at Black's Beach in the winter when tides are lowest. Fishing license is required. △ Fresh Eastern seafood and live lobsters from the following companies will be shipped to you overnight: **Atlantic Seafood Direct**, (800) 227-1116; **Clambakes to Go**, (800) 423-4038. △ If you have a pool, use it to raise fresh water fish and shrimp. Call the Marine Biology Department of local universities

for a graduate student interested in aquaculture to work on your pool as a project.

Happy Hours

Happy Hour is a special period in the afternoon, generally too late for lunch and too early for dinner, when restaurants offer reduced prices on drinks and an array of complimentary (or low cost) hors d'oeuvres in order to lure in clientele, who, under normal circumstances, probably wouldn't be there. Happy Hour is usually held Monday through Friday from about 5–7 p.m., with some restaurants observing 3–6 p.m. or extended hours, 4–8 p.m. Speaking of drinking, yes, of course you are expected to purchase a beverage to go along with the complimentary munchies, but your beverage doesn't have to be alcoholic. There are a number of non-alcoholic cocktails on the market today, in keeping with health-conscious times. You can order a *Virgin* Margarita, *Virgin* Pina Colada, etc, (with the alcohol left out), or Diet Coke, Perrier or even coffee! Later in the week, many restaurants provide live music for dancing during happy hour, and these restaurants become some of the "happening–est" places in town, packed with patrons. A few restaurants offer Happy Hour on weekends, but they are truly few and far between.

Here are some of the best happy hour spreads in San Diego, at the time this book was printed, based primarily on the array of food provided and drink specials. Nothing is cast in stone, so call first.

∆ **Carlos Murphy's**, 3890 Twiggs, Old Town, 260-0305; build your own nachos, mini–burritos, taquitos, veggies, chips, dip, rice, beans. Lots of it. 4–7 p.m.

∆ **Charlie Brown's** (sternwheeler), 880 E. Harbor Island Drive, 291-1880. From 4–7 p.m., there is complimentary food featuring three hot dishes, fruit, veggies, salads, drinks at happy hour prices.

Δ China Camp, 2137 Pacific Highway, 232-0686. Thursday, Friday, 4:30-8 p.m., chicken wings or meatballs, veggies, chips, dip.

Δ **Fundido's**, in the Hilton, 1755 East Mission Bay Drive, 276-4010, 5-7 p.m. Bountiful complimentary buffet on Fridays; the rest of the week is half price appetizers from menu. Drink specials.
Δ **Skies at the Sheraton Inn**, 8110 Aero Drive, 277-8888; Friday, complimentary full buffet, lots of food, drink specials, 5-7 p.m.

Δ **Humphrey's**, 2241 Shelter Island Drive, 224-3577, Monday through Friday, 4:30-6:30 pm. The California Riviera view plus complimentary hors d'oeuvres, special drink prices. Big Margaritas, $2. Monday: carved roast beef sandwiches; Tuesday: 75¢ peel-your-own shrimp; Wednesday: 50¢ seafood bar; Thursday: nachos with all the fixings; Friday: spicy chicken wings and fresh fruit. Piano bar 5:30-8:30 p.m., *Sunday Happy Hour/ jazz/food, 6-7 p.m..*

Δ **Any Tio Leo's**, several locations including 6333 Mission Gorge, 280-9944; 4-7 p.m. tons of food, best bean dip & chips in town.

Δ **Mr. A's**, 2550 Fifth at Laurel, 239-1377; 4-7 p.m., 12th floor view, fancy little mini-pastries, quiches, etc. Jacket required here.

Δ **Old Bonita Store**, 4014 Bonita Road, 479-3537; best happy hour in South Bay with the whole works, plenty of people, 4-7 p.m., Monday through Friday.

Δ **94th Aero Squadron**, 8885 Balboa Ave., Clairemont, 560-6771; outdoor patio on the airstrip, great spread. Daily specials from: free mini pizzas, buffet, baby lobsters-75¢, free carved roast beef, free taco bar, 3:30-7 p.m., Monday through Friday.

Δ **Quail's Inn** on Lake San Marcos, 1035 La Bonita Drive, 744-2445; the best happy hour in North County, 4-6:30 p.m.! Tons of great food, Monday through Friday; dancing at 7:30 p.m. daily!

Δ **Acapulco Restaurants**, 4060 Clairemont Mesa, 483-9222, and 2467 Juan Street in Old Town, 260-8124; buffet with chimachanagas, bean tacitos, spinach dip, veggies, chips. Menu appetizers, half price; drink specials, festive atmosphere, 4-7 p.m.

Δ Most of your better hotels have good happy hour food and drink specials in the bar.

Birthday Freebies

Δ Many restaurants give free champagne or dessert if it's your birthday. Chart House give you the world's yummiest mud pie (for two), when dinner is ordered.

Δ The President of the United States will send you a signed birthday card, upon request. Send request to: Birthday Wishes Request, The White House, 20500. Give a couple months notice.

Chapter 11

RESOURCES &
WHERE TO FIND MORE BARGAINS

"Two−For−One" Coupon Books/Discount Coupons

If you want to save 50% on leisure activities, here's the deal for you: "two−for−one" discount coupon books. Whether you're young or not so young, married or single, if you like to get out and about, you'll save a bundle with *Entertainment* or *Dine−A−Mate* coupon books. Both books contain hundreds of half−off coupons for deluxe dining, ethnic restaurants, family dining, fast food restaurants, theaters, harbor cruises, fishing, sailing, major attractions, entertainment, sports, hotels, car rentals, airline discounts and much more. This year the *Entertainment* book has a new addition: a plastic Gold card that will get you 25% off on your total bill at certain member restaurants, and you don't need to use a coupon. The savings will be reflected on your Mastercard or Visa bill. This is a new plan for those who don't like the concept of using coupons, but enjoy the discount, and the privacy provided by the card.

Thousands of new annual editions are issued every September, with coupons expiring 12−14 months later. Many working couples and families eat out on a regular basis using the coupons. Some families buy two or more coupon books. Everyone is using them, especially in this economy.   Because there are so many coupons in the books, it takes a little time to organize them for maximum personal use. Try a yellow highlighter to mark special things you want to do in the index of each chapter, or tear out coupons and organize them in a 3"x5" card file with sections: Near Work, Neighborhood, Balboa Park, Old Town, Special Occasion, Brunch, Sea Food, Pizza, Things To Do, etc.

People join trading clubs to trade South Bay coupons for North County, etc. (See *Reader* classified ads under "Notices" for trading groups soon after the new editions are out.)

The *Entertainment* coupon book, $40, and *Dine-A-Mate* coupon book, ($30) are used as fundraisers (about $8 goes to the organization selling them), and they are available at school offices everywhere. Available for purchase in the office at most high schools, community colleges and adult school. They are also available from charitable and non-profit organizations including Red Cross, Association for Retarded Citizens, Kiwanis, Boy and Girl Scouts, High Schools, etc..

Entertainment also publishes the *Gold C* book, $12. It contains several "two-for-one" coupons, but mainly 25% off coupons for family restaurants, fast food restaurants, movies and entertainment, and merchandise. Available through elementary schools and charities.

A word of caution: be sure to read the fine print in the front section of each book for restrictions including blackout days, etc.

To locate a source near you that sells the coupon books, call *Entertainment* and *Gold C* at 554-1080 and *Dine-A-Mate* at 578-4800. *Entertainment* is sold at selected Mail Boxes Etc. stores.

∆ Coupon books are available for dozens of other major U.S. cities and several cities in Europe, and are available at a discount by mail (see order form in the back of the local book) or call *Entertainment,* (800) 445-4137 and *Dine-A-Mate,* (800) 428-9241.

◬ *In Good Taste* charge card, gets you 25% discount at nearly 4,000 restaurants, hotels, florists in 20 states (California, Hawaii, Florida, etc., plus Washington, DC), (800) 4IGT–USA.

Other Good Bargain Resources

◬ **Radio talk shows** are the latest rage these days. Everyone is tuning in. You can call in for advice from financial advisers, doctors, attorneys, authors, politicians, real estate specialists, or to state your opinion on timely topics. Very informative stuff. A great way to get a free consultation from doctors, lawyers, etc. Set your car and home dials to:

KOGO	AM 600	KCEO	AM 1000
KFI	AM 640 (L.A.)	KSDO	AM 1130
KFMB	AM 760	KPBS	FM 89.5

◬ *Free Stuff for Kids* by Bruce Lansky, Meadowbrook Publishers Distributed by Simon & Schuster ($5.^{95}). Published annually, this little book contains over 250 free and up to $2 things kids age 5–11 can send for by mail: decals and bumper stickers, story magazines, maps, coloring books, comic books, fun games, booklets, colorful posters, exotic stamps and more. Makes a great gift for the child in your life, and I swear it will raise your child's IQ 10 points! Check your library or book store.

◬ *Consumer Reports*, a monthly magazine ($20 per year, $30 for two years, $40 for three years, $60 for five years, includes a copy of the Annual Buying Guide ($7.^{95} value, 400 pages) with products rated by brand name, domestic and foreign cars, kitchen appliances, stereo, cameras, tools, paints, TVs, cleaning products, and personal care products. Free with subscription. You will also receive a 314–page guide to everyday health problems and health products

($6.⁹⁵ value), free with subscription. On newsstands everywhere, or call (800) 529-0551.

∆ *A Few Thousand of the Best Free Things in America*, Roblin Press, POB 152, Yonkers, NY 10710, $4.⁹⁵ postpaid. Contains free samples of products, cookbooks, recipes, travel guides, magazines & newsletters, gifts & services from Uncle Sam, toll free hotlines, etc.

∆ *Wholesale by Mail Catalog*, by the Print Project, St. Martin's Press. You can buy almost anything at 30-90% off retail prices. Available at libraries and bookstores.

∆ *Cheap Tricks: 100s of Ways You Can Save 1000s of Dollars* 400 pages, $13.⁹⁵. Call (800) 742-4847 for mail order.

∆ *AT&T Toll-Free 800 Directory* allows you to comparison shop, make travel arrangements, purchase supplies, locate hard to find items and more, over the phone using the 800-number toll-free lines, $9.⁹⁵. Call (800) 426-8686 to order.

∆ **Second Hand News**, quarterly guide to thrift stores, resale, vintage, consignment, plus calendar of rummage sales and events; $15 per year, $3.⁷⁵ for sample. Send to Second Hand News, 3120 41st Street, San Diego, CA 92105-4133, (619) 283-5245.

∆ *Bargain Hunting in the Bay Area*, by Sally Socolich, Wingbow Press, $11.⁹⁵ includes tax and postage, P. O. Box 144, Moraga, CA 94556. (Please say I recommended it!)

∆ Out-of-town phone directories including the *Tijuana Yellow Pages* are available from Pacific Bell (ask for out of town editions).

∆ The *Pennysaver*, a free weekly publication mailed to residences, distributes 84 booklets in San Diego County, with a circulation of

964,440. It's a good source of discount coupons and two-for-one coupons for restaurants, dry cleaning coupons, smog check coupons, pet supplies, and goods and services.

△ Voice your opinions on current issues through the White House Comments Line, (202) 456-1111, or fax: (202) 456-2461. Responses are tallied and delivered to the President twice daily.

△ Free photo of the President or President and First Lady, send request for photo with your name and address to: Office of Correspondence, Room 94, The White House, Washington, DC 20500. Vice Presidential photos available, too.

△   The *President of the United States* will send a note of congratulations to any citizen celebrating their 80th or subsequent birthday or any couple married 50 years or more. Send request to Greetings Office, The White House, Washington, DC 20500.

△ **Money-saving newsletters** with tons of consumer tips:

Tightwad Gazette
RR#1, Box 3570
Leeds, ME 04263
For free sample, send SASE

Cheapskate Monthly
P. O. Box 2135
Paramount, CA 90723
For free sample, send SASE

The Cheap Report
P. O. Box 394
Antioch, CA 94509-394
For sample, send $1 + SASE

Pocket Change Investor
Box 78
Elizabeth, NY 12523
Send 32¢ stamp for free issue

Frugal Times
P. O. Box 2116
Hawthorne, CA 95170
For free sample, send SASE

Bottom Line/Personal
Box 58423
Boulder, CO 80322-8423
For free sample, send SASE

◿ Enroll in any school: adult, community college and others and you will get a student ID card that will entitle you to endless discounts on goods, services, travel, and more.

◬ *Senior Citizens* can always ask if there is a discount for seniors and compare it to other promotions being offered. The senior discount is frequently not the best bargain available, so be sure to ask about all current specials.
AT&T Toll–Free 800 Directory 281
Consumer's Report 280
FBI records 285
Money–saving newsletters 282
Pennysaver 281
President of the United States 282
Radio talk shows 280
Second Hand News 281
Tijuana Yellow Pages 281
Two–For–One Coupon Books 278
Unclaimed Cash/Abandoned Property 285
Wholesale by Mail Catalog 281

◬ The *National Enquirer* wants to assist women pursuing fathers who skip out on child support. Write to: Deadbeat Dads, National Enquirer, Lantana, Florida 33464. Over 16 million children have been cheated out of $18 billion in child support. A bill was sponsored to make it a Federal crime to skip out.

◬ *How To Collect Child Support* by Geraldine Jensen with Katina Z. Jones. Send $9.40 (includes postage) to: ACES, 723 Phillips Avenue, Toledo, OH 43612.

◬ Assn. for Children for Enforcement of Support (800) 537–7072

◬ To find out how to research local public records or find out how you can remove certain things from the public record, check with your library and book store. There are several books on the topic of public records.

Δ Locate old sweethearts, classmates, relatives for $39.^{95}. Contact We Can Find Them, (800) 251-1458.

Δ *Find Them Fast* $4.95 + $2 shipping. Write to Dave Farrell, Box 252511, West Bloomfield, MI 48325

Δ Privacy Guard will help you send for your credit report from three reporting agencies, your DMV driving record and your public health record for $49 a year, (800) 374-8273.

Δ To see what is in your credit report, see chapter on "Credit."

Δ For a print out of what is in your driving record, call DMV.

Δ To find out about what your public medical record contains, see chapter on "Health."

Δ If you are receiving anonymous telephone calls and hang-ups, call the Annoyance Call Bureau at (800) 698-7223. They can put a trap on your phone for 14 days; prosecution of the annoyer is available.

Δ If you need to get in touch with any federal agency and don't know how, call the Federal Information Center toll-free line, (800) 688-9889 for assistance. You can get in touch with copyrights, government publications, passports, and many other Federal programs. Put this one on your Rolodex.

Δ For a free Consumer Information Catalog of free and low cost consumer publications, send your request to: Catalog Request, Consumer Information Center, P. O. Box 100, Pueblo, CO 81002. Sponsored by the Federal government.

Δ If you need certified copies of birth, death, marriage and divorce certificates and don't know where to write for them, call the library and they will look up the address of the vital statistics office in any state for you.

Δ To find out about your FBI records under the Freedom of Information and Privacy Act (FOIPA), write to: Federal Bureau of Investigation, ATTN: FOIPA Request, 9th & Pennsylvania, Washington, DC 20535. Your request must include your social security number, and must be notarized.

Δ For consumer complaint agencies, see Chapter 2.

Δ For grants and low interest loans for home repairs within the city of San Diego, call the Housing Commission Rehabilitation Department at 525–3649. Household income must be below national average.

Unclaimed Cash/Abandoned Property

Δ Property and cash estimated to be worth billions of dollars is sitting in federal and state treasuries waiting for the owners to make claim. Outdated bank accounts, lost checks, unpaid dividends, unclaimed interest payment, forgotten security deposits, unrefunded utility deposits, uncollected insurance benefits and **uncashed tax refunds** are turned over to the state and federal agencies' abandoned property divisions. Unclaimed money and properties (usually the result of a death with heirs unaware of assets, or a move where people forget to close an account) is held until a claim is filed. Call the California Administrator of Abandoned of Unclaimed Property's "Claim What's Yours" line at (800)–992–4647.

△ About $50 million in federal income tax returns per year remains unclaimed. You need to file Form 3911, Taxpayer's Statement Regarding Refund. Write to: Internal Revenue Service.

⊿ **Mortgages paid off early** or refinanced have created a $60 million "unclaimed" pot. Write to: Federal Housing Administration (FHA), Distributive Shares Branch, Housing and Urban Development, POB 23699, Washington, DC 20036. Include FHA policy number.

△ There are over $1.33 billion in **unclaimed U.S. Savings Bonds** issued before 1949. For info on replacing lost, stolen or damaged bonds by writing to the Bureau of Public Debt, Parkersburg, West Virginia 26106. Send social security number, approximate year of purchase, address at that time.

△ To find out how much **social security** you will receive at retirement, call (800) 772-1213. Check several years in advance because your records may not be accurate, and it takes social security years to straighten things out. Women who were married 10 years before divorce are entitled to their ex-husband's benefits. He receives them too, and so do all his other wives of 10 years! The ex-wife is eligible to receive her own entitlement, or can receive an amount equal to half his entitlement until his death, at which time she receives an amount equal to his full entitlement. Be sure to check this out.

△ For a catalog of books on how to fight and win with the IRS, get penalties reversed, obtain amnesty, and other tax related topics, contact Dan Pilla at Winning Publications, 506 Kenny Road, Suite 120, St. Paul, MN 55101, (612) 774-0678.

The End ☺